I0815998

BIG LOOSH

BIG LOOSH

The Unruly Life of Umpire Ron Luciano

JIM LEEKE

University of Nebraska Press   Lincoln

The University of Nebraska Press is part of a land-grant institution with campuses and programs on the past, present, and future homelands of the Pawnee, Ponca, Otoe-Missouria, Omaha, Dakota, Lakota, Kaw, Cheyenne, and Arapaho Peoples, as well as those of the relocated Ho-Chunk, Sac and Fox, and Iowa Peoples.

For customers in the EU with safety/GPSR concerns, contact:
gpsr@mare-nostrum.co.uk
Mare Nostrum Group BV
Mauritskade 21D
1091 GC Amsterdam
The Netherlands

Library of Congress Control Number: 2024048570

Designed and set in Lyon Text by L. Welch.

For Jane and the Traveling Riot,
whose company Ronnie would have loved

Being an umpire . . . was sort of like being a King.
Neither job prepares you for anything else.

—RON LUCIANO

You don't leave the game. The game leaves you.

—GOOSE GOSSAGE

Contents

BIG LOOSH

1 All-Star

A charity football game between collegiate all-stars and the top National Football League (NFL) team is unthinkable today. No good young player would risk significant injury at such an event. No agent would let him play. And the Las Vegas odds on a group of college players beating the Super Bowl champions would be too ludicrous even to post. But in 1959 the College All-Star Game was both possible and popular. Sponsored since 1934 by the *Chicago Tribune*, the annual late-summer classic occasionally even provided a good contest. In 1958 an outstanding batch of All-Stars had embarrassed the Detroit Lions, 35–19. This year's opponents, the Baltimore Colts, weren't about to let such a thing happen again.

Led by blue-collar quarterback Johnny Unitas, the Colts were among the finest teams ever to take the field. They had beaten the New York Giants in overtime three days after Christmas to win the 1958 championship. Many considered it the best game ever played in the NFL, and the historically minded say it was the moment that football began its ascendancy over baseball as the country's most popular sport. Now the Colts were set to play the collegians August 14 in Chicago. "We have tried to choose a team with the weight and speed necessary to meet the pro champions on nearly equal terms," said All-Star head coach Otto Graham.[1]

Tackle Ron Luciano from Syracuse University was a third-round draft pick by the Detroit Lions and a late addition to the All-Star squad. He knew that it was an opportunity to show what he could do on a national stage before joining the professionals. The game was scheduled for a Friday night at venerable Soldier Field. Seventy thousand fans were expected to fill the stands, with millions more watching from home on television. Luciano was nervous, and he privately wondered whether he was good enough to play pro ball.

The big man seemed jinxed in Chicago. In a best-selling memoir written nearly a quarter century later, Luciano recalled Vice President Richard Nixon's visit to the All-Stars' suburban practice facility. The veep was a one-time scrub on the Whittier College football team and an avid fan. Luciano wrote that his cleats slipped on the locker-room floor when he jumped up to shake Nixon's hand. He grabbed Nixon for support and brought them both down. The Secret Service quickly untangled the pair, and all was forgiven. On the field a few minutes later, Luciano wrote, he made a perfect cross-body block, hurtled out of bounds into a knot of spectators, and neatly cut Nixon's legs out from under him again. He recounted how the vice president looked at him from the ground, shook his head, and said, "You've just got to be a Democrat!"[2]

Game night was sultry, the fans sitting in shirtsleeves. Despite what he told writers, Graham doubted that his college squad could pull off a second consecutive victory. When someone proposed at a pregame banquet "May the better team win," the coach gloomily replied, "They probably will."[3] Graham had said before that All-Stars should never beat pros. The Colts were a stronger club than the Lions the previous year and had never played in the All-Star game. "On pride alone," Graham said, "they figured to be up."[4]

Coach Weeb Ewbank's Colts roster overflowed with gridiron greats and near greats: Unitas, Berry, Marchetti, Parker, Moore, Donovan, Lipscomb, Dupre, Ameche. The pros took the field in white road uniforms with the blue horseshoe logo on their helmets. The collegians wore jaunty blue jerseys with red stars across white shoulders. Looking back, it was a wonder that they actually took the field against the professionals. But nearly all were bound for the pros too and still possessed the optimism of youth.

Luciano wasn't an offensive starter. In his memoir he described going in to play tackle in the middle of the first quarter and feeling confident but not cocky. Across from him on the Colts' defensive line stood mountainous Eugene "Big Daddy" Lipscomb. Luciano was a large man, 6-foot-4 and 240 pounds, but he appeared almost petite opposite Lipscomb, who stood two inches taller and 50 pounds heavier. *Sports Illustrated* once compared Lipscomb's reach to "the wingspan of a pterodactyl."[5]

Big Daddy liked to claim that he gathered up entire backfields with those monstrous arms and sorted through them until he found the man with the ball. An Alabaman who lived the kind of complicated life Mississippi Delta bluesmen sang about, Lipscomb hadn't played college ball or even completed high school but had gone straight into the NFL after serving in the Marines. He smashed runners to the turf and then hauled them up so they wouldn't think that he was mean. Sometimes he asked, "Are you all right, Sweet Pea?"[6]

Luciano recalled in his book that because he'd successfully blocked two rushers in college, he naively thought he could handle Lipscomb. The first play went well enough, as he brushed past the Colt to block downfield. The next play was a pass. Luciano wrote that he hit Lipscomb after the snap, bounced off, and banged him again. Big Daddy then grabbed his arm like "a great grizzly bear . . . and just threw me out of the way." Luciano wrote that he landed on his shoulder, felt "thunderbolts of pain," and for the first time in his life voluntarily left a game to be rushed to a hospital.[7]

He was the first casualty in a one-sided firefight. Ten minutes into the contest, about the time Luciano's ambulance would have pulled away, Colts linebacker Bill Pellington delivered a tremendous clothesline blow to University of Houston halfback Don Brown. Convulsing and choking on his tongue, Brown "fought a life-death battle on the grass."[8] A priest rushed to his side as a doctor and trainers worked frantically to clear Brown's airway. He briefly stopped breathing, "but they finally brought him around," Coach Graham said. "I was scared to death."[9] Fifteen minutes passed before an ambulance arrived to rush the halfback away.

The shaken All-Stars immediately gave up two points on a safety and never recovered. The game was effectively over, but the carnage continued. Ohio State's Dick Schafrath followed Brown to Alexian Brothers hospital in the second quarter with a fractured cheekbone. His OSU teammate Danny James was helped off the field later with an ankle injury. The *Chicago Tribune* said the Colts' awesome line, "1,578 pounds and 46 years of pro experience," was too much for Graham's All-Stars to handle on nerve and incentive alone.[10] The collegians' sole highlight was a 51-yard run by Notre Dame's Nick Pietrosante, another Detroit draftee, but it didn't help—they failed to score all night. "I expected the worst," said University of Utah quarterback Lee Grosscup, "and it happened."[11]

Ewbank inserted his subs and rookies during the second half. Many spectators left early, and TV sets clicked off all across America. The game ended with the final score 29–0. For the Colts, the game was the first step toward a repeat championship in 1959. For the All-Stars, it was a spectacularly brutal introduction to the NFL. Big Daddy gently allowed that the collegians were good boys, leaving smashmouth tackle Art Donovan to slip in the knife. "I would say they were nice boys," Donovan rumbled. "Nice little boys. But they got an awful lot to learn."[12]

Luciano later wrote that doctors had tried to stuff his arm back into the socket, "just as you might try to push a cork back into a wine bottle."[13] It didn't work, and they eventually had to operate. His rookie season, and perhaps his pro football career, was over before it began. Big Daddy, he said long afterward, "convinced me that my survival in the game depended on not playing."[14] But the big Colt had done no such thing, or at least not directly. Luciano's self-deprecating accounts of the game over the years—how he chose to write and speak about it almost a quarter century later and perhaps to remember it as well—were almost entirely fiction. His famous injury? It came during a scrimmage.

He described the true circumstances in 1961, only two years after they happened and before he began weaving what might be called Luciano Lore. He was filling in at defensive end when Pietrosante rushed with the ball. Luciano tried to cut down two guards running interference and landed on his right side with his arm bent. "That did it—my right shoulder popped," he said.[15] Luciano never knocked the vice president down either. Nixon reached Chicago too late Thursday to watch a scrimmage in the suburbs. He did attend the game Friday night and afterward spoke with the All-Stars in their locker room, where Luciano likely met him. "You all look so big here in the dressing room," Nixon told the men gathered around in their towels. "And you looked so little out there compared with those Colts."[16]

The All-Stars had taken a pasting from one of the greatest teams ever. Who would know the truth later if Luciano claimed he'd played two unimportant downs? Or object if he added that he'd taken his stance opposite Big Daddy? Lipscomb was an incomparable gridder, and Luciano never asserted he'd bested him. Rather than craft a tale of false heroics, he devised another of faux failure that still placed him on the playing field. Once the annual contest was dead and gone, who would remember exactly which All-Star the huge Colt had humbled on a hot, humid night in 1959?

The drubbing provided grist for a great story. Surely it was too painful for Luciano to admit years later that he'd hurt his shoulder during a workout. Or that his name was omitted from the team roster in the *Chicago Tribune*. Or that the newspaper reported a day before gametime that he and a now-forgotten back from tiny Bluffton College in Ohio were the only members of the forty-nine-man squad definitely out due to injuries. Luciano *had* been a College All-Star, a heralded All-American tackle from Syracuse, No. 74 in the third row of the team picture. But somehow it had all gone wrong for him in Chicago.

What former athlete wouldn't be tempted in middle age to put a funny and bittersweet spin on the events? The injury emotionally devastated Luciano, who would have done anything to play in the NFL. That much, at least, was true.

All he could do during the fall of 1959 was report to the Lions' training camp with his shoulder in a sling and make the most of every opportunity that arose. He would learn the pro game, befriend as many Lions players and staff as possible, and generally make himself useful. In Detroit that autumn he would fight to continue his life in football. The notion of a different future in baseball likely never even occurred to him.

2 Tiger

Like many athletes before him, Luciano was a first-generation American. He thought of himself as a typical Italian American. His father was born Pierino Luciane in 1890 in Spoltore, a comune and town in the province of Pescara, halfway down the Italian boot along the Adriatic Sea. Pierino landed at Ellis Island in New York at age eighteen in 1909. Family history says his older brother Giuseppe came with him, but a manifest for the liner *Re d'Italia* shows only Pierino, albeit with other emigrants from the same area; Giuseppe perhaps preceded him. Americanization and misspelling would eventually transform the brothers into Joe Luciane and Perry Luciano.

When America entered World War I in April 1917, Joe held a job at a wood yard in northern Pennsylvania's timber country. Pierino (not yet called Perry) was two hundred miles away working as a bartender in Oneonta, New York. He filled out naturalization papers and later became a citizen, a step Joe never took. Pierino enlisted that July as a private in the New York National Guard, his bakery company soon absorbed into the U.S. Army. The outfit's captain hailed from an old hotel family well known across the state. "He will soon be ready to open his course in culinary science, and there is much interest in it throughout camp."[1]

The 101st Field Bakery Company left for France in June 1918 and served overseas for a year in the American Expeditionary Forces (AEF). "The boys are working hard every day in the construction of a mechanical bakery which we will assist in operating after completion and think we will be here for the duration of the war," a doughboy wrote home.[2] After the armistice the bakers returned with little fanfare in 1919. Private First Class Luciano came through unscathed and possessing new skills. He lived for a while with Joe's family in Pennsylvania before returning to upstate New York.

The army veteran now called Perry lived in Binghamton before marrying Josephine DiNunzio of nearby Endicott in July 1923. Josephine was the daughter of Italian immigrants. The newlyweds soon settled in her hometown, one of the "Triple Cities" with Johnson City and Binghamton. Two years later the Lucianos opened a little restaurant called Perry's Lunch, formerly Charles' Lunch. Once Prohibition ended in 1933 the couple also served beer and liquor. They renamed the place Perry's Steak Shop, then Perry's Grill. They remodeled in 1940 with lots of chrome and modern chairs, tables, and fixtures.

"Perry will now specialize in delicious butter-grilled, top grade western steak, chops and spaghetti," a news article reported. "Perry's food is known throughout the Triple Cities."[3] The place also offered live music and dancing on the weekends.

Perry and Josephine had two daughters: Barbara (called Bobbie), born in 1925, and Delores (Dee Dee), ten years later. Son Ronald Michael Luciano arrived on June 28, 1937, at Our Lady of Lourdes Hospital, a Catholic institution on Riverside Drive in Binghamton. The three girls doted on the boy, known to almost everyone throughout his life as Ronnie. It perhaps wasn't surprising that Bobbie and Dee both later became nurses.

The family lived above the business as the Great Depression slowly ended. Endicott during the late 1930s was home to twenty thousand people, many of them immigrants drawn by good jobs. Endicott endured the lean years better than many other communities. Its biggest employer, with nineteen thousand workers, was Endicott-Johnson Corporation, commonly known as E-J. The giant shoe manufacturer wasn't named for the two Triple Cities communities where it operated; to the contrary, the villages were named for E-J founders Henry B. Endicott and George F. Johnson. Community lore had it that immigrants arriving in New York stepped off the boats knowing one key phrase: "Which way E-J?" The corporation itself was unusual. "'Live and Help Live,' benevolent socialism, industrial paternalism, and the square deal policy are all associated with EJ," a local history says. "From modest beginnings, Johnson built one of the greatest shoe industries in the world."[4]

Endicott was also home to International Business Machines Corporation (IBM), which employed four thousand workers locally while quickly becoming a worldwide enterprise. Unlike many U.S. companies, IBM was able to pay workers a Christmas bonus in 1936. The *Endicott Bulletin* observed that it and E-J were "leading the way in fair treatment of their employes [*sic*] by their generosity not only this month, but their fairness every month in the year."[5] Endicott avoided most of the economic suffering endured by other American cities, the newspaper added, and local industrial jobs in 1937 meant it would "continue to prosper and to develop into a still larger village, as it has been rapidly doing the past 20 years."[6]

Perry's Grill at 1802 North Street faced a bustling manufacturing district lined by the shoe and business-machine factories. The area buzzed with activity. Blue-collar workers poured out of the plants and white-collar workers from the handsome brick IBM laboratory only half a block up the street. "More than 3,000,000 automobiles pass in front of the IBM plant on North St. annually," the *Bulletin* reported shortly after Ronnie's arrival.[7]

Josephine Luciano had family in the Triple Cities. Her brother Nicholas DiNunzio in particular became an important figure in Ronnie's life. DiNunzio was a three-sport star at Union-Endicott (U-E) High School during the late 1920s and a bantam quarterback and punter later at Syracuse University. He once knocked himself cold scoring the first touchdown in years against rival Colgate University, his drive carrying him over the goal line into the goalpost. Afterward, Nick taught and helped coach football and golf at U-E. Later still he served as a navy chief petty officer and lieutenant during World War II, in charge of physical training at various stations around the United States. He resumed teaching and coaching after the war.

His nephew Ronnie was a big kid who in 1946 stood a head taller than third-grade classmates. Josephine believed that he got his size from her father, Michael DiNunzio, who stood six feet tall and weighed 260 pounds. Ronnie's eldest sister had married by the time their parents celebrated their silver wedding anniversary in 1948. Ronnie wasn't yet twelve years old when his father died suddenly of lung cancer the following spring. Perry was buried with the military honors due a member of the American Legion and Veterans of Foreign Wars.

Except for a few paragraphs in his memoir, Ronnie rarely spoke of his father. Close friends during adulthood didn't recall his ever mentioning Perry. Once during a radio interview while in his mid-forties, he would joke, "I had a mother but we were too poor for a father."[8]

Josephine became the center of her small family. She took control of the business and a modest estate valued at $12,000. Her son was "one of those gangling, gawky skin-and-bones type of kid" at Henry B. Endicott Junior High School.[9] Ronnie bulked up considerably before his ninth-grade graduation in 1952 and entered U-E High School as a sophomore that fall.

The boy took a strong interest in sports. Endicott was Yankees country, and the Triple Cities had a New York farm club called the Triplets. Ronnie occasionally traveled down to the Bronx to catch a big league game but otherwise didn't care much for baseball. He said long afterward that he couldn't hit a curveball or catch a fastball. But he participated in track, played volleyball, and was a big fan of lacrosse.

Like his Uncle Nick, a member of the U-E coaching staff, Ronnie especially loved football. A newspaper recalled that he'd begun dashing around in a football helmet when he was eight, "but as with so many big good-natured kids he had a quality of gentleness to overcome, especially once he reached high school."[10]

Ronnie didn't letter in football as a sophomore but was more than ready to make an impression as a junior in 1953. The tousle-haired tackle with the gap-tooth grin now stood several inches above six feet and weighed 242 pounds. "A bright future is forecast for Ron if he continues his improvement as in the past year," the *Endicott Daily Bulletin* predicted.[11]

The school's head coach was Harold V. "Ty" Cobb, a laconic World War I veteran who'd arrived in Endicott in 1920. "If we lose we don't alibi," he said, "nor do we try to take any credit away from the team that beat us."[12] Cobb didn't lose often. By the time he retired in 1958, his record was 202 wins, 84 losses, and 18 ties. His teams played at En-Joie Stadium on Riverview Drive along the Susquehanna River. Rebuilt after a fire in 1949, the stadium seated over six thousand fans and was connected to the school by a twenty-foot tunnel. Ronnie took the field there during an era when footballers were still two-way players (on both offense and defense) and wore helmets without protective face bars.

The 1953 team's senior co-captain was Joseph Barbara (Bar-BAR-a), a 239-pound tackle who kept in shape by unloading trucks at the small bottling plant owned by his father, Joseph Sr. A sportswriter recalled the high schooler as a very tough player, "not dirty, just a hard hitter who asked—and gave—no quarter. Generally thought of as a 'nice guy,' he had few real friends on the team."[13] Ronnie's picture ran below Joe's in a team photo spread in the Endicott newspaper. Joe's younger brother, Pete, was a 184-pound U-E tackle.

The brothers' father kept a low profile around Endicott, with good reason. Joe Barbara Sr. was what people called connected. The *New York Times* later mentioned his long police record, "including three arrests as a suspect in murders."[14] But few locals except the Triple Cities cops realized the scope of his influence. "There was an awkward moment in 1946 when Barbara was convicted of violating wartime regulations for failing to explain how he came to possess five tons of sugar," a reporter wrote, "but otherwise, life went respectably well."[15]

The family lived in a $100,000 estate in the Tioga County hamlet of Apalachin a few miles west of Endicott. Joe Sr. was considered a fine neighbor. He drew glaring nationwide attention in November 1957, however, after his sons and Ronnie had all moved on from high school. New York state troopers and federal treasury agents raided Barbara's hilltop home to bust up what the press called a gangland convention. "There seemed more than coincidence in the fact that the Apalachin meeting took place less than a month after the slaying on Oct. 25, 1957, of Albert Anastasia, racketeer, former chief executioner for Murder, Inc., and a big wheel in the Mafia," the *Detroit Free Press* later added.[16] The elder Barbara son, known now within the circle as Little Joe, helped his dad host the meeting.

Police sealed off the road to the house and caught everyone by surprise. They rounded up sixty-five hoodlums, some of whom tried to flee through surrounding fields and woods. Residents were startled awake to the news that the Triple Cities had hosted "every ranking Damon Runyon character in America," including one with $10,000 in his pocket who told a trooper he was unemployed.[17] The police sergeant who uncovered the gathering said it "looked like a meeting of George Rafts," the kind of wisecrack Ronnie would have appreciated later.[18]

Little Joe punched a photographer as local, state, and national press descended on Apalachin. His arrest was the first step in a criminal career that saw him marry into a Michigan mob family. He led his in-laws into a lucrative waste management business during the 1960s, the man who "first whispered 'garbage' in the ears of Detroit's top mobsters."[19] Ronnie later penned a funny if exaggerated account of his friendship with the Barbara boys. But in 1953 they were all simply teammates.

Their school called its sports teams both the Tigers and the Orange Tornado. The U-E football squad opened the upstate New York Southern Tier Conference (STC) schedule October 10 at En-Joie Stadium, the Tigers battling Binghamton North to a 25–25 tie. Ronnie saved the game by dropping North's halfback short of the goal line to prevent a twenty-sixth point after the tying touchdown (teams being allowed to run as well as kick before introduction of the two-point conversion). His gridiron heroics then ended the following week when he fractured an ankle in practice, the first of several injuries that would bedevil his football career. Joe Barbara went down too, his senior season ended by a knee injury.

RONNIE RETURNED FOR HIS SENIOR SEASON in 1954 at tackle. He wore size 14 cleats and was the biggest Tiger gridder Coach Cobb could remember. During the preseason weigh-in he nearly popped a spring in the scale, registering at what *Binghamton Press* sports editor John W. Fox called "an honest-to-goodness 267."[20] Fox would enjoy an exceptionally long career and write about Endicott's favorite son for the next forty-plus years.

"Big Ronnie, by contrast to his mean appearance on the gridiron, is a soft-spoken happy-go-lucky lad," fellow *Press* sportswriter Russ Worman wrote.[21] Joe Barbara's brother Pete weighed 208 pounds, and the rest of the Tiger line wasn't much smaller. Worman recalled them as being so big that their athletic letters looked like lapel buttons on their jackets. Together, they constituted the biggest line in the conference and one of the biggest ever at Endicott.

Ronnie would say as an adult that he couldn't remember ever weighing less than two hundred pounds and add that he had notions about playing pro football while still in high school. His mother offered another reason for his phenomenal growth: "He doesn't have a girl friend, his whole life is devoted to athletics."[22] He was terribly conscious about his weight, Josephine also remembered, "and lots of reports in the papers and some kidding from the other kids didn't help much."[23] Despite his bulk Ronnie topped the U-E lineman in wind sprints once practice began.

The Tigers won their first two games comfortably before hosting speedy and tricky Vestal Central at home October 16. The two schools were non-conference archrivals situated practically within sight of one another across the Susquehanna. The Tigers had never lost to coach Dick Hoover's green-shirted Golden Bears, who were trying to prove that their little school could keep up in the STC. Remnants of Hurricane Hazel roared through the area the night before the Saturday game, downing power lines, lifting roofs, and toppling hundreds of trees. The storm proved an omen for Coach Cobb and his Tigers.

The underdog Vestal team won the "biggest plum of its 17-year scholastic football history," the Endicott paper said, a 13–0 humbling of U-E before 7,500 stunned fans at En-Joie Stadium.[24] Locals talked about the upset for decades, John Fox calling it "the village's greatest athletic moment."[25] The Golden Bears continued on to an undefeated season.

U-E won twice and lost twice more before ending its 1954 season with a traditional Thanksgiving Day game versus Binghamton Central. It was *the* game for both, with five thousand fans expected at En-Joie Park. The Tigers broke a scoreless tie with two minutes left after a fifty-yard touchdown drive. The victory gave them a 5-3 record on Ty Cobb Day, a celebration of the coach's thirty-fifth season at the school.

Ronnie's performance during the season earned U-E's mammoth senior lineman a place on the STC All-Conference second team. But fans remembered him as the overweight tackle during the Vestal upset, and some of the area's coaches "pretty much agreed that Ronnie didn't have what it took to make it at the college level."[26]

Over the winter he played guard and center in a local Catholic Youth Organization basketball league, netting 218 points and winning a spot on the All-Star team. But as graduation approached, Ronnie's natural position remained tackle. The seventeen year old hoped to go on to college. He was good at math but otherwise no great shakes academically. "It was reported that Ron Luciano had gone on a hunger strike because the school administration had forbidden him to take more than seven subjects," the student newspaper joked on April Fool's Day.[27] Josephine fretted about affording tuition but said "with football and the help of God" she might swing it.[28] But few college coaches took much notice of her son.

Endicott sportswriter Ed Casey remembered that Ronnie "wasn't a much-chased schoolboy gridder" in 1955.[29] Colgate, Syracuse, and Bloomsburg State Teachers College in Pennsylvania were interested. The latter was winning a "snail-paced race" for the tackle, John Fox added, "until Vestal's Dick Hoover pointed Ben Schwartzwalder in the right direction."[30]

Hoover knew that Syracuse coach Schwartzwalder liked big linemen. Getting a boost from the man whose Golden Bears had humiliated the U-E line perhaps surprised Ronnie. But the coach had seen enough in the 267-pound tackle to recommend him to one of the country's elite programs. That fall Ronnie followed the path his Uncle Nick had blazed more than two decades earlier, seventy-five miles north to Syracuse.

3 Orangeman

Coach Schwartzwalder was a decorated World War II paratrooper who sported a graying crewcut. His Syracuse gridders were called Orangemen, and like the Union-Endicott Orange Tornado, they mostly played both ways. Schwartzwalder believed his 1955 freshman squad was the best he'd ever had and that Luciano was the best lineman on it. The tackle shed fifty-plus pounds once trainers put him on a diet, John Fox reporting him down to "a murderous 215."[1] Bob Velie, the highly touted Vestal quarterback who had beaten U-E the previous fall, played on the same squad. The Southern Tier pair saw significant playing time.

The Syracuse frosh played separately from upperclassmen. Luciano's good season probably surprised doubters at home. He missed a late-season match after a knee injury in a game against the United States Military Academy at West Point but returned for the finale at home against rival Colgate. An Endicott columnist wrote that Velie played a whale of a game in leading the Orangemen to a 20–13 victory, but so did Luciano. "Luce played most of the way and did an outstanding job."[2]

Luciano began his sophomore year at Syracuse in the College of Business Administration before switching to mathematics. He made friends easily, especially with anyone from the Triple Cities. Before the interstate highway system quickened travel for everyone, three or four players piled into a car for weekend trips home along two-lane country roads. Josephine Luciano loaded them down with homecooked goodies to take back to school, which they usually polished off before they'd gone halfway to Syracuse.

The Orangemen suspected that their fearsome young tackle was very bright and maybe even brilliant. Schwartzwalder considered Luciano an "exceptionally intelligent boy" and couldn't recall another footballer who had scored better on the Syracuse entrance exams.[3] Velie had a memory of him hunkered in the backseat during one of their drives, helping a female friend tackle complicated premed math equations. "He was very articulate," another teammate added, "and he knew a lot of trivia, a lot about movies and the arts."[4] The pals watched films together in downtown Syracuse, always classics such as *Love in the Afternoon* or *A Farewell to Arms*.

Luciano was also a wise guy, so funny in practice that he could get Schwartzwalder to laugh before a big game. "And if you knew Ben and how uptight he'd get before the Penn State game," a coach said decades later, "you'd know that that was no small feat."[5] The big Endicotter was the team comedian, always on the verge of being a troublemaker. "But when it came time to bump heads," a teammate said, "he would rattle your skull."[6] Those big knocks got noticed. The *New York Daily News* noted that the Orange was well-fixed for sophomore reserves, "the hottest prospect being Ron Luciano."[7]

The Syracuse program wouldn't be affiliated with a league or conference until 1980. The Orangemen played in Archbold Stadium, college football's second-oldest venue behind Harvard's big concrete horseshoe. Uncle Nick Luciano had played there, once scoring a touchdown against Cornell and punting twenty-seven times versus Columbia. His nephew was thrilled to follow him. Luciano later remembered standing in the stadium as a freshman and telling himself that someday he'd be a star and hear his name announced over the PA system.

All-American Jim Brown starred for the Orange when Luciano was a sophomore. Luciano later wrote that he addressed the senior halfback as "Mister" and in return answered to "Hey, you." He also joked about Brown having the world's best physique. "He has muscles I didn't even know existed."[8] The tackle and three teammates appeared with Brown in a *Life* magazine photo, all climbing ropes together during a conditioning drill.

Luciano weighed a few pounds more than he had as a freshman, in the low 220s. He banged his right knee in a line-blocking drill during the first day of spring practice but was ready to go September 22 for the 1956 season opener. Schwartzwalder wished he had a half-dozen more like him while preparing for heavily favored University of Maryland at College Park. "Give me six like that and I'd be a lot closer to Maryland's manpower," he said.[9] The Orange stormed out to what a sportswriter called the greatest opening game victory in the school's sixty-three-year football history. Brown scored two of the team's four touchdowns in the 26–12 thumping of the Terrapins.

Luciano earned praise too. "Before his knee locked on him and forced him out, 'Loose' did his share in shoving Maryland around in his first game for the varsity," John Fox wrote for Triple Cities readers.[10]

Syracuse suffered a letdown the following week, losing to the University of Pittsburgh Panthers 14–7 in the Steel City. Luciano wasn't mentioned in game coverage and perhaps didn't suit up. After a bye week, Syracuse opened at home October 13 versus West Virginia University. Brown rushed for 165 yards in a 27–20 victory, but Syracuse's heralded second-string sophomore tackle went down again. This time, the injury was serious.

Fox reported that Luciano was carried off on a stretcher midway in the third quarter after his "trick knee began acting up again."[11] He underwent surgery for torn cartilage and was done for the year. His absence was a blow to Syracuse's reserve strength, especially with the Army game approaching. Schwartzwalder said it was the same knee Luciano had hurt as a freshman. "I suppose he should've had the operation then," the coach added.[12]

Syracuse finished the year with a 7-2 record, enough for a bowl bid. An appearance in the segregated Sugar Bowl was out of the question, so the Orange agreed instead to play Texas Christian University (TCU) in the Cotton Bowl. Luciano accompanied the team to Dallas but didn't suit up for the New Year's Day game. A Syracuse paper later speculated that his presence on the field might have changed a slim loss into a victory, the Orange losing by one point despite valiant play from their halfback. Luciano recalled that after Brown's great performance a hotel employee entered the locker room to say he could now use the front entrance. "You can guess what Brown told him about his offer."[13] According to Luciano, the team always felt that the wire services had reported the score incorrectly; it should have been TCU 28, Jimmy Brown U 27.

Luciano began 1957 with high hopes but pushed too hard during spring workouts and hemorrhaged his knee. After he recovered and resumed contact, a series of unrelated health issues brought a disappointing junior season. A throat infection, a chest cold, and minor injuries slowed him, but he played in every game. Fans who noticed him wearing a collar during the season might have figured he had a neck or back injury. Trainers actually had rigged it to protect his inflamed tonsils, which were removed after the season. Luciano was mortified to learn afterward that four hospital attendants were needed to hold him still as he emerged from the ether.

The Orangemen finished the season 5-3-1 without a bowl bid, but the Associated Press named the big tackle to its All-East second team. Luciano returned to Endicott following his tonsillectomy to spend the December holidays with his mother, who had sold Perry's Grill and now worked in the E-J sales department. Josephine's modest new home at 105 Badger Avenue was only a short way from Joe Barbara's bottling plant.

"LUCIANO WILL BE A SENIOR in 1958," a Syracuse paper said, "and wants to leave his mark in Orange football history, with an outstanding season."[14] The sentiment was fine, but the preseason proved rocky. John Fox reported that Luciano even considered transferring to another school that summer. The big senior's demotion to the Syracuse second string, Fox wrote, probably meant little more than Schwartzwalder "trying to light a fire under the gentle Endicotter."[15]

Luciano regained his fire and started the opener September 27 versus visiting Boston College. Writers voted him the game's best lineman after the Orange came from behind for a 24–14 victory. He served as co-captain the following week versus the College of the Holy Cross at Worcester, Massachusetts. The Crusaders pulled off a late 2-point conversion to win 14–13, Schwartzwalder saying afterward that except for Luciano and the Syracuse halfback, his team "didn't play smart and didn't hustle as much as we wanted."[16]

Syracuse rebounded by annihilating Cornell and the University of Nebraska at home by a combined score of 93–0. After Luciano's fourth consecutive strong game, Schwartzwalder called him a real fine ballplayer. "As a matter of fact," he said, "the other clubs have started to think pretty seriously about running somewhere else than where he's located."[17]

The old jinx then struck again. Luciano missed a big away game at Penn State, stuck in the student infirmary with a 104-degree fever and a bout of what doctors called virus pneumonia. Schwartzwalder said it was a major blow because the tackle had been his best player all season. "They ought to vote poor Ron Luciano another season of eligibility, the luck he's had at Syracuse!" the *Binghamton Press* declared.[18] The bedridden senior listened to the game with his mother as the Orange pounded out a 14–6 win without him.

Next up came the Pitt Panthers the first day of November at Archbold Stadium. Luciano delivered one of the great performances in Syracuse football history, cinematic in its drama and simplicity. The *Syracuse Herald-American* reported that the two teams "drained the last drop of nervous energy from 38,000 frenetic Archbold stadium football fans."[19] The halftime score was 10–0 in Syracuse's favor, but Luciano was suffering. His temperature had risen, and the team doctor said he should return to the infirmary. Luciano countered that he'd stay on the bench in case he was needed.

He returned to the fray shortly into the second half. The Panthers advanced the ball to the 5-yard line, where the Orangemen line stopped them with their second goal line stand of the day. Pitt came back later with a touchdown but missed the extra point, making the score 10–6 with thirty-three seconds left in the third quarter. The teams traded TDs in the fourth, Pitt taking the lead before Syracuse retook it with less than ninety seconds remaining then missing the extra point. The thriller ended with Syracuse intercepting a pass in the end zone that would have given the Panthers the victory, the final score 16–13. "Hollywood never thought up a more dramatic finish," declared the front page of the *Syracuse Post-Standard*.[20]

Luciano was named Outstanding Lineman of the Game for the fifth time that season—every game he'd played. A Pitt coach said Syracuse could have played in the Big 10 if they performed like that every week but added, "I'll bet you never see that 78 [Luciano] ever play a game like that again."[21] Schwartzwalder praised his exhausted tackle as almost unbelievable after he'd gone out with one-day's practice in two weeks and played a hell of a game. "We couldn't have hoped to beat Pitt without him," Schwartzwalder said. "He was so tired at the half he could hardly stand up, but he kept going."[22]

That evening Luciano struggled through supper with his family before going back to the infirmary. John Fox marveled at what he'd seen that day. If Syracuse played well the rest of the way, he wrote, "look for the Triple Cities' surprise package of the decade to make at least one of the major 'all' teams."[23] Fox also tagged Luciano with a new nickname, Loosh, which stuck for the rest of his life. (Fox's pronunciation had a soft consonant. Luciano preferred a purer Italian, *Lu-chee-ano*, but sometimes he also used a softer *c*, *Luce-iano*.)

Syracuse stormed through its last three games with Boston University, Colgate University, and West Virginia by a combined score of 104–12. Luciano didn't play as much as he had before his illness. Sportswriters were calling him Unlucky Luciano, punning on the nickname of deported mobster Charles "Lucky" Luciano, but the big tackle's performance was still impressive. "How many kids could lick virus pneumonia in the middle of a football season and bounce back to play great football?" Schwartzwalder wanted to know.[24]

The Orange team finished with a record of eight wins against their single nightmarish loss and awaited a bowl summons. They didn't have Jim Brown anymore, the coach said, "but we have a better line than the team we took to the Cotton Bowl two years ago."[25] The Orange agreed to play in the Orange Bowl at Miami versus the Sooners of the University of Oklahoma (often called OU) on New Year's Day. Luciano meanwhile waited to learn if he had been picked for one of the numerous All-America teams. Schwartzwalder called him probably the best interior lineman during his decade of coaching the Orange. "He's determined, spirited and has marvelous reactions."[26] John Fox remembered the Pitt game when later writing that Luciano "in that one afternoon became All-America."[27]

But the voting wasn't clear cut, and electors were fickle. United Press International (UPI), the Newspaper Enterprise Association (NEA), *Sporting News*, the Football Coaches Association, and the Central Press Association all announced first and second teams by early December. Ted Bates of Oregon State University was the only consensus All-America tackle. NEA and Central Press both named Luciano, and three other tackles made one team apiece. *Look* magazine was widely expected to choose Luciano, too, but instead named four tackles whose names didn't appear on any of the five other lists. "Imagine, a magazine representative going over the country and saying, 'You just might make our All-America, if you're lucky, so you better not make any plans for the first weekend of December,'" the *Endicott Daily Bulletin* huffed.[28] UPI later included Luciano and Army halfback Pete Dawkins on its All-East team, while the *Binghamton Press* named him its 1958 Athlete of the Year.

All such honors, however, were less important to Luciano than the National Football League draft in Philadelphia. The San Francisco 49ers were interested, and the Packers had sent him more than a dozen letters. Luciano said he'd rather play on the West Coast than in Wisconsin but hoped the Giants or Browns chose him instead. The Detroit Lions then beat everyone by making him the thirty-sixth overall pick December 1.

The *Binghamton Press* explained that Detroit had two picks in the third round because of a prior deal with Baltimore. The Lions picked Luciano at the end of the round, the Colts' position in the draft order. Detroit had traded star quarterback Bobby Layne to Baltimore early in the 1958 season, prompting Luciano to joke later that his draft swap had completed the transaction. Sometimes he even claimed he'd been traded straight up for the fabled "Night Train." Having grown up and gone to school in upstate New York, the Endicotter was surprised but happy to land relatively near home in the Motor City.

Luciano said that going to a West Coast club would have forced him to make a decision about whether to continue playing football. He was a bit disappointed not to land with the Giants, because they were closest to home. "But I'd much rather play in Detroit than San Francisco," he said. "I feel good about it."[29] Before joining the pros, however, he and the Orangemen first had to meet the Sooners at Miami.

THE SYRACUSE TEAM LEFT CAMPUS in mid-December to spend twelve days at North Carolina State University at Raleigh, the practice site for the bowl game. Players found enough snow on the ground when they landed to have a snowball fight, but the weather warmed for the rest of their stay. Several men then got airsick on the way to Florida as turbulence rocked their flight. Luciano sat up front behind coach Schwartzwalder and was first to bound down the steps at Miami. Photographers posed him on the tarmac kissing two waiting bowl queens.

"This is great," Luciano beamed, lipstick staining his left cheek. "You guys go back in the plane," he said to envious teammates, "and I'll call when I'm ready for you to come down."[30] Years later he quipped that he'd learned early always to be first in line.

The team awaiting Syracuse was another powerhouse. Like the Orangemen, coach Charles "Bud" Wilkinson's Oklahoma team had lost only once during the season, also by a point. The Sooners knew Luciano by reputation. "He's reportedly as mean as a hungry lion," an Oklahoma newspaper said.[31] But Wilkinson had his men ready, and OU entered the game a 13-point favorite.

The thermometer touched eighty degrees during the nationally televised afternoon game, torrid for January 1 even by Miami standards. An

Oklahoma newspaper described the game as one of the oddest the Sooners had ever played. Wilkinson's team scored three touchdowns, all on long plays, but was bested in rushing yards and first downs. "OU looked less than startling, and many onlookers were disappointed despite the fact that it was probably a fighting Syracuse defense rather than an OU deficiency that made the Big Red attack look weak on occasion."[32]

Schwartzwalder's team also struggled. By the fourth quarter, the coach had thirteen men down with injuries and muttered that he couldn't remember ever having one of his teams so banged up. Late in the game with three injured men at the same position, Schwartzwalder turned to the bench and asked, "Anyone here ever play left guard?"[33] With three minutes remaining, Luciano went down too.

Syracuse sportswriter Bill Reddy reported that the tackle had taken a blow to the midsection, others that he simply ran out of gas; an Oklahoma City scribe hypothesized that he was "the lone sun victim, collapsing on the sideline near the end."[34] The Sooners had oxygen tanks and masks that the Orange lacked on their sidelines. Luciano "abandoned all pretense of freshness when he came out the last time," the *Miami Herald* reported. "He drew a hand from the crowd, then laid down in front of the Syracuse bench."[35]

Syracuse managed only two field goals in a 21–6 loss. Luciano said the heat bothered both teams and that except for Oklahoma's three long runs, the Orangemen would have prevailed. "But they are too fast," he added.[36] The *Endicott Daily Bulletin* later observed that Luciano had broken his helmet almost in half late in the game and suffered a mild head injury. He made only two tackles plus an assist, but sportswriters and players alike praised his play. An Iowa writer called his tackle of the Sooner halfback the most vicious of the day. Upstate New York papers described him as brilliant and a terror on defense. "I hit him as hard as I could all day and never did move him," said Sooner senior co-captain and right end Joe Rector.[37]

Neither OU nor Syracuse earned the national championship. Louisiana State University won the vote before the bowl games were played then narrowly won the Sugar Bowl to end an undefeated season. The rankings didn't mean much to Luciano after a punishing season. The All-American flew home with only two things on his mind: catching up on course work and otherwise sleeping as much as possible. "I'm tired," he said.[38]

4 Lion

Luciano shifted his attention from collegiate to professional football. In mid-January, he said he'd probably play for the Lions but was mulling an offer from the Canadian Football League's Toronto Argonauts as well. Meanwhile, he was a hero in the Triple Cities. When had a pair of high school tackles ever made such headlines, John Fox asked, as U-E's 1954 twosome, "at left tackle All-America Ron Luciano and at right tackle, Joe Barbara, Jr.?"[1]

Ron stayed in shape over the winter playing amateur basketball for Jerry's Restaurant in nearby Oneonta. U-E High School meanwhile named his uncle Nick to replace retiring Ty Cobb as head football coach. Looking fit, healthy, and handsome in jersey and shorts, Luciano brought several former Orange teammates to demonstrate the T-formation during a clinic at the Endicott Boys Club in April. Nick DiNunzio kept the football job only one season, too nice for his own good, supporters said, but he enjoyed a long tenure as U-E's golf coach.

Luciano returned his signed Lions contract to Detroit on May 11 and was relieved not to be chosen for the College All-Star team the following month. NFL rules required drafted players to participate if selected, and Luciano told Fox he'd been sweating because he didn't want to join the All-Star team. "I told Bob Nussbaumer, the Lions scout who signed me, that I hoped they'd hold back the release on my signing until after the All-Stars were named," he said.[2] Luciano had worried that being in Chicago rather than Detroit might hinder him in catching on with the Lions.

The tackle lacked the credits to graduate with his Syracuse class in the spring but planned to complete his degree in math later and perhaps work toward a master's in education. Luciano celebrated his twenty-second birthday June 28, no doubt thinking ahead to the training camp. Ten days later, however, he got a letter from Otto Graham saying he'd been added to the All-Star roster. Workouts started at Northwestern University on July 23, the same day he was due to start rookie drills in Detroit. "Instead he'll stop in Detroit on July 20 and pick up mimeographed Detroit plays," the *Detroit Free Press* said.[3]

The Lions coaching staff fumed over Graham's taking five of their draftees. Nussbaumer said that by playing in the college game, they could fall so far behind they might never catch up. "It's a reason many never make it," he added.[4] Luciano also understood the risks. He later told Ed Casey of the *Endicott Daily Bulletin* that the Lions' front office felt the same way about it that he did. "Glad I was selected but sorry I'll have to miss so much practice."[5]

Before heading for Chicago, Luciano stopped in Detroit for quick introductions with other draftees. An earlier conversation with former teammate Jim Brown, starring with the Cleveland Browns, stuck in his mind. Luciano said Brown had told him he'd been lucky to stick in pro ball. "He said you make the grade only IF the team you're trying out for happens to have an opening," Luciano told Casey. "And then you must really prove yourself in the preseason drills, because there are a flock of candidates for every opening."[6]

CHICAGO WAS A DISASTER, the injury jinx striking again at the worst possible time. It was little wonder that Luciano later spun a tale blaming Big Daddy Lipscomb for wrecking his shoulder. He stalled before calling his mother with the bad news. Luciano was hurt on Sunday, July 26, during drills at Northwestern, the *Press* reported Wednesday, adding that he would be out of action at least six weeks. "Hospitalized since then, he didn't call his family in Endicott until after his discharge (in a splint) last night."[7] The silver lining was that All-Star Game insurance paid his full Lions salary.

The team kept Luciano on the taxi squad of non-roster men ready to replace injured players during the season. He kept quiet about his future, but his sister Dee Jester wasn't shy about speaking up for him. "When he left home he was very dubious about his chances in pro football," she said of her brother in October. "But he has plenty of confidence now. He feels he'll surely make the club next year."[8] Luciano didn't get into a game all season but thought later that he'd been lucky to ride the bench and learn, since it would have been tough to make the club in 1959. "Now I have an extra year's pro experience to back me up when I make my bid next season," he said.[9]

Luciano was cheerful and popular in Detroit, accepting ribbing from Alex Karras and other Lion veterans about getting pay for no play. Quarterback Tobin Rote kidded that he was a "regular Jesse James."[10] The sidelined rookie made himself useful wherever he could, especially in the film room. Luciano later joked about giving himself a title: audio-visual coach. "That guy could always sell himself," linebacker Wayne Walker remembered long afterward. "He was never without an idea."[11] Walker thought Luciano would have been a good pro player, although not the star he'd been in college.

The rookie missed playing for a mediocre team; the Lions finished with three wins against eight losses and a tie. Syracuse under quarterback Ernie Davis meanwhile completed its first perfect season and won both the Cotton Bowl and the 1959 national championship. Luciano found no little humor in the timing of his old school's triumph. He played amateur basketball again over the winter, and in April, along with two former Syracuse teammates, he faced Wilt Chamberlain of the Philadelphia Warriors in a charity game at the U-E gym. John Fox wrote that the 7-foot-2 basketballer "didn't appear inclined to start an argument with the 716 prime Syracuse pounds."[12] The Stilt's squad won nonetheless, 113–107.

Luciano nurtured high hopes for the 1960 football season. NFL teams of his era often let players participate in their alma mater's spring varsity-alumni games. The Lions, however, had lost an offensive end to injury during such a game back in 1957 and wouldn't let Karras or another Iowa alum play at Iowa City or allow three Michigan Staters to suit up at East Lansing. Luciano was the sole exception; Lions president Edwin J. Anderson said he needed a little action after missing the whole 1959 season. The *Binghamton Press* noted that Luciano had skipped the previous Syracuse spring game ahead of the All-Star Game and his Lions debut. "But big Loosh says he'll be in there this time, even though his NFL debut is still upcoming due to injuries."[13]

Quarterback Davis became a fabled Syracuse star who won the Heisman Trophy in 1961 before his early death of leukemia two years later. Luciano would often joke that he'd kept the Orange program from collapsing during the interim between Davis and Jim Brown. ("I was the glue that held Syracuse together between their careers.")[14] The Orange QB now led the varsity to a 21–15 victory over the alumni in the April 30 game at Archbold Stadium. The Lions surely rued letting Luciano play when he reinjured his shoulder making a tackle only eight plays after entering the game.

His injury didn't appear serious, and in late July, the second-year tackle reported to the Lions' training camp at Cranbrook School in Bloomfield Hills, Michigan. He arrived weighing about 245 pounds, down fifteen from his peak with Detroit but higher than at Syracuse. Luciano's bad shoulder, however, soon gave out again. The same day coach George Wilson cut three rookies, he saw Luciano go down for the second straight season.

A Grand Rapids paper said Luciano's probable loss for the season was a big blow to the Lions. The *Detroit News* suggested that the tackle was a casualty in Operation Reddog, "a rough daily session designed by Coach Wilson to stiffen pass protection for Earl Morrall and the other quarterbacks."[15] The *Detroit Free Press* added that the club feared Luciano might be finished. "Lion doctors are sending him to the University of Michigan Hospital to see if an operation could repair the damage enough to let Luciano try again next year."[16]

Luciano returned to the sidelines after the operation at Ann Arbor. One good bit of personal news was the marriage of his sister Dee in August. Luciano went on the injured reserve list and again missed the entire season. He recovered to the point of accompanying the team to Chicago for a November game with the Bears, but he didn't play. He meanwhile helped the staff chart games and served as what a sports editor later called "the highest priced film projector operator the Lions ever had."[17] Luciano appropriated the quip and repeated it for years. The Lions put him on waivers the following summer, having never seen him play in a real game.

THE BUFFALO BILLS of the young American Football League (AFL) were interested in making an offer, but the *Binghamton Press* predicted that Luciano "probably won't chance further injury unless it is exceptional."[18] He knew Bills coach Garrad "Buster" Ramsey from Detroit, where he had been an assistant coach with the Lions. Ramsay overcame Luciano's hesitation and signed him in late July after a club physician examined him at the Bills' East Aurora camp and gave his shoulder the okay.

The *Binghamton Press* said the lineman was now so eager to play pro ball that "he agreed to waive club responsibility if he re-injures the shoulder, his mother said today."[19] Ramsey moved him to left offensive tackle during an early scrimmage. "My legs sometimes feel like it's been a long, long two years," Luciano said during practice.[20]

His shoulder held up, but he hurt his knee during an August 25 preseason Bills game with the Boston Patriots at Providence, Rhode Island. He got hit from the side while playing on the kickoff unit. "Just call me Unlucky Luciano," he said, the old nickname then repeated on sports pages across the country.[21] Hobbled with a sprain, he received his release when the Bills cut down to their final roster in early September. A Buffalo trainer later commented that Luciano hadn't really put his heart and soul into coming back from the bum shoulder. "I think it was a big comedown for him to come to the American Football League," he said.[22]

Any club claiming Luciano before the twenty-four hour waiver deadline was liable for his medical expenses and salary while injured. Nobody picked him up, but he still wasn't quite finished. His status was "very much in the air," sister Dee told the *Binghamton Press*. A place on the Bills' taxi squad was possible. "He was discouraged, naturally," she added, "and said he wouldn't know for sure about this taxi business until next week."[23]

Luciano wore a shirt and tie instead of a Bills jersey for the first regular season game, September 10. He sat hunched at a table near the bench in War Memorial Stadium, manning a telephone for the coaches. He said years later that too many operations had done him in. "They really cut me up," he said. "Those guys are too big for me. I was a little man in that game."[24] But that didn't prevent him from pursuing his pigskin dreams a while longer.

THE UNITED FOOTBALL LEAGUE (UFL) had formed during the spring of 1961 in four adjoining states, with teams in Louisville, Indianapolis, Grand Rapids, Cleveland, Columbus, and Akron. The whole circuit cost peanuts; each team's thirty-man payroll was capped at $15,000—less than some NFL stars got individually. The average player pay was fifty dollars per game during a ten-game schedule. By autumn the six clubs reached informal agreements with the NFL and AFL.

Ramsey believed a year in a lower league like the UFL might give a green player like Luciano the experience he needed to win a regular spot with the Bills later. The club dispatched him to the Indianapolis Warriors. The *Indianapolis Star* reported that about half the roster consisted of local players "who played their college ball with Hoosier teams and who are now working and living in Indianapolis and Central Indiana, and half who are 'cuts' from both the American and National Football Leagues."[25]

UFL players had some hope of being called up to a higher league. The Warriors sent a halfback to the AFL Denver Broncos in November. An Indiana newspaper mentioned Luciano, "who Hoosier football fans may be watching on Sunday afternoon television next season."[26] After several weeks of being unable to play because of his bad knee, the former All-American finally suited up for the Warriors November 26.

He wore No. 66 during the Western Division championship game at home versus the Grand Rapids Shamrocks. A *Star* photographer captured an opponent illegally yanking the face guard to pull Luciano's helmet down over his eyes. The 24–14 Indianapolis loss ended both the big tackle's stint in central Indiana and the Warriors' first season in the UFL, which lasted only through 1964.

Luciano never publicly mentioned his time with the team. "Like all great football players, I was mo-bile, a-gile, and hos-tile," he said in his memoir. "Unfortunately, I was also fra-gile."[27] He was back home in upstate New York by Christmas, needing to make a living outside of football. Luciano started substitute teaching in the Union-Endicott school system but soon grew unhappy. He often joked afterward about discovering his hatred of children, which was absurdly untrue. What he hated was being inside teaching.

He said later that he was an easy grader, marking tests with eighty that only deserved thirty. He tried to stay in sports by emulating his uncle Nick but was too impatient to coach high schoolers. Luciano admitted he expected too much of the teens. He'd see a quarterback having trouble completing a 30-yard pass and bark, "Dammit, Tobin Rote can throw it 30, 40 yards with no problem. Why can't you?"[28] Worse still, he admitted, "I couldn't stand not to play."[29]

Luciano began promoting a string of hamburger joints and teenage dances around upstate New York. He broadcast football for Endicott radio station WENE-AM during autumn 1962 as play-by-play man for some of the same games he'd played in during high school. His voice, pleasantly soft and high-pitched, wasn't ideal for the job. "My voice is perfect for mime and my face is made for radio," he joked later.[30]

He returned to the field that fall, playing and coaching for a football team much nearer home than Indiana. The Frankfort Falcons played in the new Atlantic Coast Football League, which had teams in Portland, Maine; Paterson, New Jersey; Providence, Rhode Island; and Stamford and Ansonia, Connecticut. The Falcons weren't based in Frankfort, New York, but in nearby Herkimer and drew fans mainly from greater Utica. The Falcons succeeded in little Herkimer because the field there had lights, which allowed them to play home games on Saturday nights. The *Binghamton Press* said the names on the roster wouldn't stir much excitement among grid fans, "but there was a time when a nucleus of the Falcon ball club did some pretty good work for Syracuse University's high-ranked teams."[31]

Following its inaugural season, the semipro league expanded to twelve teams in two divisions during 1963. Luciano returned as a player-coach for the club now called the Mohawk Valley Falcons. He played anywhere the Falcons needed him and owned a piece of the league as well. "This is the bottom of the professional football barrel," the *New York Times* wrote, accurately but not unkindly, "and a man who can't make it here had just better wait until his sons grow up."[32] Mohawk Valley's halfback was a forty-six-year-old surgeon who had never played college football. Luciano knew how the situation looked. "Well, I think I'm half crazy," he admitted. "But I still want to play very badly."[33]

Years later he said he didn't remember much about the games but did recall the practices. "We'd be discussing what we were going to have to eat that night after practice," he said, "and before you know it we would call off practice and head for some Italian restaurant."[34] Luciano made a few good plays for the Falcons, scored his first ever touchdown on an intercepted pass, and earned a few brief mentions on local sports pages. Future sportswriter Paul Zimmerman lined up across from him at Herkimer as a member of a team from Mount Vernon, New York.

Zimmerman and his teammates played for the Westchester Crusaders for forty dollars a game and gas money. They lost the game on home-town officiating, he said, and nearly got run down by a train driving back to their motel. He remembered that Luciano had a big night. "What was he like?" Zimmerman later wrote. "Like a typical semipro 300-pound tackle. He'd anchor himself in a four point stance and throw punches."[35]

John Fox profiled the league sympathetically that September. "Some players are in it for more than the urge," he wrote. "There's always the chance that Someone Up Somewhere will spot them. . . . Luciano, on the other hand has no illusions."[36] The big tackle, he added, planned to attend a baseball umpires' school in Florida the following spring.

5 Arbiter

Luciano later explained his switch to baseball with a tale involving Walter Briggs, who he said owned both the Detroit Lions and the Detroit Tigers. He claimed he'd asked "Spike" for a job in sports and was offered the general managership of the Tigers' Class A farm club in Lakeland, Florida. Luciano then arrived in the Sunshine State in January before spring training began. "I went over to the baseball umpiring school just by coincidence and I said to myself, 'Hey, I could actually be back on the field.' When I told Briggs what I wanted to do, he was stunned."[1]

This account doesn't track. John Fox mentioned the interest in umpiring the previous fall, and Luciano offered his GM tale only after Briggs's death in 1970. A Detroit book reviewer said the job conversation "could not possibly have taken place."[2] The Briggs family sold the Tigers in 1956, their final link to the club broken five years later with a name change from Briggs Stadium to Tiger Stadium. As for the Lions, Briggs was only a member of the club's executive committee in 1964, not its owner. The whole tale was Luciano Lore.

Why did Luciano concoct it? Probably for much the same reason he invented his encounter with Big Daddy Gene Lipscomb. He always wanted to amuse, certainly. But his tales also cloaked a private gloominess that plagued Luciano much of his life. His motive for changing careers was simple, as Luciano admitted during his first season in baseball. "I've always been wrapped up in sports," he said. "Instead of teaching school at Endicott, N. Y., I decided to be an umpire."[3]

Two Major League pals got him to consider the possibility. His explanation varied slightly over the decades, but Luciano always credited umpires Lou DiMuro of the American League and Bill Kinnamon of the National League for inspiring him. "Football officiating looked awfully competitive, but I'd met Lou DiMuro at a Chicago sports dinner and he convinced me it was a pretty good life if you make it 'upstairs' fairly fast," Luciano said.[4] He offered a slightly different version a few years later, saying he was down in New York City to see some shows when the pair suggested that he try umpiring. John Fox added that his first meeting with DiMuro and Kinnamon came at a bar owned by teammate Alex Karras when Luciano was "an ailing Detroit Lions' candidate."[5]

Whatever the chronology, Luciano hated to leave football but concluded that umpiring was "the next best thing."[6] Bored and desperate to return to the playing field—any field, in any capacity—he abandoned the gridiron for the diamond. "What else could I do?" he asked. "Once you're in sports, and you love it, you want to stay."[7]

The Al Somers Baseball School at Daytona Beach, Florida, was the oldest and most prestigious umpiring academy in the country. DiMuro and Kinnamon both taught there. The idea of a former tackle starting over as an umpire didn't seem entirely farfetched. Although no longer a lethally conditioned All-American, Luciano was still in his middle twenties and in decent shape. He enrolled for the six-week Somers course.

Luciano already had a bit of officiating experience in college basketball. He'd once worked a big game at Hamilton College in Clinton, New York, whose hoops coach had also helped coach the Frankfort Falcons. Kenneth Patrick sensed Luciano's nervousness and skipped any pregame chitchat. The coach known as "Pat" never looked his way or said a word to him until the game ended. Then he extended his hand. "I'll just never forget it," Luciano said. "What a lesson for an official taught by a man who was sports, and everything it projected."[8]

While only one big man among many in football, Luciano was exceptionally large for baseball. He towered above nearly everyone, standing at what he later joked was "5-feet, 16-inches."[9] He weighed more than most others too, struggling and usually failing throughout his umpiring career to keep his weight down to 250 pounds. An umpire had to be heard across the diamond when working behind home plate, so Luciano also needed to work on his voice, once described as "three parts gravel and two parts gravy."[10]

Luciano often said that the first thing he learned at the Somers school was that an umpire was God on the field. "I said to myself, 'I didn't want to teach school, I didn't want to play football. I wanted to be God my whole life.' . . . I really, after a while, thought I was."[11] But he later rejected treating baseball as a religion, coming to believe that umpires who acted that way "end up in the cuckoo house."[12]

He considered much of the curriculum absurd too—unraveling the mysteries of the balk rule, for example, or learning never to turn his backside toward the fans when whisking off home plate. "I thought about a real good Shakespearean course I had at college and I thought, 'Now look at you,' but on the other hand, a lot of it is trickier than you'd expect."[13] He also appreciated that he didn't have to worry any longer about getting hurt or hearing coaches yell at him. "I could be part of the game," he said, "yet I didn't have to be concerned with winning and losing."[14]

His roommate at school was Danny McDevitt, a thirty-one-year-old former lefthanded pitcher with a 21-27 record in six seasons pitching for the Dodgers, Yankees, Twins, and Athletics. McDevitt had also made the last pitch ever thrown at Ebbets Field in Brooklyn. Dave Phillips, a classmate and future Major League umpire, remembered the pair as the stars of the Somers camp. McDevitt had grown up only twenty-five miles from the Triple Cities in Hallstead, Pennsylvania, while his father worked for IBM, but he had never met Luciano. He too wanted to return to professional sports, and umpiring seemed a likely route.

The harsh reality was that only a handful of entry-level positions opened each season, and the Somers school could produce few jobs for its sixty-five students. The ex-pitcher and former tackle nonetheless both landed spots in the Class A Florida State League (FSL). Luciano got ready for the season by working spring training games at Tigertown, Detroit's farm base at Lakeland, which perhaps inspired his tale of a GM job offer from Spike Briggs.

Luciano got his first outing when a AAA umpire scheduled to work a Detroit intrasquad game couldn't make it. Detroit righthander Frank Lary took the mound with the newcomer behind the plate. "I missed about 100 out of 102 pitches," Luciano recalled. "At least he thought so."[15] He also worked a game at Lakeland between two AAA clubs, the Syracuse Chiefs and the Indianapolis Indians. When an Indy batter angrily tossed his bat against the screen after a called third strike, the rookie ump promptly tossed him. Syracuse sports editor Bill Reddy remembered that the ejection caused considerable consternation, since "such things almost never happen in spring games."[16]

Only two officials worked games in the eight-team Florida State circuit. When the 1964 season began, the league initially paired Luciano with McDevitt. They remained roommates and drove to assignments in McDevitt's powder-blue convertible. FSL umpires were "notoriously low paid," the *Miami News* said, "and in terms of pride their jobs would seem much more enjoyable if they were allowed to stuff several swatches of Grade A cotton in their ears."[17] Umpires received a monthly salary of $375 to $400, plus seven cents per mile for the owner of a car. Luciano gave himself six seasons to reach the majors but figured his partner might make it after four. McDevitt had always felt as a pitcher that umpires should pay their way into a park but said, "Now I know it's no easy job."[18]

The two made their regular-season FSL debut April 21 before a small crowd at Lopez Field in Tampa. Luciano admitted that he and McDevitt were a little apprehensive. Someone asked how tough he planned to be on the young Lakeland Tiger and Tampa Tarpon players. "Well, let's hope that my size does scare them a bit," Luciano replied. "The way they throw the ball in this league it's a little different than having Big Daddy Lipscomb coming at you," he added with a wink.[19] (The great Colt had died a year earlier. The rookie arbiter wouldn't begin offering his tale about Lipscomb rearranging his shoulder for several more years.)

Luciano got a harsher introduction to umpiring when the Tarpons faced the St. Petersburg Saints before 162 fans June 5 at Tampa. A sportswriter called it "a rain delayed game that, once begun, turned into a Mack Sennett comedy."[20] Luciano tossed the Tarpon manager and catcher for disputing his limit of five pitches or one minute for warmups, after which Tampa played under protest. When a Tarpon hitter later lingered too long in the dugout, Luciano told the St. Pete pitcher to start throwing anyway. He called two quick strikes with no one at the plate.

"The batter was still on the way to the box when the third came by," Luciano said. The hitter threw his bat at the ball while on a dead run for strike three. The ump also had trouble from the Saints, who protested a double down the line in left. When a Saint's pitcher unwisely rolled a ball in from the mound for inspection, Luciano angrily bounced it back. He knew he'd made a mistake the instant the ball left his hand. "I let my emotions get the best of me. Just for a minute," he said. "Then I got hold of myself."[21]

The game lasted nearly to midnight as tempers grew short all around. The exhausted ump finally told the two teams to fight *each other*, since "they should know they can only lose by fighting me."[22] St. Pete finally won, 8–7, Luciano managing to ignore constant catcalls from the box seats. After playing pro football, he said, "you don't listen to that sort of thing."[23]

He had more trouble in Tampa late that month. He tossed the Orlando Twins' manager during the eighth inning of a scoreless game for racing out to second base and disputing an out call. The boot was the ump's sixth in his last three appearances at Lopez Field. It was hard for even a close observer to see Luciano give someone the thumb, "for he never actually makes the sweeping gesture," a Tampa sportswriter observed. "At best, according to Tampa players (who know best) it's usually 'You're through.'"[24]

Despite such travails, Luciano earned good overall reviews in the FSL. The owner of the Daytona Beach Islanders called him a good umpiring prospect. "McDevitt has had to toss a few guys out of games, but all I've seen of Luciano he's been able to avoid being a bouncer," he said.[25] After the season, Luciano returned home to Endicott to work as a substitute eighth-grade-math teacher.

Minor leagues bought and sold umpires much the same way teams did players. That November, the Class AAA International League (IL) purchased Luciano's and McDevitt's contracts. Most writers expected both men to go initially to the lower AA Eastern League (EL), but McDevitt made the leap all the way to AAA, probably thanks to his Major League experience. He said he'd learned more baseball during his one year of umpiring than during twelve years as a player. But McDevitt didn't survive the season, abruptly quitting in August. Luciano later said a former big league teammate and friend then playing in the IL had screamed and cursed at McDevitt on a team bus following a game. Something in the ump broke. "When the bus reached the airport," Luciano added, "he got on a different plane and flew home."[26]

Luciano spent the 1965 season getting further seasoning. He was far better off financially working in the Eastern League than in the Sunshine State. "I couldn't come close to breaking even down there," he said.[27] He was also nearer his family in Endicott. The EL had a team at Elmira, New York, only fifty miles west, and none of the other five clubs was more than two hundred thirty miles away.

McDevitt meanwhile began running a federally funded training and economic development program in his wife's hometown of Greenwood, Mississippi. Decades later he said he was probably best remembered there as "the guy that came down and put all this government in front of the Ku Klux Klan," an indication of just how tough umpiring actually was.[28]

LUCIANO LEARNED A FEW MORE THINGS about the job's challenges in the Eastern League. That spring he first encountered the man who would be his antagonist for the rest of his career. Earl S. Weaver was then in his fourth season managing the Elmira Pioneers, a Baltimore Orioles farm club. Opposing skippers considered him a hot dog and an agitator. "According to the media, I am famous for three things: arguing with umpires, battling with players, and winning ball games," Weaver wrote long afterward. "Well, you can't have the latter without the first two, I'm sorry to say."[29]

Weaver argued loudly and at length about anything. A Minor League second baseman who never made the majors, he once got ejected for complaining about a called third strike while still in the on-deck circle. ("The cotton-picking pitch was obviously high and outside," he insisted years later.)[30] A troubled franchise in Knoxville promoted him to player-manager in August 1956, six days before his twenty-sixth birthday. He lasted only until his sixth game before an umpire gave him the thumb.

The hotheaded skipper left a trail of managerial fines and suspensions from the Deep South to the Great Plains to the Empire State. Weaver's arguments went beyond umpires when he reached the Eastern League in 1962. EL president Rankin Johnson fined him fifty dollars for yelling "embarrassing remarks" at *him* during a game at Williamsport, Pennsylvania.[31]

One of the most infamous stunts of Weaver's long career came a season later when he stole third base—and kept it. The plate umpire tossed him during the fifth inning of an August road game with the Charleston (West Virginia) Indians. Weaver reappeared at the top of the sixth to coach third base as if nothing had happened and refused to go when told he'd been ejected. The skipper and ump jawed for several minutes, Weaver walking into left field then sitting on third base as the ump pleaded for him to leave. "He finally picked up the bag and walked to the Elmira bench," a Charleston paper said. "The bat boy finally brought the bag back to the field and play was resumed."[32]

Weaver's temperament never softened. During 1964 the league suspended him for three days and fined him $100 for pushing an umpire. Early in the 1965 season, the thirty-four-year-old Elmira skipper led the Eastern League in what *Sporting News* called the "'tossed-out-of-games' department for the last three years."[33] Despite his many faults (and perhaps to some degree because of them), Weaver also was a consistent winner. A local sportswriter placed him atop all Elmira managers. "Earl's had two second-place finishes, one pennant winner and another Governor's Cup victor—and no one can match that."[34]

Weaver explained his combative ways by saying that some umpires just weren't good enough. "Unfortunately, there's nobody rich enough to pay a $25,000 bonus to hire a good one," he said. "I've been in this business 17 years. I feel I've got a right to say something when an umpire who's been in baseball just three or four years makes a mistake."[35] Luciano was at a disadvantage working with Weaver in the EL; he was seven years younger and had only one summer's professional experience at baseball's lowest level. Things predictably went badly when they met.

"The first four times I saw Weaver in the Eastern League, I had to run him," Luciano said in 1973.[36] He told variations of this tale for over two decades, sometimes recounting a particular offense and the inning of departure. Sportswriters happily wrote it all down; once Luciano even tried to convince Weaver of the scenario. "The first time we met I threw you out in Reading [Pennsylvania] in the Eastern League . . . ," he began. "It wasn't Reading," Weaver snapped. "You worked about four of my Elmira games before then."[37] Luciano beamed as if delighted at being caught.

Weaver was correct. The pair first met May 1 during a series at Dunn Field in Elmira. Luciano worked the plate and didn't eject the skipper, but he did toss his catcher for arguing too strenuously that he'd been hit by a pitch while batting. "Pioneers manager Earl Weaver also squawked, but this time the scrappy pilot was outdone in the beefing department and he remained on the scene," a newspaper said.[38] The Pioneers traveled to the Keystone State ten days later for the series that Luciano later mentioned so frequently and inaccurately.

The Elmira skipper survived the opening game with the Reading Indians, although Luciano ejected the opposing manager for arguing about a walk. He made it through the second game as well before blowing a gasket in the third. A third strike for the third out in the top of the fifth inning didn't go the Pioneers' way. "Weaver got the gate from plate umpire Ron Luciano in the bottom of the fifth for protesting from the dugout."[39] The pair argued about five minutes before the manager departed. The fourth game provided no further dramatics and the series ended with only the single Weaver ejection. The four boots during their initial encounter were pure Luciano Lore.

THE PAIR SQUABBLED AGAIN LATER in May as Elmira faced the Springfield Giants in Massachusetts. The Pioneer catcher again protested, this time over a foul tip, and once more got the Luciano boot. "Elmira manager, Earl Weaver, a bantam rooster-type standing about 5-6, argued some, but never got into the pushing stage. It's just as well, because Luciano is 6-4 and weighs 245. He's not the budging type."[40] The ex-Lion next ejected the Elmira skipper June 9 at home following a series of arguments at the plate. Luciano bounced Weaver for the second time that year then warned the Pioneers when he suspected them of talking to him over the field telephone.

Weaver wasn't Luciano's only foil in the EL. Pittsfield (Massachusetts) Red Sox manager Eddie Popowski contested an out too hotly during a game in early August. Luciano gave him the thumb, but Popowski got the last word. "The trouble with you," he said, "is that when you were making all those tackles, your head hit frozen ground too often."[41] The crack so amused Luciano that he repeated this too as his own for years afterward.

Popowski's club was in a tight pennant race with Weaver's. Luciano's partner, umpire Dick Vollmer, later complained that fans noticed only the stresses exerted on players, never on arbiters. During the last six weeks of the 1965 season, Vollmer said, he and Luciano called games involving either Pittsfield or Elmira or both. "That was a lot of pressure."[42]

Luciano clashed with Weaver again in late August, after tossing Pioneers shortstop Mark Belanger for flinging a helmet toward him after a called third strike. Belanger's ejection brought a "lengthy and loud protest" from both him and Weaver, the *Elmira Star-Gazette* said. "It was to no avail."[43] The umpire later conceded in his memoir that Weaver was probably right in his insistence that a batboy had tossed the helmet toward the dugout, but he said it came too late. Luciano was always fond of Belanger and once attended Catholic mass with him on the road; he never ejected the shortstop once they both reached the Majors. "It was like throwing Bambi out of the forest," Luciano said.[44]

Weaver's Elmira club finished the season in second place, one game behind Pittsfield. Luciano felt the toll of his confrontations with the Pioneer skipper. "It was the only time since I got in this business that I seriously thought about throwing it in—quitting," he told John Fox a few years later.[45] The ump wound up his season the first week of September at Springfield, where Pittsfield pitcher Bill MacLeod was going for a record eighteenth consecutive win and twenty-second over two seasons. "I could hear him behind me all night," MacLeod remembered after a quarter century. "He was rooting for me. He would say, 'come on Bill, you can do it.'"[46] Despite some squabbling over a double play call the ump didn't make during the ninth inning, MacLeod got his record.

Luciano headed south after the season as one of twenty umpiring prospects selected to spend the winter in the Florida Instructional League. "Eastern league managers, reluctant as they are to put in good words for ANYONE in a blue suit, voted him the league's best this year," Fox reported.[47] Luciano got the welcome news in February he was moving up from the Eastern League to the International, which Fox said was "next-door to the majors."[48]

He would get more field support in the IL, where umps worked in three-man crews rather than in pairs. It was familiar ground, too. The far-flung AAA league stretched from Canada to Florida, but three of the eight teams were in upstate New York, at Syracuse, Buffalo, and Rochester. Before the 1966 season began, the league sent Luciano to work spring training at Tigertown. "It's a good break for the big fellow from the Southern Tier," Bill Reddy wrote, "because he'd work some Major League exhibition games before the Syracuse Chiefs' spring opener March 21."[49]

Weaver also went up to the IL, promoted by Baltimore to lead the AAA Rochester Red Wings. The manager always claimed no ill feeling toward Luciano and said many times that he'd recommended him for the Major Leagues while still in the EL. But Weaver was no less combative toward umpires while heading the Rochester club. A sportswriter in Columbus, Ohio, surmised that the manager's middle initial *S* stood "probably for 'Stormy.'"[50] A writer in Richmond, Virginia, called Weaver an earthmover for his habit of excavating basepaths with his shoe during rhubarbs. "He approaches from the rear and begins digging before opening the debate. Umpires hint that they are not very impressed by the dust and dirt clouds."[51]

The skipper surprised people in 1966 by managing a winning ballclub composed largely of rookies. Weaver and his kids drew over a quarter million paying fans into Red Wing Stadium and delivered Rochester's first pennant in thirteen years. Luciano had a good season too, and longtime IL umpire Augie Guglielmo predicted that the Endicotter would become a Major League umpire within two years. "He's a real prospect," Guglielmo asserted, "a hustler, and a great guy, too."[52] The *Binghamton Press* likewise thought Loosh stood an excellent chance of working in the majors by 1968.

Luciano skipped substitute teaching or umpiring in Florida after the season and instead took a temporary job with IBM. Both he and Weaver reported to the IL in 1967, the latter as the league's only returning skipper. The manager's beefing continued, but nothing remarkable involved Luciano as Rochester fashioned another good season, finishing a game behind the Richmond Braves. Weaver's performance earned him a promotion to a big league coaching job in Baltimore as first base coach the following season. Luciano meanwhile finished the year by working in the IL semifinal and championship games.

He returned to the league for a third season in 1968, a make-or-break point of his umpiring career. "Once you've made it to Triple A, you've only got two places to go—the big leagues or home," recalled IL ump Mike Schirmer Jr., who eventually did go home to South Dakota, where he became a sportswriter and broadcaster.[53]

Luciano realized he wasn't enjoying life on the diamond and began to question his approach to the game. "All I was doing," he remembered, "was getting in trouble because a manager would come out, say something profane and I'd say, 'That's it,' and throw him out." A fellow umpire told him that despite what they'd learned in Daytona Beach, an ump wasn't really God and that he had to let the players play. Luciano revised his approach and let people see more of who he was out on the field. Suddenly, the job seemed to open up. "I started to enjoy the game and watch it," he said. "Mundane games were no longer hours of nothing."[54]

A Florida sportswriter later recalled seeing "Man Mountain Luciano" polishing his act in the IL. "First, he was a good umpire. Second, he could entertain without inciting either the fans or players."[55] Colleagues noticed a change too. One night at Jet Stadium in Columbus, Ohio, Luciano got tangled up at first base with a runner and knocked him flat. "As an infielder raced toward the kid, Luciano leaned over and said, 'Sorry about that. But unless you can get back to first you're going to be out any second,'" Schirmer recalled. "He was the kind of a guy who'd do so many crazy things that nothing would surprise you."[56]

The Major Leagues expanded by four teams in 1969, with the American League adding Kansas City and Seattle and the National League adding teams in San Diego and Montreal. With both leagues needing more umpires, IL president George Sisler Jr. thought Luciano was ready to move up. Learning that the head of the National League planned to attend a game in Rochester with a handful of big league execs, Sisler juggled his umpiring crews to make the stars align and place Luciano behind home plate. A Rochester paper said the ex-Syracuse footballer responded with "one of his usual outstanding performances."[57]

Sisler's tactic worked, but not within the circuit he intended. The American League announced in July that it had hired three AAA umpires for the expansion season. Among them, Ron Luciano, "whose shoulder and knees couldn't take the strain of major-league football, was approved yesterday as having the eyes, the composure and, when called upon, the thumb necessary for administrating major-league baseball," the *Binghamton Press* said when Loosh got the call.[58]

6 Gunfighter

Ron Luciano traveled to Florida for his sixth spring in baseball, his first in the Major Leagues. His early months in the bigs were strangely connected with the Washington Senators. As a Yankees fan during boyhood, Luciano felt no great fondness for DC teams—neither the earlier one that was now the Minnesota Twins nor the current one that replaced it. But as an athlete and an American, he was unusually deferential toward the Senators' first-year manager, former Red Sox slugger and U.S. Marine flier Ted Williams. Their first encounter came during 1969 spring training when Washington faced Baltimore at Miami.

When the Splendid Splinter made an unannounced pitching change, Luciano strode toward the Senators' dugout calling, "Mr. Williams. Mr. Williams, is that Bosman pitching for you?" For all his prickliness as a player, the Washington skipper was highly regarded for rarely beefing with umpires. He confirmed to Luciano that his hurler was indeed Dick Bosman. "Sorry, I'm sorry, but I got so excited I forgot to tell you," Williams apologized. "I guess I thought the guy we had pitching was going to pitch forever."[1]

Teddy Ballgame repaid the ump's courtesy at the end of Washington's 3–2 loss after Senator Hank Allen was tagged at the plate trying to score from second on a single for the final out. Allen started to argue until his manager intervened. "You've lost the ballgame, now just shut up and head for the dressing-room.'"[2]

For the regular season beginning April 7, the league assigned Luciano to the crew of senior AL umpire Jim Honochick along with veterans Bill Haller and Frank Umont. They worked Opening Day together in Washington, the Senators hosting the Yankees. Luciano's old acquaintance Richard Nixon, newly inaugurated as president of the United States, threw out the first pitch, then two more for good measure. The Yankees looked on without

No. 7, retired after eighteen seasons in pinstripes. "Hello, Mickey Mantle, wherever you are," the scoreboard said.[3]

Luciano almost missed the opener along with the Mick. The *Binghamton Press* said the league's tailor had mistakenly sent his gray slacks and size-fifty extra-long blue blazer affixed with league insignia and emblems to Miami Beach instead of Washington. Luciano's International League uniform wouldn't do, because it was black and AL umpires wore blue jackets. Hank Soar rushed in to replace him at first base, but Luciano got a last-minute reprieve when AL president Joe Cronin decided that Loosh's civilian blue blazer would suffice.

The rookie pinned a Major League Baseball (MLB) centennial insignia to his jacket, changed into regulation gray slacks that had arrived in the interim, and hit the field—to the puzzlement of fans and sportswriters who had no idea why he was there. "The unidentified 260-pound object down the left field foul-line at Washington's Robert F. Kennedy Stadium wasn't a secret-service man, but Ron Luciano," the *Press* gleefully reported. The lonely ump said he put up his right arm only once all afternoon, and then not very far, "because an umpire's coat has a lot of extra room for stretching and I wasn't that confident of what would happen."[4] His presence brought no luck to the Senators, who lost 8–4.

Luciano's next moment with the Senators came a month later at the top of the ninth inning of a sloppily played game in Oakland. His costar was Frank Howard, the mild-mannered left fielder and first baseman who was one of the few ballplayers even bigger than the umpire. At issue was whether "Hondo" had swung at a curveball on a 2-1 count with the game on the line. Luciano was already tense, having lost track of the count on an A's batter the previous half inning, perhaps misled by an incorrect scoreboard. He also believed that a checked swing was an umpire's hardest call.

Washington's 6-foot-7, 270-pound outfielder was positive he hadn't swung. "Unfortunately for him, 6-foot-5, 250-pound rookie umpire Ron Luciano thought he did," the *Oakland Tribune* said. After flying out to left, Howard flung a few furious words toward the plate from the dugout steps. "Luciano gave him the thumb, the hand and the mask, all in one violent motion," the *Tribune* added.[5] A *Washington Post* writer who'd never seen such bad temper from Howard wrote that "the ground shook as he walked to the clubhouse."[6] The next batter struck out to end another Senators loss, 5–4. The ejected Nat fumed about Luciano afterward.

"This man is taking bread out of my mouth, out of our mouths," Howard said. "The ball was a mile outside and it wasn't even close to being a check swing."[7] Manager Williams knew something about hitting and thought Hondo was mostly mad at himself for flying out. Sportswriters nearly dropped their notebooks when the man who'd thrown the pitch agreed that Howard had gotten a bum deal. "I don't think he swung," Oakland reliever Paul Lindblad said. "He's so big he undoubtedly blocks the plate-umpire's view."[8]

The boot was the first for Howard, who had broken into the big leagues with the Dodgers in 1958. "Now Hondo will not be able to tell his children that he was never tossed out of a major league game," *Sporting News* chirped.[9] The *Washington Post* added that the last time Howard had left a game early was when he'd fouled out playing basketball for Ohio State University.

Howard was ejected only twice more during sixteen seasons in the Majors and once more as a manager. The ejection during his twenty-fifth game was the first in the majors for the umpire too. "I told him to shut up," Luciano said, "but he was way out of line—when he kept yelling, I had to throw him out."[10] The *Post* suggested that there must have been a full moon because "there seems to be an extraordinary number of players and managers ejected from games this year."[11]

The Senators often made Luciano's first season memorable. He worked a day-night July 5 doubleheader at Boston when the Red Sox saluted Williams as the greatest player in their history. He made the occasion doubly remarkable by doffing his cap (without actually tipping it) to the crowd. After winning the afternoon contest, Williams's Nats were losing the nightcap badly. Luciano was behind the plate when a brushback war broke out during the eighth inning of what a Boston sportswriter called "one of the wildest games ever seen at [owner Tom] Yawkey's house of thrills in years."[12]

Boston starter Sonny Siebert plunked Howard and threw close to Ken McMullen at the top of the frame. During the bottom half, Washington reliever Bob Humphreys buzzed Carl Yastrzemski before walking him then threw twice over the head of Reggie Smith. The *Boston Herald Traveler* said it was a trifle questionable why Siebert had hit Howard, "but there's little doubt Ted ordered Reggie's trip to the dirt."[13]

Luciano started out toward the mound. Smith dropped his bat and headed out behind him. The benches and bullpens emptied, Frank Howard holding off five Red Sox himself and tucking one under arm. But it was a typical baseball scuffle with more shoving than hitting. "Both managers and the umpires had a long chat," the *Washington Star* reported, "but it appeared that Luciano, a rookie ump, had permitted the situation to get out of control."[14]

Despite the drama nobody got the thumb, which wouldn't have been the case later in Luciano's career. In his report to the league the ump credited crewmate Frank Umont, working third base, with getting the situation under control. "Mr. Umont restored order almost immediately and took both managers aside, telling them this must stop. . . . No other pitch came close," Luciano wrote.[15]

The rookie ump already knew the terrible effect an injury could have on an athlete's career. Now he knew how to stop suspected headhunting, always one of his top priorities from then on. The next incident came only three nights later as Detroit played in Beantown. Luciano's suspect this time was Tiger star southpaw Mickey Lolich, who sent Yastrzemski sprawling with a pitch during the fourth inning.

Lolich said later that he was pitching Yaz up and in, across the letters, not trying to hit him. Luciano, unconvinced, walked out to the mound. "I don't know if that was intentional or not," he said, "but don't come close again." Lolich couldn't believe it. "He didn't even warn me," the pitcher exclaimed. "He wouldn't have come out at all if the third base ump hadn't told him to."[16]

One paper applauded Luciano's quick action and his work throughout the series. "He gets there, and he did not get any beefs on balls and strikes," the *Boston Herald Traveler* said. "He also gave quick warning when a dusting match started Tuesday night. It stopped."[17] During a series in New York later that month, Yankees pitcher-turned-broadcaster Whitey Ford also gave Luciano "a strong verbal medal for his unruffled handling of a hot-night of gripes."[18]

The moment that moved and touched everyone, however, came during a day game at Yankee Stadium on Sunday, July 20. The Yankees and Senators were tied 2–2 at the top of the eighth inning when plate umpire Luciano suddenly called time. Stadium announcer Bob Shepherd told a Bat Day crowd of nearly thirty-three thousand that *Apollo 11* had landed on the moon. "The youngsters and oldsters roared their approval while waving their bats in triumph."[19] The sound system played a recording of "America the Beautiful," after which the scoreboard flashed WE'RE ON THE MOON. The Senators, of course, went on to lose the game 3–2 in eleven innings.

ON EARTH THREE WEEKS LATER, Luciano saw firsthand what a ball to the head could do to a player. The lesson never left him. He was behind the plate at Detroit when Tiger Earl Wilson unleashed a fastball that struck California Angel Tom Egan just above the left cheekbone. Although Egan had homered earlier, the pitch was clearly accidental. Wilson trotted in and kicked at the dirt in anguish as the batter lay crumpled. Medical crew carried catcher Egan off on a stretcher and rushed him to an area hospital.

Angels manager Harold "Lefty" Phillips had no doubt it was a brushback pitch but didn't think hitting Egan was intentional. "When a guy throws as hard as Wilson sometimes it's kind of tough to see the ball," he said.[20] The Tiger pitcher fretted about the fallen Angel, saying he was trying to keep the ball up. Wilson said Luciano told him afterward that Egan "sort of froze on the pitch. . . . I hope he's all right."[21] Fortunately, Egan suffered no fracture, only a mild concussion.

Luciano worked the rest of the 1969 season relatively unnoticed. He felt healthier, having given up smoking along with colleagues Haller and Umont (Honochick didn't smoke). Luciano used his thumb only once more, in late August, tossing White Sox second baseman Bobby Knoop for arguing a third strike versus the Indians. The boot became part of perhaps the first bit of Luciano Lore, the ump telling John Fox later that Knoop was the second in a trio of ejections during three consecutive games—supposedly preceded by Duke Sims (on a day when Luciano didn't work) and followed by Ken "Hawk" Harrelson (who played the entire game).

There was also his reacquaintance with Earl Weaver, now managing in Baltimore. Luciano told Fox the Orioles skipper was unbelievable but added that since he didn't curse on the field, "you don't have grounds to throw him out except for the rule—for which I thank baseball!—prohibiting dispute of balls and strikes!"[22] Luciano failed to note that despite working twenty-five games with the Birds that season, he didn't chase Weaver even once.

DESPITE GAINING FIFTY POUNDS after he stopped smoking, Luciano grew more spirited on the diamond during his second American League season in 1970. Increasingly, in a process he later called "jazzing it up," Luciano was becoming the true Ronnie his family, friends, and former teammates had known all along.[23]

The *Chicago Sun-Times* said Luciano was nothing short of glorious in calling a strike. "The index finger goes straight out and then, as the arm comes back, Ron pivots spectacularly and jams his fist in the general direction of the batter's dugout. This umpire wants everybody to know."[24] The *Los Angeles Times* ran four photos across its sports page, presenting Luciano as a "study in emotions as he moves around first base" during an Angels game at Anaheim.[25] The *Chicago Tribune* said he'd made one of the quickest and most favorable impressions of any new Major League umpire. "Rushed to the majors last year because of the latest expansion, the colorful, 33-year-old bachelor from Endicott, N. Y., has become one of the American League's most respected arbiters."[26]

Inspiration for this vibrance came partly from August Donatelli, one of his officiating heroes. A small man with a big reputation, Donatelli was a National League umpire from 1950 through 1973. Luciano said that now, if a call was correct, people didn't care how an ump made it, but during the 1940s and earlier, all umpires' calls were more mechanical. "Augie changed all that," Luciano said. "He put his hand on the catcher, put one leg way back, and was very demonstrative in his call."[27]

Donatelli understood his admirer's unorthodox style and thought that despite appearances, Luciano was as serious as he could be. The older veteran didn't regard a few extra gestures added to a call as showboating. "He was that way, so that's the way he umpired," Donatelli said later. "It was natural; he never took his eye off the play."[28] But it had taken Luciano six seasons to relax this way. "I certainly wasn't a character in the minor leagues and during my first full season in the majors," he would write. "I was so nervous about getting each call correct that I didn't dare do anything even slightly out of character. Or what was later to become in character."[29]

During 1970 Luciano worked mainly with Bob Stewart, Merle Anthony, and John "Red" Flaherty, an AL umpire since 1953. He again saw firsthand the dangers inherent in baseball while working the plate May 31 for an Orioles-versus-Angels game at Anaheim. A fastball got away from reliever Ken Tatum during the eighth inning and struck Baltimore center fielder Paul Blair in the face. "It made a 'splat' sound like someone slapping jello," the horrified ump recalled.[30] The pitch broke Blair's nose and fractured the bone below his left eye. Luciano thought Blair was dead and frantically signaled for help.

Blair's mother lived in Los Angeles and rushed weeping out of the stands. Manager Earl Weaver tried to comfort her as teammates carried the stricken Oriole off the field on a stretcher. Blair missed three weeks of play following surgery. The beaning traumatized Luciano, who later considered it the worst sight he'd ever seen on a ballfield. "I was never the same umpire—after seeing Blair lying unconscious in the dirt I couldn't tolerate pitchers trying to hit a batter in the head," he wrote.[31]

CROWD ROWDINESS ALSO PLAGUED the 1970 season. Troubles began Opening Day when dozens of young fans flooded the field at Pittsburgh's Forbes Field, fistfights broke out in the stands at Chicago's Wrigley Field, and sixteen beatings and robberies were reported at Cleveland's Municipal Stadium. During a mid-April doubleheader in New York with the Indians, fans whom the *New York Daily News* called "the 'yoot' of America" warmed up by booing commissioner Bowie Kuhn before pelting players and the bullpen with paper, cups, balls, and cans.[32]

The umpires huddled with stadium security personnel several times to try to get the situation under control. The yoots stormed the field at the end of the second game, mistakenly believing it was over when a throwing error actually had tied the score and prolonged play. The behavior embarrassed the Bronx club on the day it dedicated centerfield monuments to two Yankee icons. The *Daily News* opined that instead of plaques for Joe DiMaggio and Mickey Mantle "the Yankees should have hung some of the kids on the centerfield wall at the Stadium yesterday."[33]

Luciano was officiating when the Indians returned to the Bronx for a Wednesday afternoon doubleheader in late June. Yankee outfielder Bobby Murcer hit four consecutive homers, three during the second game with

Luciano behind the plate, but his heroics were a mere footnote to other events. Cleveland left fielder Vada Pinson punched Yankee pitcher Stan Bahnsen after a tag play at home ended the top of the fifth inning. Luciano ejected Pinson but let the hurler stay, prompting a protest from normally mild-mannered Indian manager Alvin Dark.

The crowd was stirred up when play resumed during the Yankee half of the fifth. A firecracker exploded at home plate beside Cleveland catcher Ray Fosse, narrowly missing the ump, who mistook it for a rubber ball tossed from the upper deck. Luciano suspected that the cracker was meant for him and said it probably would have hit him if he hadn't had his chest protector up. Fosse saw the projectile too but didn't have time to react before it hit his spikes. "All of a sudden it went off, and I felt a stabbing, burning pain in my foot," he said.[34] Fosse reflexively reached up to protect his eyes before he felt his right foot hurting; he considered himself lucky to escape worse injury.

An usher grabbed the bomber as a Cleveland trainer rushed to treat minor burns to his catcher's foot, instep, and sole. Fosse continued the game after a six-minute delay. According to the *Daily News*, the crowd of nearly thirty-two thousand "cheered wildly when it was announced that the fathead who has done this foolish thing has been apprehended."[35] In an echo of the Blair beaning, Luciano's mother was watching from the stands. As they rode back downtown, he asked if she had been scared. "I've seen you on the football field enough," Josephine replied, "why am I going to get scared now?"[36]

The rest of the season passed without serious incident. Luciano again completed the schedule without ejecting Earl Weaver, but he certainly knew by now that a combative manager wasn't his only challenge. Umpiring was a tough profession. Gone was the close camaraderie of playing on a large football team. True, he had three crewmates now in the American League, more than in the Florida State, Eastern, or International, but every umpire lived under continual pressure. Travel alone was a constant irritant, more serious in the Majors than in the regional circuits.

A Minneapolis sports editor wrote that Luciano, DiMuro, John Rice, and Larry Barnett had traveled to the West Coast seven times during the 1970 season. "Once in 1969 Luciano worked back-to-back doubleheaders in Baltimore and Seattle and slept in an airport during the trip."[37] The task of arranging all that rushing around fell to the umps themselves. They paid their own daily bills out of a per diem allowance that sportswriter Edwin Pope said was "better suited to sparrows." Pope had once heard a World Series umpire shout during checkout, "I hope your bleeping hotel burns down!"[38]

The *New York Times* wrote some years afterward that the style of travel for umpires during the expansion era differed greatly from the ballplayers'. "The players never have to make a plane reservation, check in or out of a hotel, pay a bill, or do anything so burdensome as lift their own luggage."[39] Umpires enjoyed none of those privileges and instead were their own travel agents, typically divvying up responsibilities for booking planes, rental cars, and hotels.

It was a strange and often lonely existence. After the relaxed atmosphere of spring training, umpires spent the season on the road without vacations, working 162 games and sometimes more to make up for another crew's rainouts. They routinely flew 100,000 to 125,000 miles during a season, going commercially rather than on a club's charter flight. AL ump Larry Napp considered travel the worst part of his job. "I'm married 30 years and it seems like I've been married 15," he said,[40] Doubleheaders were especially rough, he added, because umps had to leave right away, fly across the country, and be ready for another game the next night.

Home life suffered too. Married umpires missed birthdays, anniversaries, and everyday chores. AL umpire Bill Kunkel once got a call from his wife saying their lawn needed mowing. "I can't reach it from here," he told her. "There's no lawn mower in the world that will reach from Milwaukee to New Jersey."[41] Many umpires were divorced, and just as many drank too much. Quite a few became devotees of TV soap operas. "'One Life to Live' *is* fantastic, though," Luciano allowed.[42]

Barred from socializing with ballplayers or managers, they relied on each other, but even close-knit crews sometimes grew bored of one another's company. Longtime AL umpire and future Hall of Famer Nestor Chylak said they didn't sleep together or call each other for breakfast at nine o'clock every morning, "but we will have dinner when possible."[43]

Luciano tried to relax by reading. He claimed that nobody in America had cried harder over the passing of Agatha Christie. He'd also loved Shakespeare since his Syracuse days and estimated he'd read *Macbeth* forty times; the *Binghamton Press* said "a compact volume of the tragedies is part of his all-summer traveling ensemble."[44] The American League later exaggerated by listing Luciano in a press guide as a Shakespeare scholar.

The ump also watched birds to help cope with life on the road. He said he'd learned from a cousin, ironically while toting a shotgun to hunt them. Luciano explained that when he missed, he still enjoyed watching a bird fly away. He claimed to tote the heaviest luggage in the league, filled with volumes of Shakespeare, notebooks, bird guides, and several pairs of binoculars.

"I'm an ornithologist. That means I study birds," Luciano said.[45] He added, however, that birds tended not to appear in the mornings when he was staying on the thirtieth floor of a New York City hotel. A Syracuse newspaper called him "quite possibly the biggest bird watcher east of the Mississippi," but Luciano managed to hide his avocation for several seasons.[46] He confessed to colleagues only when his binoculars led to suspicions he was a Peeping Tom. Afterward, crewmates knew he was only a harmless "orni-something."[47]

During a subsequent season Luciano would appear on the NBC pregame show *The Baseball World of Joe Garagiola*. He'd talk about birdwatching and compare everyday players to robins and umpires to eagles or perhaps a hornbill, "which is ugly, but very, very big and domineering and carries a lot of weight."[48] A *Baltimore Sun* writer followed up by asking who most resembled a noisy blue jay. "Manager!" Luciano chirped, without naming names. Yankee Graig Nettles reminded him of a yellow bellied sapsucker, "a bird who goes about his daily occupation with hardly a commotion." The woodpecker? "A player who keeps beating on the side of my head. Talker. Constant noise, noise, noise."[49]

Major League umpires all developed coping mechanisms away from the field. But on the diamond they supported one another unconditionally, no matter their foibles, quibbles, or disagreements. At the end of the 1970 season, they closed ranks and briefly went on strike, demanding better pay for umps working the postseason. The leagues balked and hired Minor League and former Major League umpires to work the first games of the playoffs. An unnamed longtime ump told the *New York Times* he was shocked and angry. "It was like saying they didn't care for us," he said, "that any garbageman could do our job."[50] The umps and management soon hammered out a new four-year contract, however, paving the way for a tranquil World Series, which Earl Weaver's Orioles won in five games over the Cincinnati Reds.

LUCIANO WORKED WITH RED FLAHERTY again in 1971, along with Bill Kunkel and John Rice. The season was uneventful aside from two incidents that enhanced his growing reputation as a good umpire with an imposing presence. The first event was accidental.

The Endicotter worked second base during an Athletics-Yankees game June 1 in New York. Oakland's phenomenal young lefthander Vida Blue won 5–2 during a complete game in front of over thirty thousand fans. But what the *New York Times* called a "freakish accident" to Yankee shortstop Gene Michael during the ninth inning sidetracked the post-game chatter about the game's newest drawing card.[51]

Yankee catcher Thurman Munson threw wide as Oakland runner Joe Rudi broke for second base. Michael ran to cover the bag then reached left in a vain attempt to stop the ball from bouncing into center field. "Stick" crashed into Luciano, slashing his lip and suffering whiplash to his neck when his face hit the ump's elbow. No one blamed Luciano for the collision. After x-rays at Lenox Hill Hospital Michael went home wearing a neck brace and missed two games. He didn't remember what had happened. "I got hit, then my head started hurting," he said. "I couldn't figure it out."[52]

The Yankees and A's met on the opposite coast twelve days later, with Blue again on the mound. Luciano worked first base as Oakland rapped twenty hits during a 13–3 shellacking before thirty-five thousand fans. Yankee first baseman Johnny Ellis began beefing with Luciano during Oakland's five-run fifth inning. Ellis thought he had tagged Sal Bando, who slid around him for an infield hit. The 6-foot-2, 220-pound former high school fullback and linebacker unwisely shoved the former All-American. Luciano pushed back.

"However, both cooled off quickly, the kid apologized and Luciano didn't kick him out," the *Daily News* said.[53] The paper later added that Ellis was "slammed back by Luciano's hamlike hand and quickly cooled off. Luciano didn't kick him out, and his report to the league will not be severe."[54]

The *Newark Star-Ledger* in New Jersey reported that Ellis backed off and the ump let the whole matter drop, "so let's hear it for Luciano."[55] The ex-Lion didn't realize at first that he'd even put his hands on the Yankee. "I guess 15 years of football makes me react to charge 'unconsciously,'" he said, adding that the same thing might have happened with Stick Michael. "He was coming towards me, I reacted and I moved towards him and we collided."[56]

The pressure of working big league games affected him. Despite all his reading and birdwatching, Luciano developed stomach problems. He'd never had them before, and the only difference now was umpiring. He was also drinking more than was healthy, building toward a fifth a day before he cut back several seasons later. Alcohol was a common problem among umpires, who told each other that if you couldn't umpire while hung over, you couldn't umpire. "I didn't have to drink every night when I was umpiring," AL ump Don Denkinger said later, "but I did."[57] Luciano thought Bill Haller was probably the only Major League ump who didn't drink at all. "This job is perfect for broken marriages and alcoholism" became something of a mantra for the Endicotter.[58]

Most of the time, however, Luciano put on a jovial face for sportswriters. He polished his quotes and revised his curriculum vitae as he attracted more and more attention. An early bit of Luciano Lore appeared during the summer in a wire article from the Associated Press. "I was playing for the college stars in Chicago and Big Daddy Gene Lipscomb almost tore my arm off," Luciano said. "I was an offensive tackle, but he took the offense out of me." He then added more truthfully, "Umpiring—this is the most enjoyable thing I've ever done. I like the pressure and the action."[59]

THE AMERICAN LEAGUE assigned Luciano to work the 1972 season with Umont, Jim Odom, and Denkinger, an umpiring partner back in the International League. A players' strike the *Chicago Tribune* called "baseball's darkest stretch since the Black Sox scandal" delayed opening day by two weeks.[60] It also shortened teams' seasons by six to eight games apiece and delayed pay for AL umps, who didn't receive their first scheduled checks on April 1. Once games finally got under way, Luciano pasted Oakland pitcher Johnny Lee "Blue Moon" Odom in the face, much as he had done to Stick Michael.

The accident happened when Luciano called Angels' outfielder Mickey Rivers safe at the plate during a May 23 game in Oakland. Odom insisted that Rivers was out by three feet. "Luciano wasn't in position to call it," he said. "I tried to get in there and say something and he was waving his arms and he hit me in the mouth."[61] Luciano told one writer he'd felt the pitcher's hands on his shoulders, spun around, and inadvertently smacked him, fortunately without injury. "Odom grabbed me from behind and I pushed him away," he told a different scribe.[62] Oakland catcher Dave Duncan said all he knew was the pair had collided "and Luciano's a lotta beef."[63]

Clearly it wasn't wise to get anywhere near the former All-America tackle during a close or fast-developing play. Odom later apologized and conceded that he shouldn't have touched the man behind the plate. Luciano apologized in turn for unintentionally smacking him. "Everyone got excited," Odom said. "He's usually a very good umpire, the best in the league, but he missed that one."[64]

Beside almost literally killing players, Luciano began killing them figuratively as well. He soon became famous for "shooting" runners out at first base, using his forefinger and thumb as a pistol. He wrote later that he began the practice in 1972, although wire photos showed him pointing at runners earlier, if perhaps not yet pulling the trigger. "Ronald Luciano looks more like an old Western gunfighter rather than an umpire as he goes through the contortions of calling Minnesota Twin Rod Carew out at first base," an Ohio paper had said the previous September.[65]

A shooting gesture like Luciano's would instantly be condemned and banned today. But fans during the 1970s had grown up watching movie and TV westerns starring Gene Autry, Roy Rogers, Hopalong Cassidy, and the Lone Ranger. The good guys in white hats never killed anyone, only winged them or shot six-shooters out of their hands. *Oh, Pancho! Oh, Cisco!* Big Loosh delighted people by duplicating what everyone had done a million times in their own backyards. Bang-bang-bang-bang! Out-out-out-OUT! The total of his consecutive *Out!* calls varied in the telling. Luciano claimed a personal record of eleven, which in time grew to twenty-one, before he settled on sixteen during interviews and in his memoir. Whatever the real number, it was extraordinary. Luciano Lore is fuzzy on specifics, but the ump always claimed that Amos Otis was his first victim.

Luciano knew the Kansas City Royal outfielder from the Jacksonville (Florida) Mets back in the International League. He often claimed that after initially calling fleet Otis out on every close play, he overcompensated and couldn't call him out at all. The embarrassing quirk continued when both reached the Major Leagues. Finally, according to one of the many accounts Luciano offered to sportswriters over the years, Otis hit a little tapper back to the mound.

The ump ran down the first base line screeching, "I gotcha you, I gotcha you." Then someone in the KC dugout yelled, "Why don't you shoot him?" Seconds later Luciano did. "I thought about it and I made a pistol out of my hand and started shooting him. The fans went wild."[66] Otis later confirmed that he was the first runner slain. "The way Lucie would shoot you is that you'd hit first base and run about five feet past it and you knew that you were out," he said. "He'd cock his gun and then shoot you. He'd make a lot of noise so the fans could hear him . . . 'Pow, pow, pow, pow!'"[67]

Luciano sometimes also blew imaginary smoke from his forefinger before slipping his weapon back into invisible leather. Sometimes players told him where to put the gun "and it was not in the holster."[68] Some accounts say he occasionally blew up a baserunner using an invisible hand grenade instead. Many players and umpires disliked the pantomime. Commissioner Bowie Kuhn and the American League didn't care for it either, but they didn't prohibit Luciano from doing it. Fans generally loved the performance. *Us* magazine noted that most umps made a fist, pumped the arm once, and were finished. "Luciano has been known to pump 26 [*sic*] times, while traveling about 13 feet laterally and yelling 'Out!' with such conviction that his mouth opens like the entrance to the Lincoln Tunnel."[69]

Umpires didn't like his habit of chatting with players, either. Arbiters weren't supposed to be friendly with anyone else on the ballfield. But Luciano was a cheerful chatterbox who approached players, coaches, fans, and vendors alike. Hall of Fame and former National League umpire (1941–65) John "Jocko" Conlan understood. He was a former player who like Luciano hadn't set out to become an umpire. An ump certainly might vow never to talk with players on the field. "But it isn't your nature to be that way," Conlan wrote. "And I did have the faculty, or the reputation, of being able to talk to a fellow and still throw him out of the ball game, if he deserved to be thrown out. So that my conversation with players had nothing to do with me umpiring the way I was supposed to umpire."[70] Luciano never expressed it exactly that way but was even more voluble than Conlan.

Despite his friendly and apparently carefree nature, Luciano was increasingly bothered by stomach trouble as the season wore on. He admitted later that he drank too much and neglected his diet. "That plus the tremendous pressure gave me ulcers."[71] He lost weight as his condition worsened. He felt so lightheaded September 13 that he fell asleep in a cab on his way to a game at Yankee Stadium. A visiting Red Sox coach thought he looked bad and wondered if he was all right. Luciano ran onto the field to begin the game, but he turned away and staggered into the home dugout, where he almost passed out. An ambulance rushed him away to Lenox Hill Hospital with internal hemorrhaging, still dressed for the game.

The doctor who attended Luciano was a baseball fan. "What are you doing here?" he asked.[72] The ump's sister Dee spoke with the *Binghamton Press* the following day. "Ron, who isn't careful about his diet, apparently had been eating less and less and feeling worse and worse," she said, "and when Don [Denkinger] told him he ought to take last night off, he wouldn't hear of it because the commissioner was going to be there."[73]

Doctors admitted Luciano to intensive care as his crewmates worked the game without him. The American League activated retired Hank Soar to take his place for what little was left of the season. Luciano remained hospitalized for two weeks before Dee's husband drove him back home to Endicott. The *Binghamton Press* said he was eager to get outside with a new English pointer called Jack, but physicians had ordered at least another week of bedrest. Luciano scoffed that other people were more worried about his ulcer than he was.

He gave a chatty interview during the World Series to the *Press*, which noted that his condition had improved "and he feels he could start working games this month, although he won't."[74] An appearance by Joe Rudi at an IBM awards dinner that November doubtless cheered the recuperating ump. The A's outfielder said he'd never had any problem with Luciano. "He's one of the best in the league," Rudi said. "He's concentrating out there all the time—he's in the game 100 per cent."[75]

Luciano finally was able to go hunting for a couple days at the end of the year. Best of all, the Boston Baseball Writers Association announced that it was presenting him with its annual Umpire of the Year Award at a dinner in January. A suburban newspaper noted Luciano's love of ornithology and the Bard, avocations that seemed unlikely for a big tough former tackle. But that's what made him different, the paper said. "And they may explain, in part, why he brings so much desire to succeed to his occupation as a baseball umpire."[76] The ump meanwhile was at home on the lookout for an escaped Monk parrot, an exotic South American bird spotted near the local airport. "It's something to think that a bird could be brought up here from a 100-degree plus climate and survive," Luciano said. "It's fascinating."[77]

He had ample time for reflection over the winter. For all that he'd gained from becoming an umpire, he also knew he'd lost something vital. Luciano began wondering how much longer he could continue wearing the mask. He gave an honest answer to a *Boston Globe* interviewer who asked about the difference between playing and umpiring. "For me it's the loss of glory, the sense of being a part of things," Luciano said. "If you win you get complimented, your spirits soar. If you lose, you are depressed and have to get yourself back. Those highs and lows are missing as an umpire."[78]

7 Showman

Luciano began the 1973 season in Arizona after nine previous springs in Florida. He later claimed that the league sent him there because he'd been a bad boy, although it seems unlikely for the umpire of the year. He loved working in the Cactus League with its fewer teams and freer atmosphere. He said it was a lot more fun because none of the teams out there played as if in a pennant race, as they did in Florida. "So every year I plead with the office," he explained. "'For heaven's sake, you're not going to send me to Arizona again, are you?' It always works!"[1] He missed a few calls in Mesa, but as a fan noted, it was spring training for umps too.

American League umpires faced two changes once the regular season got under way. The first was sartorial. The arbiters no longer ruled their domain "looking like refugees from a settlement house—Messrs. Doom, Gloom, Tomb and Broom," the *Boston Globe* quipped.[2] Decked in double-knit maroon blazers and blue trousers, they looked now as if they might have stepped from pages of *Gentleman's Quarterly*. They continued wearing the maroon jackets the rest of the decade, whenever conditions were too cool for shirtsleeves. The Yankees paced them by becoming the last Major League club to switch to double-knits, although they retained their pinstripes.

The bigger change in the AL—but in not the NL for nearly another half century—was the designated pinch-hitter rule, which created the position known now as the designated hitter. The AL umpires sat through a two-and-a-half-hour briefing during the preseason to understand the innovation. Luciano thought it was about time. "After all," he said, "it's been 81 years since they made a major rule change in the game."[3] He wrongly predicted that within two years, baseball would see speedy designated runners as well.

Luciano's 1973 crewmates were Haller, veteran Marty Springstead, and Dave Phillips, working his third season in the AL. Haller was de facto crew chief because of the illness of Larry Napp, an AL umpire since 1951. Despite having to swig antacids to control his ulcer, Luciano took charge of the crew's supper arrangements. If someone wanted stroganoff that night, the son of café owners called around until he found a good restaurant that served it. "Ronnie was a wonderful person to spend time with," Phillips remembered.[4]

Even when ill or tired, Luciano was a showman. Phillips recalled watching him trudge wearily up the steps to the field at Cleveland's mammoth old Municipal Stadium. He paused at the top before throwing his arms wide as if signaling a touchdown. "And he turned around to all the fans like, 'Here I am,'" Phillips said. "The people just loved it."[5] He considered his pal an entertainer equal to famed baseball clown Max Patkin. Luciano once got so distracted behind the plate that he began a game without wearing his mask. He was often so besieged by fans, friends, writers, and people wanting tickets that he took hotel phones off the hook and shoved them in drawers simply to get some peace.

The first half of the season passed with the usual minor disputes. Luciano made a controversial call at first base on May 2 in Yankee Stadium, a two-run double that swung the game in the Royals' favor. "When the ball landed, I said to myself, 'it landed foul so it must be foul,'" Luciano explained. "But it went over the bag, so it must be fair."[6] Objections from Yankees manager Ralph Houk did no good.

Luciano's animated performance later that month in Texas sparked more criticism. A Fort Worth paper said he signaled an out like a man with St. Vitus' dance, "a shuddering series of righthand thrusts into the ozone." The paper added that the gestures were offensive to old veterans such as Hank Soar, retired now and serving as an umpire scout. "I think the greatest compliment that can be paid an umpire is obscurity," Soar said.[7] But Luciano was exactly the man Rangers manager Whitey Herzog wanted behind the plate for the Major League debut of eighteen-year-old pitcher David Clyde.

The Rangers, formerly the Senators, were the second team to leave the nation's capital. They were awful, having lost a hundred games the previous season on their way to losing 105 this year. Clyde was the country's top draft pick, a $125,000 bonus baby who had tossed nine no-hitters during high school in Texas. He had graduated less than a month earlier, and

Herzog feared that Clyde's parents, the Rangers, and the pitcher himself all expected too much too soon. He was glad Luciano would be working the plate on June 27. "A lot of these old heads like to put the squeeze on a kid like Clyde," Herzog said. "But Luciano will call a fair game for him."[8]

Herzog sent the kid to the plate with the lineup card the night before his debut. It gave him the chance to talk with Luciano about balks and not touching his fingers to his mouth while standing near the pitching rubber. Again the skipper was happy, because Clyde had gone to his mouth on every pitch while throwing batting practice.

His debut drew the first sellout crowd in the club's brief history. The teenaged lefty "also packed the parking lots, the Turnpike, the Turnpike exits, the concession stands and the press box," the *Fort Worth Star-Telegram* said.[9] The Rangers pushed the first pitch back fifteen minutes to 7:45 to give fans time to filter into the park. Among the crowd were nine of Clyde's relatives plus his girlfriend, high school coach, and principal. American League president Joe Cronin called it the biggest debut since Bob Feller's.

The youngster's first offering was low and away, but the crowd booed Luciano for calling it a ball. When Clyde fired a strike, the ump "nearly pulled 71 muscles and you would have thought these Rangers were going to stop the game and hold an on-the-spot ceremony to retire Clyde's number"—32, worn by Sandy Koufax before him.[10] Clyde struck out the side after walking the Twins' first two batters. He threw 112 pitches over five innings, struck out eight, and walked seven. Clyde gave up only one hit (a two-run homer) and was the winning pitcher in the 4–3 final.

The Rangers didn't stir from last place that season, but as a Texas newspaper later said, the rookie proved that "metroplex people could be attracted to baseball."[11] He ultimately made eight-four appearances over five seasons with the Rangers and Indians, winning eighteen games while losing thirty-three.

According to the ump, Clyde showed a decent fastball but no composure during his first outing. Luciano wrote that it was "obvious after a few pitches he shouldn't have been pitching in the major leagues."[12] The Twins didn't offer much praise either. Second baseman Rod Carew walked three times and wasn't impressed at all. Outfielder Bobby Darwin went 0 for 3 but said Clyde "ain't no Nolan Ryan that's for sure."[13]

RYAN WAS A NATURAL WONDER. The California Angels star had thrown his first no-hitter two months earlier at Kansas City and was building a fearsome reputation as a flamethrower. Luciano later said and wrote that he sometimes had to call Ryan's fastball by sound because it was too fast to see; sometimes, he added, it seemed literally to explode because it tricked the eye and the brain. This was more Luciano Lore, but not by much. California catcher Art Kusnyer also remembered the sound of Ryan's pitches—the fastball went *Whoosh!* while the curve was *Whoosh-ppt!* because it broke sharply downward.[14]

Ryan was glad to see Luciano behind the plate July 15 versus the Tigers in the Motor City. He knew the ump heard criticism from people who disliked his showmanship and colorful ways and believed that some arbiters envied the attention he drew. "I always thought Ron was a dynamic guy and a fine umpire," Ryan later wrote. "When Ron umpired behind the plate, he gave me a good effort, although there were times when he could get distracted."[15]

One distraction this day in Detroit was first baseman Norm Cash. Ryan pitilessly mowed down the Tiger batters in front of forty-one thousand fans. The Angel battery constantly changed signs, suspecting the Tigers of stealing and relaying them via the scoreboard. If so, the tactic was a bust. Ryan struck out seventeen, the most ever in a no-hitter, and walked only four. "My God," Kusnyer heard Luciano say, "No one's gonna touch him today."[16] When Cash strode to the plate with two outs in the bottom of the ninth, he asked whether Luciano was going to check his bat.

The ump glanced over and stepped away laughing. The Tigers' last hope stood at the plate clutching a leg from a clubhouse table. It was "square and knobby," recalled Kusnyer, whose fingers were purple from fastballs popping into his mitt. "I might as well use this," Cash said of his cudgel, often remembered as a piano leg in Tiger lore.[17] After Luciano ordered him to get rid of it, the slugger popped out to end the second of Ryan's seven no-hitters.

Ryan said Luciano was "very, very good" behind the plate. "He didn't have many borderline calls, and that made it easier for him."[18] Luciano in turn said Ryan's fastball and curve were so tough that one or the other ought to be outlawed. He never worked another no-hitter and regarded the game in Detroit as the finest game he ever umpired.

THE AL SWITCHED AROUND its umpiring crews at midseason. Haller and Luciano began working beside Jerry Neudecker and Merle Anthony. Anthony said no reason was given for the change. Luciano also received an honor due a veteran umpire and worked the left field line at the July 24 All-Star Game in Kansas City. The first-time ump received instructions to be extra careful and tolerant on the field while Nestor Chylak worked the plate.

The event was a thrill for the players and for Luciano, who came away with a couple of autographed All-Star Game balls. It was fairly ho-hum for everyone else. The *Kansas City Star* called the nearly three hour affair a "dose of Nodoz and not so much a game as a parade," with fifty-four players playing in the 7–1 National League win.[19] Had he worked first base instead of the line, Luciano still wouldn't have been able to "shoot" out AL starting centerfielder Amos Otis. The Royal played four innings, stroked two singles, batted in a run, and stole second base off the NL starter Claude Osteen and catcher Johnny Bench.

If practically unnoticed during the All-Star Game, Luciano attracted a flood of ink throughout the summer. As complaints about umpiring continued, a Texas sportswriter wrote that American League umps fell into two categories: "Nestor Chylak and Ron Luciano, and the rest."[20] The scribe regarded them as by far the best in the league, the others ranging from incompetent to adequate. Players and managers never rapped Chylak or Luciano, he added, because they hustled. The *National Observer* likewise called Luciano the AL's leading impresario, "who performs at once like a tackle, an Indian doing a war dance, and a radio broadcaster."[21]

Haller praised his pal too. "Ronnie could work with the devil—he's that good," he said. Haller added that if Luciano had a fault it stemmed from playing football at a high level, which meant he could "find himself sympathizing with a ballplayer."[22]

As his fifth Major League season wound down, Luciano still hadn't ejected Earl Weaver. He shared his tale about throwing Weaver out of their first four games back in the EL but added truthfully that he hadn't yet run the Oriole skipper in the big leagues and thought he had somewhat mellowed. "I think he [Weaver] finally realized that if he hollers and screams on every pitch, he makes us nervous."[23] The harmony between them finally vanished during the second game of a doubleheader on September 29, the last day of the regular season.

The Orioles were bound for the playoffs for the fourth time since Weaver had taken the helm. They dropped the first game of the twin bill but won the second, despite an incident that the *Baltimore Sun* said saw Weaver ejected by one of the umpires, "apparently without the other three or a great majority of the fans aware of it." The lone ump naturally was Luciano, who had gathered with the others to hear Weaver's objection about a fan interference call during the home half of the fifth inning. Concluding his lecture, the *Sun* said, "Weaver returned to the dugout, and hardly a few seconds passed when third base arbiter Luciano was observed pointing to the runway from the bench to the clubhouse."[24]

The ejection was so quiet that writers in the press box sent a message to Neudecker behind the plate asking if the skipper had really been tossed. Neudecker had to check with Luciano to learn that he had. The phantom thumbing provided no hint to the wild and infamous antagonism that later developed between the umpire and manager. The Orioles went on to lose the league championship to the Oakland A's, who were on course to win the second of their three consecutive World Series titles.

THE AMERICAN LEAGUE announced the retirement of four umpires a month later. Their unexpected exit was the opening salvo in a battle over the Major League umpires' contact due to expire at the end of the year. The four departing umpires—Red Flaherty, Jim Honochick, Frank Umont, and John Rice—all were in their mid-fifties and former crewmates of Luciano's. Umont didn't go voluntarily, and it was unclear whether he'd been retired or fired. "No notice. No nothing," he said. "I just get a form letter for 20 years service."[25]

The league promoted three umpires from the Minors and took options on two others. The Major League umps reached a new three-year deal the first week of the following March, but the loss of eighty-five years' combined experience was apparent throughout 1974. Dick Butler, AL supervisor of umpires, said the league had a trio of first-year umpires and only seven who had been on the job when he'd arrived only five seasons earlier. "People forget that one of the things that helps make a good umpire is experience," Butler said. "It takes five years to sell himself."[26]

The new season brought more of the fan violence plaguing Major League baseball. The worst was the Dime Beer Night riot June 4 at Municipal Stadium in Cleveland. Drunken fans invaded the field at the bottom of the ninth and fought with visiting Rangers players and the Indians who raced out to help them. Twenty Cleveland squad cars roared to the scene, broke up the brawling, and arrested a dozen troublemakers "They were uncontrolled beasts," growled crew chief Nestor Chylak, a wounded veteran of the Battle of the Bulge during World War II. "I've never seen anything like it except in a zoo."[27]

Luciano was more concerned with reducing the type of violence that had felled Paul Blair. A ball that accidentally got away was regrettable but understandable. An intentional high-and-inside brushback pitch was something very different. Luciano tangled with Rangers manager Billy Martin over the issue during a July 14 doubleheader at Milwaukee. Martin had replaced Whitey Herzog and was managing his third club after the Twins and Tigers before going on to lead the Yankees (hired and fired five times) and the Oakland A's. The game in Milwaukee was the beginning of Martin's long rocky relationship with Luciano, who suspected him of ordering a pitcher to throw dangerously close to batters on purpose.

The two had clashed earlier during an April game at Arlington, when Luciano ruled a Texas runner out for intentionally letting a ball hit him to avoid a probable double play. Martin protested the game but wasn't upheld. Luciano was now working the plate during the first game of a Sunday doubleheader. Martin got upset before the game even began, believing that the Brewers had thrown at his shortstop on Saturday. As he delivered his lineup card, Martin told the umpires and Brewer manager Del Crandall that his pitcher would knock down Brewer shortstop Robin Yount the first time he came up.

Martin said later he'd never order a pitcher to hit a batter but that a brushback was part of the game. "I have to protect my player, who was thrown at four times."[28] He added afterward that he was simply being honest.

Luciano had no patience with such sentiments after seeing Blair accidentally hit and bleeding in the dirt. Jocko Conlan had felt the same way. To Conlan's way of thinking, a beanball pitcher wasn't throwing a baseball but wielding a weapon. "It's like having a knife and a gun," he wrote.[29]

The fireworks in Wisconsin didn't begin immediately, Yount hitting safely his first three times up opposite Jackie Brown on the way to a 9–3 Brewers win. But when a pitch whizzed close to Yount's head his fourth time up in the sixth inning, Luciano warned reliever Pete Broberg. Martin told him that Broberg was just wild. "Fine, but don't let him get wild around his head," the ump retorted.[30]

Luciano warned both skippers when Brewer starter Ed Sprague sent Texas batter George Scott diving to the dirt at the top of the seventh. He told them to knock it off or they were gone. An inning later Broberg threw a pitch behind Milwaukee center fielder Bob Coluccio's head. The ump heaved the pitcher and his manager. Martin claimed that Broberg was simply a wild pitcher, "but I didn't like him being wild around guy's heads," Luciano said. "Maybe I was wrong."[31]

Martin agreed that he was. "He's never been wronger in his life," the skipper said. "I'd always considered him a good umpire."[32] Broberg said he tripped delivering his pitch and later apologized to Coluccio.

The chaos continued during the second game as Luciano worked at third base. He thumbed Martin again during the first inning for arguing that the Brewers were now throwing at the Rangers. Two innings later he also tossed Rangers coach Frank Lucchesi and second baseman Lenny Randle for arguing his call when Randle was thrown out at third. Plate umpire Art Frantz capped the day by ejecting Crandall during the fifth for arguing an out call at home. Although the clubs split the double bill, a wire story said the Rangers were well ahead in one statistic, "personnel thrown out of the game."[33] Luciano remembered the double bill as perhaps the most unpleasant day he ever spent on the diamond.

Former Yankees general manager Lee MacPhail, now president of the American League, backed his ump's actions during the first game by handing Martin a fine and a three-day suspension. Oddly, after throwing the famously volatile manager out of both ends of the doubleheader, Luciano never ejected Martin from another game. Instead, he soon got into hot water himself.

Luciano worked third base during the second game of an A's-Twins twinight doubleheader August 4 at Metropolitan Stadium in Bloomington, Minnesota. The night entered Luciano Lore because of the man standing beside him, Oakland third baseman Sal Bando. The two Italian-Americans doubtless chatted during the game. As Luciano repeated the tale for years, Bando was in a batting slump and asked what he was doing wrong. Luciano supposedly suggested he was standing too far off the plate.

Bando actually was on a tear, however, "off and running for most valuable player . . . an uncanny RBI man."[34] He'd blasted his fifteenth homer of the season a day earlier and needed no advice from a former football lineman. When he stepped to the plate during the sixth inning with two outs and Claudell Washington dancing off first after a single, Bando parked a pitch from righthander Bill Hands in the left field pavilion for home run number sixteen, a two-run shot that gave him twenty RBI over his last fourteen games. Luciano clapped like a schoolboy.

"Salvatore, attababy *paisano*," he shouted as Bando rounded third base. Luciano never really explained cheering for Bando, except to say he was a fan who appreciated the outstanding plays he was privileged to see as an umpire. He wouldn't have been surprised had MacPhail sent him a letter of reprimand, but *Sports Illustrated* said the AL president should save the postage. "The time to send all your 'Dear Mr. Luciano' letters is when Mr. Luciano begins to take the game, its people and its environs too seriously," the magazine advised.[35]

Luciano's applause for Bando's homer boosted his appeal to fans but lowered it among colleagues whose more traditional values favored a more impartial—and less demonstrative—approach behind the plate. Years later the NL arbiter who took over the Somers umpiring school said that lack of dignity set Luciano apart. "He doesn't care about dignity," Harry Wendelstedt said. "He is his own bombastic element."[36] Bill Haller understood Wendelstedt's point but defended Luciano.

"I loved the guy," said Haller, who treated Luciano like a younger brother and tried with little success to curb his excesses and prevent repercussions. "I'd say, 'Listen, Loochie, if it was up to me I'd fine you so often you'd owe money to the league.' I always thought Ron was using umpiring as a vehicle to other things."[37] Luciano spoke about paying frequent fines throughout his career, but Haller remembered only four or five being levied.

Earl Weaver stood with the many baseball men who didn't appreciate Luciano's shenanigans. The pair met again at Baltimore during a September 11 doubleheader with the Yankees. Unsurprisingly, they clashed on a checked-swing call as Luciano worked at first base. The *Baltimore Sun* said Weaver got the boot after he "apparently gestured for divine guidance, looking to the sky with his arms held wide before finally disappearing into the dugout."[38] Luciano dryly explained that with his cap off and arms raised, Weaver appeared to praying "Please throw me out."[39] So he did.

Despite what Wendelstedt or Weaver thought, players across the American League rated Luciano highly. As complaints against AL umpires multiplied, Yankee Sandy Alomar said that Luciano and Chylak were the only umpires who admitted when they missed a call. The second baseman wondered why others didn't do the same. "That would end the argument," he said. "They can't change it, but at least they can admit it."[40]

Alomar wasn't the only player who respected the pair, including some of Weaver's. Luciano and Chylak were the only AL umpires rated excellent in a poll conducted late in the season by the Major League Baseball Players Association. Haller rated right behind them as above average, while Lou DiMuro was merely average. In the National League, only veteran umpire Doug Harvey, like Chylak, a future Hall of Famer, was rated excellent. Luciano likely took the survey's only knock against him as backhanded praise: "Showmanship may detract from otherwise excellent judgment and attention."[41]

The evaluation was supposed to stay confidential. But according to a newspaper that reported on Chylak's hometown, a reporter covering the Indians saw the poll on a bulletin board in the Cleveland locker room and wrote a story. *Sporting News* picked it up and covered the furor that followed. The sports publication said MacPhail was extremely upset that the material hadn't been kept confidential and called it "a real tragedy and very unfair to the umpires."[42] The paper had also reported on a rating system unknown to the umpires during the 1973 season. The umps were understandably furious over the new poll, saying the players weren't qualified to make such judgments and that failure to keep the survey private was a serious error.

Luciano surely was pleased by players ranking him beside the dean of AL umpires. "Nestor Chylak is so much better than I am it's ridiculous," he said a couple of years later. "And so is Bill Haller."[43] But as the regular season edged toward its close, he for once did the wise thing and said absolutely nothing. He didn't want to add to his colleagues' embarrassment. Besides, he was scheduled to work the World Series.

LUCIANO HAD MIXED FEELINGS about the A's-Dodgers World Series in 1974, which he called the worst ever. He said later the most exciting part was guessing when Oakland's Herb Washington would steal a base. "So what happens? Mike Marshall picks him off."[44] Washington's blunder while pinch-running for Joe Rudi, famously foreseen by TV broadcaster Vin Scully, ended Game Two in a 3–2 Oakland victory.

Umpires appreciated Oakland manager Alvin Dark as polite and rational. Luciano loved working with the church-going, Bible-carrying skipper, who somewhat offset the Series' lack of suspense. The ump thought Dark outmanaged Walt Alston over the five games, making moves to bring in ace reliever Catfish Hunter to face a particular Dodger batter, for example. "All of a sudden it would happen," Luciano said. "Dark manipulated things perfectly."[45]

Luciano and Dodger third base coach Tommy Lasorda were two of baseball's great chatterboxes. The pair became the surprise stars of the annual MLB film about the series, a producer considering them far better than Alston or Dark to enliven things. *Sporting News* called the movie the Tom and Ron Show. "What do you think of the designated hitter?" Luciano asked during Game Three. "We don't like it in our league," Lasorda replied. "Well, you better because it's going to be in your league, too, pretty soon," Luciano shot back—wrong by nearly five decades.[46]

Lasorda talked so incessantly during the series it didn't seem to matter to him whether anyone listened. "Will you stop talking to yourself?" Luciano yelled. Lasorda took a nervous step forward and another back again. "That's not too bad, Ron," he said. "It's when I start answering myself that you are really in trouble in this game."[47]

Always a faithful Dodger, Lasorda took over the club when Alston retired before the last four games of the 1976 season. He then managed it until mid-1996 on his way to induction into the Hall of Fame. Luciano meanwhile returned to the small farm outside Endicott where he lived and raised quail and chukar partridges during the offseason. He worked with his beagles and English pointer, gulped antacid medications from the bottle to control his ulcer, and considered his career in sports.

"I'd like to get into baseball administration," he'd said during the summer. "As an umpire I never get the winning feeling I had as an athlete."[48]

8 Windmill

Luciano's profile and persona expanded as publicity continued to surround him during the 1975 season. "The man making like a crazed windmill with a hot foot" wasn't inventing a new dance, the *Kansas City Times* quipped. "It is only Ron Luciano, the umpire, who leads the major leagues in animation, calmly turning in another routine call."[1] The umpire must have *felt* like a windmill, constantly twirling amid winds of criticism, praise, and controversy.

Fans and writers often compared him now with Emmett Ashford, the first African American umpire in the Major Leagues. A former postal clerk and World War II Navy veteran, Ashford had worked three seasons in the low minors before signing with the class AAA Pacific Coast League (PCL) in 1954. He rose to umpire-in-chief during a dozen years in the PCL before breaking the Major League color barrier for umpires at age fifty-one. Ashford called himself "the wandering minstrel of baseball who finally made it to Broadway."[2]

Ashford reached the American League in 1966, nineteen years after Jackie Robinson's debut as a player with the Brooklyn Dodgers. *Sporting News* said that for the first time in baseball history, fans might buy a ticket to watch an umpire. "Although effecting the shape of a blue-suited pear," it said, "Emmett has the speed, grace and agility of a ballerina."[3] The ump explained his upbeat approach by quoting former Dodger catcher Roy Campanella's observation that there was a little boy in everybody who played. Ashford felt the same way about umpires. If personality and enthusiasm shone in his work, he said, he was just being himself. Besides, "it's something for the fans to see, and I think it helps the game."[4]

Critics called Ashford a vaudevillian or worse. Two months after the ump's arrival in the bigs, a *Washington Star* sportswriter wrote that he was already starting to overdo it. "His showboating is not appreciated by the losing clubs, by most of the fans, or by the other umpires."[5] The same scribe dismissed Ashford months later as downright boring. This was a minority view, however. Like Ashford, longtime Negro Leagues and PCL umpire Bob Motley also was known for his energy and liveliness. He called Ashford the best umpire he'd ever worked with, "a showman extraordinaire" who made no apologies for his techniques, antics, or dapper dress. Motley wrote that Luciano was a near match for Ashford, but "Emmett's style set the pace."[6]

Ashford had been positively elderly for a rookie. His first crew included Luciano's later friend Bill Haller, and he was still working when the Endicotter came up in 1969. But Ashford's stint in the AL was brief, and he retired at the end of 1970. When the 1975 season began, he called Luciano the most colorful arbiter in the game and proficient to boot. "Some guys are good enough umpires that they can put a little frosting on the cake," Ashford commented. "Sometimes you overlook how good the umpire is because of it."[7] A few years later he said Luciano had all his old moves down cold plus "a few that I don't even want to know where he found."[8]

Luciano appreciated the praise but said the similarity of their on-field style wasn't intentional. He added that he'd go to sleep if he didn't stay active. "I'm not trying to be Emmett Ashford; I'm trying to be myself," he said.[9] Writers and fans compared them anyway. "Ron Luciano, my dears, was Emmett Ashford's heir as king of the soft-shoe baseball umpires; the man who played shamelessly to the gallery and hammed it up for the television cameras at every opportunity," a Maine journalist remembered.[10] Veteran National League umpire Tom Gorman largely agreed, writing that while many people criticized Ashford and Luciano, "their antics never bothered me and the fans certainly enjoy them."[11] More important, he said, both were good umpires.

BUT EVEN GOOD UMPS got mixed up in controversies no matter how much they tried not to, and they didn't back off once the rhubarbs got started. Luciano got embroiled in three doozies during 1975. Not surprisingly, two involved Billy Martin and Earl Weaver. The first came April 12 before the start of NBC's Saturday *Game of the Week* from Arlington.

The Rangers skipper started arguing with the umps before the first pitch versus Oakland. Sportscaster Joe Garagiola, an ex-Major League catcher, told viewers that Martin was wired for sound and recording everything. "Billy wants his own evidence of these conversations, it seems," he said. Garagiola then observed with a smile that the Central Intelligence Agency and Martin both made recordings. "The big question now is, will his records play at 78 or 33 1-3?"[12]

Luciano laughed about the incident years later, saying that he nearly tossed Martin for what fellow ump Joe Brinkman called GP or general principles. "But even then I couldn't resist a microphone."[13] The Texas skipper declared that he wanted a recording because Luciano had gone out of his way to get him fined, adding that he was tired of president MacPhail receiving one-sided reports from umpires. Martin wanted a recording of any conversation with Luciano, he said, "so that Lee can get both sides of the story."[14] He added that he wasn't out to get the ump merely fined, "I'm out to get him fired."[15] The comment didn't "move MacPhail to hilarity," Red Smith wrote in the *New York Times*, "but it would have warmed the cockles of the late John J. McGraw, who regarded umpires as tribal enemies."[16]

The silliness splashed across sports pages all over America. *New York Daily News* columnist Dick Young reported that the only thing wrong with the wonderful tale was that it wasn't true. The microphone was a dummy, "connected with absolutely nothing, no recording device, no tape, nothing but Martin's fertile imagination."[17] But if Martin's aim was to get MacPhail's attention, he succeeded. "No manager is going to get any umpire's job, ever," the AL president said.[18]

The guerrilla warfare between umpire and manager continued. A Long Beach, California, newspaper quoted Luciano in early June saying that attempts to intimidate arbiters were "why we hate Martin and Weaver."[19] He softened his language a bit in the *Los Angeles Times*, saying that umpires hated managers trying to intimidate them, "and that's why we dislike Weaver and Martin so much. They're yelling on every pitch. They're continually on us."[20]

The remarks went down badly with both managers. Martin said that Luciano had "opened his mouth too wide this time" and that the story would go up to the league office. "How can a man hate you and be impartial as an umpire?" he asked.[21] The ump always maintained, however, that he much preferred Martin to Weaver, and he later came to regard Martin as a friend. He told the *New York Times* that Martin wasn't as wild as he might seem but instead was a terrific manager and possibly "even a better actor."[22] Luciano told another writer that Martin would approach him the day after an explosion and say, "Wasn't that something? I really gave the fans their money's worth, didn't I?" Weaver, on the other hand, remembered that "you swore at him back in 1970 and holds it against you."[23]

Luciano's next encounter with Weaver came five weeks after the kerfuffle with Martin and involved a phantom home run as comical as any imaginary tape recorder. The stage was a mid-May Saturday night game with California at Baltimore. Angels left fielder Tommy Harper stepped to the plate at the top of the fifth inning with a regular-season-record forty-eight thousand fans in the stands. With nobody out, runners on second and third, and the score tied 3–3, Harper drilled a liner into the left-field seats near the foul pole.

Luciano, the league's "most flamboyant umpire and acknowledged as one of the best," according to the *Los Angeles Times*, was working third base.[24] He ran halfway to the fence when Harper smacked the ball, jumped up, and gestured it fair, meaning a home run. There was one problem. The ump later admitted that he hadn't seen the ball but had to call something. "I figured I had a 50-50 chance of being right," Luciano said, "but when all those Orioles surrounded me and started screaming I got to feeling I might have blown it."[25]

The fifty-fifty defense was a favorite that he used several times during his career. But what must have galled him this time was giving Baltimore's skipper a solid reason to complain. Manager Weaver exploded from his dugout to join left fielder Don Baylor, shortstop Mark Belanger, third baseman Brooks Robinson, and catcher Elrod Hendricks in what the *Baltimore Sun* called "ferocious objections near the left-field line."[26] An Oriole fan sitting near the pole in foul territory later said the ball flew six to eight inches wide.

Luciano trotted off to consult with his crewmates. "Ron, if you want the God's Honest truth, it was foul," Haller told him.[27] Luciano overruled himself and reversed his call. Seeing an umpire admit a mistake astounded *Sporting News*. "Diogenes, the mythical Greek who spent his life searching for a completely honest man," the publication said, "could have found one in the umpires' dressing room May 17 at Memorial Stadium."[28]

Angels manager Dick Williams, no less shy than Weaver about berating an arbiter, popped out of his dugout. Luciano conceded the skipper had a legitimate beef. "He saw me call the ball fair and then I had to tell him that I was changing it."[29] The argument continued too long, and Williams had to go as well. Williams said he wasn't leaving until Luciano signaled his ejection as energetically as he had the mistaken homer. "I wanted him to make it real good for television," Williams said.[30] Harper afterward struck out with the score still tied. Luciano didn't blame the Angels for being furious that he'd taken three runs away from them. He was relieved when they rallied later to a 6–3 victory.

Luciano's third big dispute during the season was more serious than the earlier two. One of Weaver's ex-sluggers, Frank Robinson, was the new player-manager of the Cleveland Indians. The first African American skipper in the Major Leagues, Robinson was proud and prickly and not hesitant to say that he felt that Luciano and other AL umpires treated him differently from other managers. His dispute with the arbiters began the same day Luciano reversed his home run call in Baltimore. In a game in Chicago, the Cleveland skipper raced from his dugout to argue that a White Sox triple off the right field wall should have been a double because of fan interference. During the brouhaha that followed, Robinson shoved first base umpire Jerry Neudecker, Luciano's former crewmate.

Robinson said he wasn't really upset on the field, that it was the ump who had "provoked the whole thing with his actions."[31] According to the manager, Neudecker hadn't run into the outfield to make the call, hadn't asked the second base ump for help, and had shoved Robinson first when the argument got heated. Robinson, however, got his first ejection as a manager.

Neudecker said they had only brushed rather than bumped, and he allowed that they might have been equally to blame. If Robinson had cooled off, he added, the whole thing might have ended without a boot. "But then he started cursing and pushing," Neudecker said.[32] MacPhail suspended Robinson for three days and fined him $250.

Luciano gave Robinson his second heave-ho June 11 in Kansas City. The KC catcher appealed a checked-swing during the fourth inning. Luciano signaled from first base that the batter had gone around and struck out. The first base coach objected and Robinson came out to join him. "That gleam in umpire Ron Luciano's eyes tells you he's about to put another notch in his chest protector," the *Kansas City Times* said beneath a photo of the confrontation.[33] The one to bite the dust was Robinson. The manager kept a diary he later adapted into a book, in which he offered this account of their exchange:

> "We can't be fair with you," Luciano said. "You won't let us be fair with you."
>
> "What are you talking about?" I said. "What do you mean, you can't be fair?"
>
> He couldn't explain what he meant. Instead, he started talking about how I'd been out there long enough. I reminded him that if he hadn't been arguing with my coach, I wouldn't have been out there at all.[34]

Luciano said Robinson didn't swear and that he didn't want to eject him. "Please don't make me run you," the ump said he told the manager. Robinson denied it, saying that every time he went on the field, the umps were "very conscious of the time I'm out there."[35] He added that if anything, Luciano did all the cursing. Robinson got the heave but his coach stayed in the game.

Robinson later told a luncheon audience that AL umpires were trying so hard to appear impartial that they were too hard on him instead. Umps claimed that he continually argued and stayed on the field too long, but he'd seen managers go out for "seemingly a lifetime and not get thrown out of the game," Robinson said. "I just want them to be fair to everybody."[36]

Luciano clashed with Robinson again during late June at Boston. After what one area newspaper called a "reverse force double play," Luciano disallowed an Indians run that even Boston writers thought should have counted.[37] Robinson said the ump didn't bear down and was distracted by everything going on. He blasted Luciano again later at Cleveland over his constant bantering with players, which the manager didn't find amusing or funny. "He's just bad," Robinson fumed. "He's not doing his job."[38]

A few days later Robinson went off on AL umpires in general. He told the *Cleveland Plain Dealer* that he wasn't saying the umpires were prejudiced. "But I am saying they are so aware of my situation, with all the hoopla that goes with it, that they are determined to NOT let me get away with anything, to keep me in place."[39] Robinson insisted that all he wanted was to be treated like every other manager. He listed ten AL umpires he thought did a good job or at least weren't bad. Chylak, Denkinger, and Kunkel made the list. That left fourteen others "in Robinson's unspoken opinion, who are not credible," the *Plain Dealer* said.[40]

Earl Weaver heard about Robbie's list. He knew what Robinson meant by umpires taking things out on his team because he was tough on them, he said. "My players feel the umpires are against them, too, because of me, because I holler so much." But Weaver surprisingly disagreed with placing Luciano among the noncredible fourteen. He was a good umpire, the Baltimore skipper said, "even though he says he hates me."[41]

Robinson later backed away slightly from his criticism. He told the *Los Angeles Times* that personality was more of a factor than race in his problems with umpires, since they generally disliked managers who were intense and volatile. The paper noted, however, that he "seemed to be saying that the umpires were finding it hard to ignore his race."[42] Luciano said little during the season but claimed many times afterward that Robinson imposed a fine of $200 on any player he caught talking with him. "Ever wonder why a guy who was M.V.P. in both leagues ended up with five different teams?" Luciano asked. "He is very difficult to get along with. I can't understand why they ever made him a manager."[43]

Once the Robinson uproar died down, Luciano again had to contend with Weaver. The ump had ejected him for the third time in the big leagues June 28 for arguing balls and strikes at Detroit. Perhaps it was Luciano's present to himself on his thirty-eighth birthday. The most famous episode of their epic feud then occurred August 15 during a Friday twi-night doubleheader at Baltimore. The games with the Rangers made national sports news, entered Luciano Lore, and is still noted today in countless this-day-in-baseball columns. The *Baltimore Evening Sun* said Weaver might have set a Major League record that day: "fewest number of innings seen by one manager in a doubleheader."[44] Luciano of course was the reason.

Frank Lucchesi now managed the Rangers, who had fired Billy Martin a month earlier. (In a spectacular miscalculation, Martin doubted any return later because "my reputation precedes itself no matter where I go."[45]) Lucchesi knew the Baltimore manager from the Eastern League, where Weaver had once been bounced for drop-kicking an umpire's whisk broom down the third base line. Then managing the opposing Williamsport Grays, Lucchesi had retrieved the broom, used it to brush off his cap, then smilingly handed it back to the ump. But he now quickly departed the first game in Baltimore, tossed by second base umpire Armando Rodriguez for disputing a call at the top of the first inning.

Luciano's trouble with Weaver started at the top of the fourth when he ruled that Oriole first baseman Tony Muser had missed the bag, negating the initial out of a probable double play. The ump appeared to signal the out, "but he could have been merely indicating the ball was fair," the *Washington Star* said.[46]

Weaver stormed out of the dugout, yelling that Luciano hated him and called plays against him and declaring that he wouldn't be allowed to work any more Baltimore games. "He told me I would be driving a garbage truck and not umpiring," Luciano reported to the league after he ejected Weaver. "He told me I was a showboat and cared more about talking to the press than umpiring."[47] Between games the Oriole manager repeated his claim that Luciano hated him.

"He told me on the field he hates me," the skipper said. "MacPhail should get him away from us. He's killing our team."[48] Weaver didn't last long in the second game either. "To show Weaver there were no hard feelings," according to a wire story, Luciano tossed him from the second game too—during the exchange of lineup cards.[49] These were the skipper's sixth and seventh ejections of the season, the second and third by Luciano, and the fourth and fifth of Weaver by Luciano overall.

Weaver said he really didn't know why he was tossed from the second game. "I just reminded him of four idiotic calls he made against us this year." Luciano said he wasn't the least bit biased against the Orioles, called them as he saw them, and threw Weaver out of both games because of his allegations of prejudice. "He repeated the same remarks before the second game so I had to throw him out again," Luciano said.[50] He later called the second ejection a preemptive strike.

A sports editor in Massachusetts placed Luciano among the Majors Leagues' most improved umpires, writing that fans loved his colorful capers, "and he leaves no doubt as to how he calls a play nor will he stand for abusive treatment."[51] But a Florida sportswriter later took the contrary view, calling Luciano "baseball's Greek chorus gone completely amok" and saying he was "more than willing to rearrange the basic building blocks of the game."[52] Having tossed Weaver from the first game in Baltimore, he added, the ump threw him out of the second on principle. Luciano later called the double ejection a personal high, apparently more satisfying than even his double-boot of Billy Martin a season earlier.

People remembered the dual ejections for years. Writers noted that the manager avoided a third consecutive ejection on Saturday by attending his daughter's wedding in St. Louis. One reporter later commented that the antagonists' connection was "not unlike that between Groucho Marx and Margaret Dumont."[53] Luciano often mined comedic nuggets from the relationship for interviews and books. But the feud, *Washington Post* sportswriter Thomas Boswell later wrote, was "genuinely heartfelt, not a gimmick."[54] And the worst was yet to come.

LUCIANO HAD MISSED the 1972 AL playoffs because of his ulcer but worked the 1975 Boston-Oakland playoff series along with DiMuro, Kunkel, Denkinger, Jim Evans, and Hank Morgenwick. A New England sportswriter called him "the closest thing to perpetual motion since Hoyt Wilhelm's knuckle ball."[55] The Red Sox swept the A's and moved on to the World Series versus Cincinnati. When umpiring controversies marred Boston's tenth-inning 6–5 loss in Game Three, Carl Yastrzemski wished Luciano had stayed to work the Series games too.

Luciano often shared Yaz's supposedly brusque response to his chattiness at the plate: "Listen, you bleep, my wife is okay, my kids are okay, I'm okay, I don't know any good eating places in town and keep your mouth shut."[56] But the Boston left fielder appreciated umpires like Luciano and Chylak, who bore down and got the job done. "They should be working here," Yaz fumed as the Sox battled the Reds during one of the most thrilling World Series ever. "If you are going to rotate the umpires, rotate the teams, too. Let the worst teams in baseball play."[57]

Cincinnati's "Big Red Machine" triumphed in seven games to end the 1975 season. Luciano fulfilled his mother's longtime hopes a month later by finally marrying at age thirty-eight. He joked awkwardly that he'd finally caught a woman dumb enough to agree. "I would have married an Italian from Endicott," he said, "but the town only has 11,000 people—10,900 are relatives and the other 100 are men."[58]

His wife, Polly Dixon, was a marketing director for Trans World Airlines in Chicago. A divorcée reared and educated in Indiana, she worked closely with the Cubs and White Sox and occasionally assisted Major League umpires as well. An NL ump had introduced her to Luciano in 1970. She called him Ron, not Ronnie like so many others. "We had a whirlwind courtship," Luciano wrote. "Five years after we met we rushed into it."[59] His ex-crewmate Dave Phillips thought Dixon would be "a nice partner for his life. She seemed to be that person."[60] Luciano kidded friends that he wasn't inviting anybody to their November 14 wedding in Dayton, Ohio. But before the nuptials, he first had to visit New York to tape an appearance on a popular television program—*To Tell the Truth*.

Dixon left her job after twenty years with the airline because Luciano didn't want his wife to work. Once married, they spent the winter in a rented place in Apalachin, site of a mafia conclave in 1957. The arrangement wasn't convenient once the 1976 season began. Luciano also took an apartment for his wife in Chicago so he could see her more often. But during the summer he said he'd only been there four days altogether. "I agree with the other guys that this is a lonely job, now," he said. "And I understand why umpires get upset so easily."[61] His pal Bill Haller called the bride Julia Child "because, he says, she can barely manage to boil water."[62] Dixon in turn called Haller a male chauvinist, a label the traditionalist happily embraced. She sometimes vacationed without her absent husband.

"An umpire's wife must be strong," Luciano's sister Barbara Walton said later, noting that he and Dixon were around forty years old when they wed. "They both were very independent. He likes bird-watching and hunting and fishing. After a year of living in [Apalachin], and with Ron gone for seven months of the year, she told him, 'Ron, I want to go back to my type of life.'"[63] Luciano shared little about his marriage. He told the Associated Press they had two winters and a summer together. "The winters were great. It was the second summer that did us in."[64] Sometimes he feebly joked about their difficulties together. "After being married for less than a year, I came home at the end of the baseball season and my wife asked, 'Ron who?'"[65]

As with many of his colleagues, one of their problems was Luciano's life on the road. He once said he'd left home the first week of March 1977 and hadn't returned until the end of June, and then only for a day. They had talked about the difficulties when they married, but neither realized how difficult their lives would become. "Nobody does at first," Luciano said. "It boiled down to my having to make a choice between my wife and baseball."[66]

They divorced in August 1977. He so rarely spoke of Dixon afterward that friends had difficulty remembering her first name. But his ex-wife still spoke highly of him decades later, and the big ump was never certain he'd been right to choose baseball over her.

9 Nemesis

If run-ins with umpires were recorded on rap sheets, Earl Weaver would have been a career criminal. Thomas Boswell came to believe that the contempt American League umpires felt for Weaver amounted almost to hatred. He wasn't a showman to them, he wrote, but "the symbol of the professional disrespect, the cruel and unusual punishment they encounter everywhere."[1]

Luciano in particular seemed destined to butt heads with the Oriole manager. A *Washington Times* sportswriter thought they could never get along, because they saw two different things. "Weaver looked and saw empire," he wrote. "Luciano looked and saw stage front of a Milan opera house where he is gloriously rolling over a high C. Ron Luciano saw only make-believe."[2] The pair's feud peaked during 1976, a season when Luciano worked with Bill Haller, Larry McCoy, and Al Clark.

AL umps jointly chased Weaver ninety-eight times during his career. Luciano claimed fifty-four of them himself, including once for lighting a cigarette during the national anthem. None of it was true, although his pal Haller *had* tossed Weaver in 1969 for smoking in the dugout and then swearing at him during a televised game at Minnesota. Luciano thumbed Weaver for only the sixth time May 25 under the lights versus Cleveland at Baltimore.

Weaver squawked after Luciano called Jim Palmer's first pitch at the top of the third inning a ball. The angry skipper got the thumb before he could leave the Oriole dugout but came out anyway. He cupped his hands, screamed into Luciano's face, then kicked dirt over the plate. "He's a bad umpire and he's getting worse," Weaver said. "He's not trying to improve himself. If MacPhail has any sense, he'll keep Luciano away from us."[3]

The umpire only laughed and said he'd told Weaver not to yell at him from the dugout. But Weaver had then come out, stood too close to him, and declared, "I'm going to yell at you from right here."[4] Luciano admitted he'd been tempted to leave the plate covered in dirt, but he brushed it off when Palmer seemed about to do it himself. Weaver wished he hadn't. If Luciano had let Palmer clean off the dish, he said, MacPhail would have been forced to fire him, "which he should have done long ago."[5]

The crucial and most humiliating episode in the pair's long history, however, wasn't an ejection. It was an off-the-field remark made weeks earlier on May 2 in Chicago, when the Tigers–White Sox doubleheader was rained out on Bat Day. With no game to call, Luciano sat around his hotel room talking with Tom Fitzpatrick of the *Chicago Sun-Times*. Their chat resulted in a June 13 article on the life of an umpire in which Luciano spoke freely about his salary, homelife, the danger of alcoholism, and the comparative intelligence of baseball and football players. He even mentioned his four supposed ejections of Weaver at Reading.

Fitzpatrick wrote that Luciano was a delight to talk to and that he held nothing back. But one of his quips proved explosive: "I don't care who wins the pennant," Luciano said, "as long as it isn't Baltimore."[6] He added that the situation was so bad with Weaver that the league arranged his crew's schedule to keep them apart as much as possible. Jim Palmer recalled what happened next.

Weaver had been waging a one-man crusade against American League umpires for months, Palmer wrote, especially Luciano. Then came the *Sun-Times* interview. "He and Luciano have escalated to near-global nuclear warfare, and Luciano has just pushed Earl's ballistic button."[7] Fitzpatrick's article ran a week later in Baltimore, and someone showed it to MacPhail. The AL president said he planned to talk with Luciano. "First I want to find out whether he was properly quoted," MacPhail added, "but the statement seems very inappropriate."[8]

The head of a Minor League in Georgia had once pleaded to Baltimore farm director Harry Dalton, "Mr. Dalton, can't you do something about your man Weaver? He gave my umpires such a bad time last night."[9] The Orioles now flipped the question on MacPhail, complaining about Luciano. MacPhail called him on the carpet, although no fine or reprimand ever became public. The *Baltimore Evening Sun* reported that Luciano then set about to "defuse potential fireworks" before his crew's next Orioles series.[10]

The ump called the team's traveling secretary to request a meeting with the Baltimore press before the July 9 game with California at Anaheim. Luciano met the sportswriters in the umpire's room. According to the Oriole skipper, the mea culpa was MacPhail's doing. "He made Luciano make a public apology in front of the press to me and [Billy] Martin, which I didn't want," Weaver later wrote. "You know, it just made matters worse. And he was dishonest. He definitely would make calls that were against us."[11]

Weaver attended the session with Oriole general manager Hank Peters, AL umpire supervisor Dick Butler, several writers, "and the long shadow of American League president Lee MacPhail," according to the *Los Angeles Times*.[12] The ump contritely offered a non-apology apology with plenty of humble pie.

"I've got a big mouth," Luciano said. "It was a dumb, heinous statement to make but I'm at the top of the ladder when it comes to saying dumb things."[13] He insisted that he never wished ill of the Orioles and asked how anyone could root against a team that included Brooks Robinson, Mark Belanger, and Bobby Grich. "I don't care who wins the pennant," he said. "I'd just like the public to know I'm not against Baltimore or for another club."[14]

Weaver told skeptical reporters he wasn't mad at Luciano and didn't believe he would intentionally do anything to affect the outcome of a game. "Ron used to be a good umpire," he said. "I recommended him for his job." His Orioles then went out and beat the Angels 4–3, but Weaver didn't last the game. Bill Haller tossed him during the fifth inning for arguing over a checked swing. "We've got no chance with this crew," Weaver huffed, the truce already shattered. "Evidently Luciano will stand back and let the others get me."[15]

At the end of the month, MacPhail shifted Luciano off all Orioles games. He went to another crew whenever Haller's umps worked in Baltimore, initially replacing Dale Ford alongside Springstead, Barnett, and Denkinger. Luciano didn't work another Oriole game until the following June. The upside to this professional slap was that he didn't have to listen to Weaver complaining for almost a year. "That was some terrific punishment," umpire Ken Kaiser later wrote. "There were long lines of umpires trying to sign up for that one."[16]

THE UMP AND THE MANAGER couldn't stand to be in the same ballpark. Despite years of jokes and quips, Luciano realized that the rift harmed the sport. "He didn't manage as well when I was working the same game; I didn't umpire as well," he said long afterward.[17] Luciano respected his nemesis even if it wasn't always reciprocated. He would tell an interviewer in 1988 that a manager couldn't hit, throw, or do anything to help his team win except inspire players to perform better than they knew how. "And a perfect example is a guy like Weaver."[18]

Fans loved watching both men. Luciano entertained them with antics around the bases and behind the plate. Weaver got them yelling with tirades from the dugout or on the field against Luciano and nearly every other umpire. Nestor Chylak was the only major exception to the turmoil. The longtime ump was proud that he'd never booted Weaver from an AL game. Indeed, the future Hall of Famer issued only thirty-two ejections in over twenty-five seasons. Fellow umps grew critical of Luciano's much different performance. "He was trying to make people laugh," Augie Donatelli sniffed later when he was an assistant supervisor of NL umpires. "Baseball isn't played for laughs."[19]

Luciano claimed he sometimes didn't realize he was gesturing or "shooting" runners until he saw the replays on TV, that such antics came naturally as he got caught up in the rush of a game. "The calling of a close play should be more than just a humdrum thing," he said. "Why shouldn't the umpire add to the flavor, the excitement?"[20] He was hurt by criticism from people like Donatelli that he fooled around too much on the field. "But if you're serious 90 per cent of the time, you'll go crazy out there."[21]

The ump tried to rebuild bridges to players also offended by his *Sun-Times* interview, during which he'd said he spent little time with them because they weren't nearly as smart as football players. He told a Dallas sportswriter he didn't mean *all* ballplayers, and he pointed to Rangers players Mike Hargrove, Toby Harrah, and Jim Sundberg as among those he admired. Luciano added, however, that ballplayers often were pampered and immature when they reached the big leaguers. He wasn't trying to make a case for pro football players, but he noted that most were older when they turn pro. "They've been exposed to four years of college and some of them do take advantage of their educational opportunities," he said. "Generally they're more humble when they move into the pros."[22]

Despite his troubles, Luciano remained a fan favorite, the "most popular umpire in the big leagues today," according to a Connecticut sportswriter, who astutely added that the Endicotter would "undoubtedly write a book one day detailing his experiences as a major league ump."[23] Russ Worman of the *Bingham Press* likewise observed of Big Loosh, "In a game still burdened by archaic rules and yawning moments, Endicott's Ron Luciano is a Raquel Welch at a matrons' meeting, a Barrymore among bit players, daring to be a superstar in a profession that prides itself on anonymity."[24]

Luciano arguably had peaked as an arbiter by the 1976 season. After the *Sun-Times* fiasco, a Massachusetts sportswriter wrote that he was a "damned good umpire. He had to be in order to get away with the stuff he pulls, on and off the field."[25] In an unusually introspective interview with *Referee*, a magazine for sports officials, Luciano acknowledged that many fellow umpires disliked his approach. "They think it belittles them, that I'm a clown out there." He knew that detractors believed fans were laughing *at* him, not *with* him. "I think if I had it to do over again," he added, "I'd try something else."[26]

His performance and reputation slipped further as the decade waned. Luciano "became known for being known," a Bay Area sportswriter later wrote. "He became a personality, a good quote, an abrasive, self-important gasbag. In short, Luciano became a mirror image of many of the ballplayers he monitors."[27] Some managers agreed. Whitey Herzog had been glad to see Luciano work David Clyde's first game in Texas but ultimately remembered him as "a good umpire until he became an act."[28] Luciano's emotions swung in a slow pendulum arc from enjoyment to melancholy and back again, although he was largely unaware that his restlessness was so apparent on the field. "I was still having as much fun and everything was going good," he recalled. "But I guess, deep down inside, I really wanted to get out."[29]

THE 1977 SEASON BROUGHT CHANGE for both Luciano and the Major Leagues. The umpires wanted a new contract because their old one had expired at the end of the previous year. The American League was expanding to fourteen cities with new teams in Toronto and Seattle, and the winter was predictably rocky.

League officials told umpires in January that baseball was on an economy drive and that they wanted to cut crews from four umpires to three. The umps naturally were opposed. "The umpires are about to pull a strike. I kid you not," *New York Daily News* columnist Dick Young warned.[30] He added that they'd been haggling with the league presidents in New York for several days with little progress. Luciano said a lockout threatened by team owners was a power move to get the umps to sign prematurely. "We're making about 1-1,000th of what the modern player is making, and we'd like to at least get it up to 1-2,000th," he added with a chuckle and bad math.[31]

AL president MacPhail dropped the idea of three-man umpire crews during early March and the umps agreed to a five year contract with a substantial salary bump. The pact hiked their starting salary from $15,500 to $16,500 in 1977 and 1978, $17,500 in 1979–80, and $18,000 in 1981. It also provided larger automatic boosts for umpires after three, six, nine, thirteen, and fifteen years' service.

Despite his improved pay, Luciano continued to patronize a seedy hotel near Times Square whenever his crew came to the Big Apple for a Yankees series. He explained that during his first season in 1969, when his per diem didn't extend nearly as far as it did later, the proprietors had "put us up for a good price and took care of us."[32] He patronized the place long after fellow umpires shifted to better accommodations elsewhere.

Luciano reported to 1977 spring training in the Cactus League, which in addition to Arizona offered an exhibition game between the Angels and new Seattle Mariners at Palm Springs, California. A columnist there was delighted to see Luciano work and wrote, "A huge bear of a man, who shuffled around the infield, he makes calls preceded by ballet steps, and arm gestures of a symphony conductor."[33] The ump clapped his hands, appeared to cheer good plays, and chatted with infielders. The scribe wrote later that Luciano became his wife's favorite man in blue when she noticed his friendly banter with a batboy.

The spouse's high regard for Luciano reflected his popularity among baseball's little people. Another batboy, in Milwaukee, thought the ump was aces because he'd once handed him ten bucks to take his car to the airport. The field announcer at Cleveland, who sat near the visitor's dugout, always felt intimidated until Luciano walked over between innings one day and asked him to place an outside call. "I want you to order me a pepperoni pizza and tell them to be sure to have it delivered immediately after the game," the ump said sternly. "Got it?"[34] He returned to the plate, lifted his mask, and winked at his new pal.

Haller, Kunkel, and rookie Ken Kaiser were his crewmates during the season. Luciano knew some chief's wouldn't have him on their crews. "Thank God for Bill Haller," he said. "He doesn't like what I do. He's totally against it. But he tolerates me."[35] Luciano also realized the effect he could have on an impressionable young umpire such as Kaiser, an outgoing, barrel-chested, ex-professional wrestler from Rochester, New York. Luciano would say a couple of years later that if umpires had become less self-righteous, "I'm partly responsible for it—and I'm ostracized for it."[36]

Kaiser soon became a pal and protégé, Luciano often joking that the younger man looked like his illegitimate son. He claimed that the man he called Kenny had started his career as a banker. "Well he wasn't really a banker," Luciano said. "He was a repossesser [*sic*] for the bank."[37] Kaiser fit easily into Haller's crew, which the rookie said must have been the biggest one ever, averaging 6-feet-1 and 225 pounds. "When we go out to home plate before a game, we don't exchange lineup cards," Kaiser said, sounding like Luciano. "We weigh in."[38]

The four umps worked the very first game at the Kingdome in Seattle. It was also Kaiser's debut in the Major Leagues after twelve seasons in the minors. Luciano claimed the tyro asked him to leave twenty-three tickets for the April 6 night game, later writing, "The man had been in the city one night, not even a full night, just a few hours."[39] Nearly fifty-eight thousand fans filled the gray mushroom-shaped stadium to see Mariner righthander Diego Segui face Angel southpaw Frank Tanana. The *Seattle Times* said the new club greeted fans with bunting, bands, and politicians to boo. "The wildest boos were given to Bowie Kuhn, commissioner of baseball, who shrugged with both arms outstretched."[40] Then they booed the umpires too.

The Kingdome had a state-of-the-art scoreboard capable of showing video replays along with photos and messages, technology not yet available in every ballpark. Entertainer and movie star Danny Kaye was one of the new team's owners. During the second inning the team showed a replay of Luciano's out call at second base after Seattle's Leroy Stanton tried to stretch a single into a double. Kaye burst into the video booth and ordered no more replays, worried that upset fans might get out of hand. The Mariners considered it merely a case of a neophyte owner overreacting and said they would be judicious about running future replays.

Luciano wasn't bothered—he was used to booing—but admitted to wondering whether he'd missed the call after watching the video. He thought the camera angle might have distorted reality. "At some point in the future instant replay might be used in conjunction with the officials," he said.[41] But he added that it would require five or six cameras to be effective, and he didn't know if that was feasible. Luciano mentioned trouble at Yankee Stadium the previous August, when fans threatened umpires after replays on a new $3 million scoreboard, but downplayed any serious concern about Seattle.

Tanana tossed a 7–0 complete game shutout to spoil the Mariners' debut. But opening night still ended on a Hollywood note when a team official introduced Seattle DH Dave Collins to actor Martin Milner, costar of the TV police procedural *Adam-12*. "Officer," Collins said in the clubhouse, "will you arrest Tanana, please?"[42]

LUCIANO FACED ANOTHER equipment-related situation two weeks later in Anaheim, at the start of the Angels' April 21 game with the White Sox. For the first time in "no one knows how long," said a newspaper in Pomona, an American League game was called because of darkness.[43] Perhaps inevitably, Luciano was the one who both called it and explained it all later.

Problems started at 6:10 p.m. during batting practice when a fire in a control panel blacked out all the stadium lighting. Everything soon came back on except a bank between home plate and first base. Oldtimers said the lighting was still worse in the Minors, and California outfielder Joe Rudi, a former Athletic star, said it was always that bad in Oakland. As gametime approached, plate umpire Luciano had twelve thousand people in the stands with the lights not yet totally working. He conferred with managers, player reps, and the Angels' president, who all agreed they should try to play.

Chicago leadoff hitter Ralph Garr stepped to the plate at 7:45, fifteen minutes beyond the scheduled start. He immediately started jawing about the conditions. "It was mean out there," Garr said afterward. "If he'd throwed [*sic*] at me, it was good night."[44] Luciano suspended play once the batter grounded out, which the *Orange County Register* said should go down as the shortest contest in Major League history. "Time of game: Three minutes. Duration: Five pitches."[45]

Fans booed and lingered in the stands, reluctant to leave, but Luciano felt he'd had no choice because he couldn't see the ball clearly. "If I could see it, we would have played the game no matter what the players said," he said. "It was strictly my decision."[46] An ump who protected batters from beanballs and purpose pitches could hardly let shadows and bad lighting endanger anyone now. It wasn't worth playing if someone got badly plunked. "There was one outside pitch that I could barely see," Luciano said. "You could see the ball, but there was no way you could see the rotation."[47]

He was sorry he'd been forced to shut down the action. "I know it costs money just to open the park and that there was a good crowd," Luciano said. "But I didn't want anyone getting hurt. Especially myself."[48] Angel starter Paul Hartzell got the last laugh by saying, "That might be the only no-hitter I throw all year."[49]

THE 1977 SEASON SAW other odd episodes that live on today in Luciano Lore. Metropolitan Stadium in Bloomington, Minnesota, where he had applauded Sal Bando's homer three seasons earlier, supplied another performance to thrill the excitable ump on June 4.

Luciano worked third base during the nationally televised Saturday game, Twins versus the Red Sox. Boston led 4–1 in the bottom of the seventh inning when Minnesota right fielder Dan Ford smashed a four-hundred-foot drive to deep center. Boston's Fred Lynn was hampered by a bad left ankle and had badly misplayed an outfield ball only a day earlier. Fifteen thousand fans screamed, believing Ford's ball was long gone. But the center fielder raced back to show why he'd been the AL Rookie of the Year and Most Valuable Player two seasons earlier.

Lynn tracked the ball all the way; it was headed over the fence, but he knew he had it. "I went straight up, caught the ball and then hit the wall," he said, adding that if he'd smacked into a wire fence he'd still be hanging from it. The theft was so astonishing that right fielder Bernie Carbo rushed over to examine his teammate's glove for the proof. "The ball was actually out of the park and he pulled it back in with his glove," Carbo exclaimed.[50]

This Week in Baseball showed Lynn's robbery for years. It still ranks among the best homer-denying catches ever. The catch was so sensational and Luciano so grateful to see it that he applauded when the young star ran past him at the end of the inning. The ump later called it "the greatest catch I've ever seen."[51] Such on-field exuberance from anyone in blue surprised Lynn. "I laughed because I couldn't believe Luciano clapped," he said, "but I thanked him anyway."[52]

Luciano returned to Baltimore the following week for the first time since his *Chicago Sun-Times* comment and apology a season earlier. He hadn't seen Earl Weaver in all that time and said he and the Oriole manager weren't "exactly social buddies." The June 11 game with the White Sox provided no explosions, but the Bird skipper pointedly didn't deliver his lineup card to the plate beforehand. Why not? No comment, said Weaver, "and I don't very often have no comment."[53]

Life remained fairly quiet for Haller's crew until August 25 at New York, where Minnesota manager Gene Mauch suspected Billy Martin and his Yankee club of skullduggery in the House that Ruth Built. The Associated Press said Mauch thought someone was stealing signs from the center field bleachers and somehow relaying them to batters. "It's more than their talent that makes them 42-19 at Yankee Stadium, I'll tell you that," Mauch snapped after a 6–4 loss, New York's eleventh win in a dozen games.[54]

The Twins skipper had complained earlier during the game. "He just said there was a door open out there behind the center-field fence and he wanted it closed," said Luciano, who worked first base. "He didn't say anything about stealing signs."[55] The Yankee manager claimed he had no idea what was happening until Luciano came over to tell him. Haller booted a stadium security officer and a non-uniformed spectator from the bleachers and told Yankee bullpen pitchers to stop leaning on the fence. Mauch changed his club's signs and the crisis ended.

A New Jersey writer pointed out that stadium cops numbered among Martin's close friends, but Billy the Kid only grinned. "C'mon," he said. "I don't know anybody out there who would understand the signs if they saw them."[56]

Luciano got through the rest of the season without serious incident aside from taking a foul tip off his right knee during a September 11 doubleheader at Anaheim, a painful reminder of his football days. The *Los Angeles Times* reported the former All-America tackle "hitting the ground with a thud which had to register on the Richter scale."[57] Luciano finished the first game but didn't work the nightcap.

Divorced since August, Luciano took his first step during the offseason toward a life after baseball. He established Ron Luciano's Sports World with his sisters, Bobbie and Dee, a sporting goods store in a furniture showroom next to an antiques center on Upper Front Street in Binghamton. Dee's husband, Don Jester, later became involved as well. They opened ten days before Christmas 1977. Their ad in the *Binghamton Press* invited shoppers to come in and meet the umpire. "Take advantage of the great buys on: Games, Sporting Gift Items, and so much more."[58]

Opening so late during the holiday shopping season showed Luciano's lack of business acumen. He later admitted knowing as much about retailing as "Jackie Onassis knows about couponing."[59] But he loved hanging around the place, greeting new customers, and chatting about anything or nothing. A local magazine asked if he planned to remain an umpire until retiring. Luciano said no, he was taking it year by year. "I'm just up to here with traveling," he said. "We'll just have to play it by ear."[60] A few months later he added that he'd get out of umpiring as soon as he paid off the store.

Having missed most of the Christmas rush, Luciano held an open house and sale during mid-February 1978 before heading to spring training in Arizona. He advertised appearances by Yankees Mickey Rivers and Roy White along with umpires Haller, Chylak, and Clark but worried about one of the invitees. "Luciano is sweating over an incommunicado Rivers' appearance," John Fox wrote. "(And THERE'S a pair; if one's the hot-dog of umpires, the other's the 'with everything' of Yankees.)"[61] Rivers famously didn't show, providing Luciano another item later for his memoir.

10 Huckleberry

The American League shifted Luciano off Bill Haller's crew for the 1978 season. He partnered instead with Chylak, Rich Garcia, and second-year man Vic Voltaggio, an ex-Marine and police officer from Vineland, New Jersey. Chylak characterized them as "a Ukrainian, two Italians and a crazy Cuban."[1] Luciano loved Haller, his best friend on and off the field for years, and wanted to know the reason behind the change. He asked MacPhail, who replied, "It wasn't me, it was Butler."[2] He meant AL supervisor of umpires Dick Butler.

Dave Phillips said decades later the league shifted Luciano onto the tough old veteran's crew to "get his act cleaned up." The pairing raised eyebrows among fellow arbiters. They learned of it during a regular umpires meeting and began laughing. "Everybody knew there was going to be an absolute head-on collision," Phillips recalled. "Chylak wanted all the attention and didn't care to share that at all with Ron. And Ron didn't care about Chylak."[3] The crew chief would be sorely challenged to control the incomer.

A Scranton, Pennsylvania, sportswriter who knew Chylak well wrote that the shift was made "to prevent rookie umpires from copying Luciano's style."[4] Luciano believed this was true as well. Butler conceded that he frowned on some of Luciano's antics but added that he admired one thing. "He always looks as if he's enjoying himself on the field," Butler said. "That's an image I'd like to see in every umpire."[5]

Chylak's crew began the season without major confrontations with players, managers, or each other. As summer neared, the quartet had made only two ejections, both by Garcia. Then an Oakland–New York game at Yankee Stadium on June 13 produced an odd moment that briefly bemused everyone. The issue, as in the Kingdome a season earlier, involved the increasing use of video screens in baseball, who could see them, and when.

After a play at the top of the seventh inning, plate umpire Luciano said and did absolutely nothing, which alone should have alerted Yankee manager Martin that something was seriously amiss.

Oakland pinch-runner Mike Edwards raced home from second on a single, somehow missed touching the plate, and disappeared into the visitors' dugout. No Yankee noticed. But Luciano did and rightly made no signal, saying later that the runner had missed by a lot. "At that point, having passed his final destination," he added, "Edwards could only be called out by the Yankees appealing."[6]

The Bronx scoreboard didn't show the play. Both leagues had banned TV sets from dugouts because of concerns about replays, so nobody saw it there either. Broadcaster and ex-Yankee shortstop Phil "Scooter" Rizzuto, however, saw what had happened on a monitor up in the booth. "Hey, that huckleberry didn't touch home plate!" he squeaked.[7] Rizzuto tried to call Martin on the bench, but the line was busy, and he couldn't get through. Luciano overheard a Yankee say something about the runner missing the plate on TV, probably viewed in the clubhouse.

Yankee relief ace Rich "Goose" Gossage was tossing warm-up pitches as Luciano visited third base to tell his crew chief what was happening. "Get out of here," Chylak barked.[8] But he added that if the Yankees appealed, Luciano should go with his judgment, even if it meant denying their plea. Martin didn't appeal, perhaps unaware of the situation, perhaps unwilling for once to complicate things. The next batter eliminated the problem since a protest was then no longer permissible. Luciano admitted he couldn't have said whether Gossage's first pitch was a ball or a strike. "I was just glad to see a pitch."[9]

The Associated Press reported that if the Yanks had appealed and been upheld by Luciano and Oakland in turn had protested the intrusion of television, the whole mess would have fallen into the lap of the AL president. "And MacPhail said he would have backed Luciano."[10] But the Yankees were leading the game and won anyway, 5–3.

CHYLAK WAS STRUGGLING and didn't need any protests to complicate his season. Major League baseball had changed drastically during his years on the diamond. The *Scranton Times* noted that during his first season, in

1954, eight AL teams played from the East Coast to the Midwest and moved mainly by rail. Since then Chylak had traveled over two million miles by air while the league expanded west beyond the Mississippi River and north into Canada. He disliked many other changes that came with modernity. "Fan violence and the news media are the things that bug him most," the newspaper said, "and not always in that order."[11]

Instead of going home during the midsummer break, the umpire was scheduled to work his sixth All-Star Game. His family accompanied him to the crew's final series beforehand, Tigers-Rangers at Arlington Stadium. Luciano had swapped places with Lou DiMuro so each could get home quicker for their precious days off. Sports pages mentioned hundred-degree heat in Texas, but Chylak remembered it as 116 degrees on the field. Afterward, he, his wife, and their son flew to San Diego for the All-Star Game, which the National League won, 7–3.

With Luciano back, the family stayed in Southern California for a series in Anaheim before flying east to Chicago. The family continued on home, but Chylak's crew went up to Milwaukee for two short series. Then it was on to Toronto, where after delays, the plane landed at two in the morning. The umps had a doubleheader that day and another game the next night, Saturday July 22. Chlylak worked second base with Luciano at third.

Chlylak felt strangely fatigued in Toronto and later conflated the three games there in his memory. He did recall standing alone behind second base after the final out on Saturday. Blue Jays manager Roy Hartsfield noticed his strange behavior and walked out to ask what he was doing. "Umpiring a baseball game, what else?" the ump answered.[12] Hartsfield shook his head and walked Chlylak off the field.

The American League later said he had suffered a mild stroke and been briefly hospitalized. Chlylak said it was nothing serious and that his medication consisted of four aspirin a day, but he conceded that he'd then gone to New York for treatment. "I did spend four days in Lenox Hill Hospital before coming home," he said. "After 25 years in the biggies and over two million miles of traveling I just need a rest."[13] His wife said he hadn't suffered a stroke at all but fallen ill after being hit by a batted ball. "Chylak's departure from umpiring caused confusion at first," a Scranton paper added, "because it was not until two days after he was struck by the foul ball that he suffered any ill effects."[14]

The ailing arbiter initially hoped to return to the field by September 1, then perhaps by the following season. But in November he faced reality and accepted a job on Dick Butler's supervisory staff, never to call another Major League game. Chylak later said he'd simply run out of gas and was exhausted. "When I was in Texas this year," he added, "it was the first time in my life that I had ever admitted to my wife that I was tired."[15]

Chylak's crew worked a man short until Hank Soar flew in to take his spot. A series of reassignments soon followed, which resulted in Luciano flying back across the country to rejoin Bill Haller's crew. From Binghamton, John Fox offered what was probably an accurate opinion. "Quick deduction (despite Loosh's fondness for Haller): umpiring supervisor Dick Butler, not a Luciano fan, didn't want to leave Ron as crew-chief of the Chylak group, as he'd have become on seniority."[16]

AILING CHYLAK MISSED the last big controversy of 1978. According to their lawyer, John Cifelli, the Major League umps had only grudgingly signed a five-year deal before the previous season. That spring NL veteran and Major League Baseball Umpires Association president Bob Engel headed a committee that told Cifelli in effect that they "needed to take more drastic steps to get what they wanted."[17] The group fired Cifelli and hired attorney Richard G. Phillips.

The son of a police officer, "Richie" Phillips bragged that as a teenager, he'd led a walkout of altar boys after a priest reduced their tips for working weddings—"thirteen years old and he was leading a strike against God," Ken Kaiser wrote.[18] Phillips had also worked for both the public defender and the district attorney. Sportswriter Red Smith said Phillips "looks like an umpire, dresses like an umpire and talks like a Philadelphia lawyer."[19] Among Phillips's first successes for the umpires was delivering a five-year, $150,000 promotional shoe deal with Converse. A third of that went into his pocket, which some umps thought excessive. Luciano thought differently. Before Phillips landed the Converse package, the umps were getting "100 percent of nothing," Luciano said. "We had a deal with Adidas and all we got was a free pair of shoes."[20]

AL umpire and association vice president Dave Phillips (no relation to Richie) was involved in hiring the brash attorney. He said the group's earlier lawyers had figuratively told Major League Baseball they held a gun but never used it. Attorney Phillips looked Umpire Phillips in the eye and said if the arbiters stayed strong and worked with him, "I will not only show you the gun, but also pull the trigger and blow their f****** heads off."[21]

The attorney previously represented the National Basketball Association (NBA) referees when their union had struck at the end of the 1977 regular season. The umps envied the refs, and like the NBA men, they still had a contract in place. The Associated Press reported that the motive for the basketball strike was apparently more psychological than physical, "an attempt by Phillips and the referees to show the NBA that the union means business."[22] The league and refs reached an agreement after eleven days, and Phillips sensed a similar opportunity now in the Major Leagues. His clients threatened to strike at the end of August, wanting a higher per diem package and vacation breaks during the regular season.

The AP said the umpires had a contract that ran through the 1981 season and that the league refused to reopen negotiations. "Phillips, however, said the umpires' demands covered items not included in the contract and therefore are appropriate for negotiation."[23] The umpires' stance was easily understandable to fans. Their current $51 per diem sounded good but didn't stretch nearly far enough to cover big city hotels, meals, and transportation. "The other day I stayed in the New York Sheraton overnight," sportswriter Dick Young wrote. "It cost me $61, single, and the Sheraton is not exactly the Ritz."[24]

Regular breaks during the season were equally important to many umps. Association president Engel called their grueling schedule "a 180-day road trip."[25] Luciano, for one, said he was less interested in a higher per diem than in getting a summer vacation. Phillips added that at one time or another during the previous season, eleven umpires had been out with injuries. "And we see these injuries as a partial result of the exhausting schedule."[26]

The umps began a strike Friday afternoon, August 25, after a vote by telephone that morning. Their only previous strike was the one-day stoppage at the start of the 1970 playoffs. Bill Kunkel's crew in Toronto was the first to walk out.

Both leagues brought in amateur umpires, retired pro umps, and collegiate officials to call the games in their places, and their presidents planned to continue using them until the regulars returned. The *Detroit Free Press* said instead of Luciano, Haller, Kaiser, and Mike Reilly, "The men in blue when the Tigers took the field to battle the Milwaukee Brewers Friday night were Doug Cossey, Joe Kavulich, Rico Zuccaro, and Leo Turner."[27] The quartet normally worked as an administrative aide, vocational counselor, physical education instructor, and athletic director at area high schools, respectively.

The strike hardly got going before a federal judge issued an injunction to halt it pending a hearing six days later. Although the amateurs called their night in the big leagues a dream come true, some sympathized with the professionals. An optometrist who worked a Cardinals game at Atlanta said that every one of the strikers was a friend. "I sympathize with them 100 percent," he said. "I know exactly what they want and I hope they'll get it."[28]

Richie Phillips told broadcaster Howard Cosell during halftime of an NFL exhibition game that he'd informed his clients they should work the following day, "out of respect for our judicial system, not out of respect for the order issued."[29] He insisted the current contract wasn't valid, but that even if it was, the National Labor Relations Act allowed the union to renegotiate any item that was negotiable in the first place. Luciano, Kaiser, and Reilly returned to the field Saturday in Detroit, working without Haller who had gone home and was unable to get back in time. Kunkel's crew in Toronto worked one man down as well. Other umps kept fairly quiet, but not surprisingly, Luciano was quoted on many sports pages.

He said all the umps wanted was for the league to talk with them. "But they haven't talked to us for 108 years, so why should they start now?" Luciano asked. "The league president, the players, the managers—everybody in baseball—consider us as necessary evils."[30] AL umpire Vic Voltaggio said the strike was necessary and demonstrated "a cohesiveness to the leagues which our association had never shown before."[31] Long afterward, Dave Phillips said nobody had liked the strike, which produced "terrible publicity in some respects."[32] The umps took considerable criticism for their walkout but were especially upset by remarks from commissioner Bowie Kuhn.

Kuhn said it was incredible that umpires responsible for baseball's integrity on the field had "so little regard for the integrity of their agreement with the leagues." He added that he hoped they would "rethink a very unwise decision."[33] The jibe set off a rare flare of anger in Luciano, who sputtered to Thomas Boswell that integrity and honor were all an umpire possessed.

He pointed to Chylak, who had wanted to return to the field three weeks after illness put an end to his umpiring career. "I guess if Nestor had just a little integrity," Luciano snapped, "he'd have been back the next day."[34]

The arbiters finished the season without further confrontation. Luciano afterward worked the New York-Kansas City ALCS with DiMuro, Garcia, Kunkel, Phillips, and Terry Cooney. An Arkansas sports editor said he didn't know who the umpires for the World Series were, "but it's not likely they'll be as colorful as the crew which worked the American League Championship Series." He quoted another writer who said he didn't care if Luciano blew a thousand calls, "I think he's great for baseball."[35]

Royals fans seemed to agree when they cheered upon hearing Luciano's name announced before Game One. "Yeah, I guess they like me," the ump allowed. "I think they can sense how much I enjoy what I'm doing."[36] The *Kansas City Star* noted during the series that he had "never been known to settle for one motion when nine or ten would suffice."[37]

Garcia was behind the plate during Game Two when the crew almost allowed the Royals an extra batter. George Brett stepped to the plate during the long seventh inning with three men already out and the Yankees still on the field. A Long Island sportswriter dryly noted that the same rules applied during the playoffs, "although comedian Bob Newhart once posed the question, 'But why three outs, Gen. Doubleday?'"[38] Yankee broadcaster Phil Rizzuto wondered what was happening. "Holy cow!" he chirped. "Do those huckleberries want four outs?"[39] Yankee coach Yogi Berra, who more often delivered malaprops than pertinent game information, finally shouted to Garcia that there were three outs. Luciano was amused by the field-wide amnesia and was delighted by New York pitching coach Clyde King's crack, "I knew you guys couldn't count to three."[40]

Endicott's favorite umpire took the plate when the playoffs shifted to the Bronx tied at one game apiece. The Triple Cities were Yankees Country, and everyone up there was either watching Game Three on television or listening to the radio. What they saw or heard during the home half of the fourth inning raised quite a few roofs. Yankee runner Lou Piniella was standing on third base with two men in and one out when batter Graig Nettles lofted a fly to medium left field. Royal Clint Hurdle made the catch and fired toward home as Piniella took off. Royal catcher Darrell Porter corralled the ball and applied a swipe tag on an extremely close play.

Luciano showed vintage form, leaping to signal the out with a dozen quick gestures, as if "shooting" the dish rather than a runner at first base. Piniella predictably went nuts. Yankees surrounded Luciano as "Sweet Lou" shouted, pleaded, and protested the call. It all reminded one observer of Jimmy Cagney riddled with bullets, staggering down the street in *The Roaring Twenties*, "collapsing and rising again in anguish only to die on the steps of a church."[41] Nettles said the performance probably would land Piniella a role in a movie. The Yankee right fielder insisted he'd touched the plate with his ankle, knee, and thigh before Porter's tag. "Piniella will forever argue that he scored Yanks' run number four on the ensuing play," one sportswriter observed.[42]

Video seemed to support his argument. Sports pages around the country said replays were either inconclusive or showed Piniella safe. The Yankees in their clubhouse were less critical of Luciano's call than how quickly he had made it. "Luciano is a large man, one of the umpires who provide entertainment via the forceful exaggerated flair he uses to indicate his decisions," a Florida columnist wrote. "Some Yankees thought Luciano had sacrificed some function to form, a classical violation of any art form."[43]

The ABC Sports broadcast team of Keith Jackson, Howard Cosell, and moonlighting Baltimore pitcher Jim Palmer backed Luciano, however. They narrated replays from several angles on either side of a commercial break between innings and both before and after Royal George Brett slugged his third consecutive home run to lead off the fifth. The broadcasters agreed that Piniella's lead foot bounced off the dirt and was in the air above the plate when Porter tagged him.

JACKSON: "He missed it!"
COSELL: "Yes, sir! Good call by umpire Luciano."
PALMER: "Bad slide by Lou Piniella."
COSELL: "Right, and he'll [Luciano] brook no nonsense from anybody, that gentleman."[44]

Piniella soon said he shouldn't have indulged in the theatrics at the plate because Luciano had always been a good umpire. "But if you don't get excited on a play as close as that," he added, "you don't belong in baseball."[45] Catcher Thurman Munson homered in the eighth inning to bail out the Yankees, who went on to take the AL playoffs in four games and win the World Series from the Dodgers in six. But it was Luciano's family who suffered the blowback from the Piniella call, especially after Yankee broadcaster Rizzuto hinted that just possibly, the ump might have erred. Luciano's sister Bobbie Walton watched the call from the stands and called the whole experience awful.

"The language all around me was unbelievable," she said. "It had been bad throughout the game, but after that call it got worse." Sister Dee Jester was literally at home minding the store—Ron Luciano's Sports World in Binghamton. The first telephone call came from an irate woman who mentioned castration. Dee took the receiver off the hook after a second female caller suggested Luciano do something anatomically impossible. The next morning, the answering-machine tape was full, and a customer in the store wondered why he had bothered to come after what her brother had done in the Bronx. "I just wish I'd saved that telephone tape instead of erasing it," Dee said. "We could have played it at parties."[46]

Luciano himself laughed off the whole thing. "Once I heard Howard Cosell said I'd been right," he wisecracked, "I knew I must've been wrong."[47]

Fig. 1. Ron Luciano was a 267-pound tackle at Union-Endicott High School during his senior season in 1954. © Press and Sun-Bulletin—USA TODAY NETWORK.

Fig. 2. Slimmed down to 225 pounds and wearing number 78 for Syracuse, Luciano was named an All-America tackle in 1958. Courtesy Syracuse University.

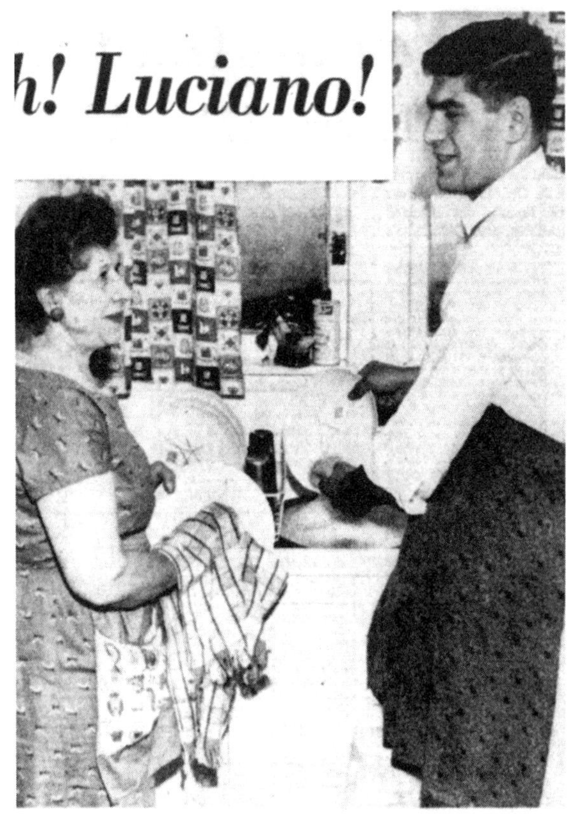

Fig. 3. Showing a delicate touch, Luciano washed dishes with his mother, Josephine, at home in Endicott, New York, before leaving for the 1959 Orange Bowl in Miami. © Press and Sun-Bulletin—USA TODAY NETWORK.

Fig. 4. The American League hired Luciano as an umpire in 1969 after five seasons in the Minors. He remained in the circuit for eleven seasons. Courtesy National Baseball Hall of Fame and Museum, Cooperstown, New York.

Fig. 5. Luciano flashed his form during a Twins–Red Sox night game in Bloomington, Minnesota, in August 1974. Here he calls one runner safe (*top*) and "shoots" another out at first base. Courtesy Associated Press.

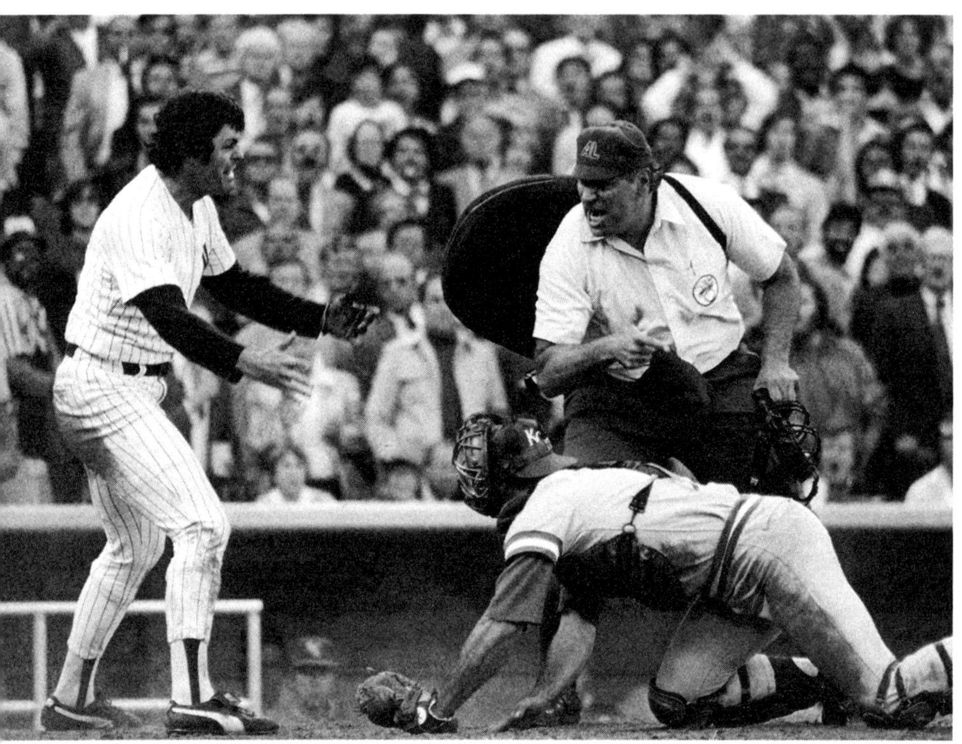

Fig. 6. Yankee Lou Piniella objects to Luciano's out signal at the plate during Game Three of the 1978 AL playoffs, as Royal catcher Darrell Porter looks on with the ball still in his glove. Courtesy Associated Press.

Fig. 7. Always a fan favorite, Luciano obliged teenager Charlie Vascellaro with a photo during spring training at Hohokam Park in Mesa, Arizona. Courtesy Charlie Vascellaro.

Fig. 8. Luciano exchanged his mask and chest protector for a microphone in April 1980, working with Merle Harmon for two seasons on *Game of the Week*. Courtesy NBC Sports via Historic Images.

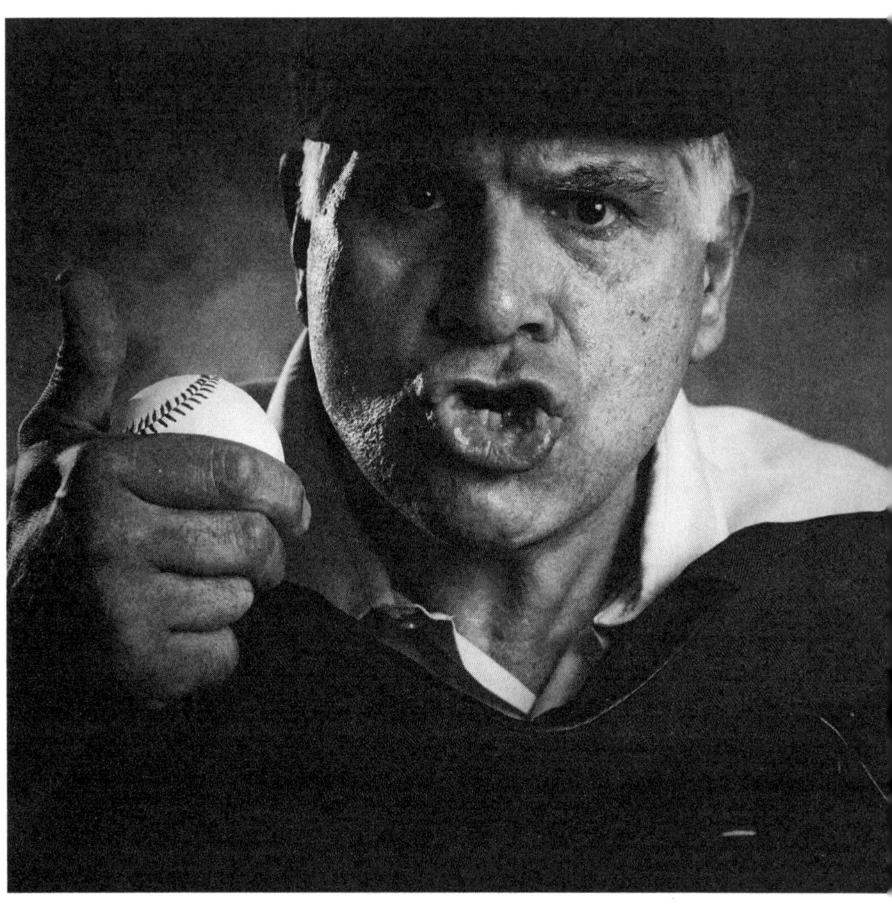

Fig. 9. Following his umpiring career, Luciano was a pitchman in numerous print and television advertising campaigns. Here he mugs for the camera after an ad shoot in the early 1990s. Courtesy robdoda.com.

11 Organizer

Luciano began the postseason goose hunting in Delaware, where he "put a stop to razzing about his eyesight by proving his shooting ability on a fat honker early in the morning hours."[1] He didn't have far to travel afterward to attend a meeting of the Major League Umpires Association in Philadelphia the first weekend of November. The three-day conclave ended with the unexpected announcement that he was the new president, replacing Bob Engel, a change not hinted at beforehand.

The new prexy claimed he'd left the room to hit the john and returned to learn he'd been elected. "I guess they figured they'd pick the dumbest guy," Luciano said.[2] It's unclear whether he actually ran as a candidate on his own or was encouraged by Richie Phillips, as seems likely. Ken Kaiser wrote that the umps elected him because "we figured no one else knew more about getting this picture in the paper than Ronnie."[3] The group's lawyer saw through Luciano's jovial facade and recalled him as a sensational guy, nothing like a run-of-the-mill umpire. "He was very funny, very bright, bordering on genius," Phillips recalled. "You cut through those antics, he did a great job."[4]

Luciano's first act as president was to appoint an eleven-man committee to study the operations of Major League Baseball, including possible rules changes. He promised Phillips to take an aggressive posture in dealing with baseball's hierarchy. Luciano also told writers his study would be done by the first of February and that he would recommend "necessary and long overdue reforms."[5] It was only a shot across baseball's bow, however, since no conclusions were ever made public. Luciano also said his committee would have nothing to do with the recent one-day strike. In fact, the umps had withdrawn their complaint with the National Labor Relations Board days earlier, knowing they would lose. Now that the season was over, Phillips said, "the matter is kind of moot."[6]

The association's new president had sometimes parted ways with the group in the past. He had supported the brief playoff strike in 1970, his second season in the big leagues. As what the *Binghamton Press* had called an "umpire-turned-labor-negotiator," he, Haller, and five other umps attended a bargaining session at commissioner Kuhn's office in New York.[7] The hard-nosed, eight-hour session resulted in a four-year contract. But Luciano quit the association the following season, feeling it was "not being run for the benefit of its members."[8] Although he resumed membership once the association got a new lawyer and served on its board of directors and as chairman of its negotiating committee, he didn't consider it well led until Richie Phillips's arrival. Together the pair now represented all fifty-two Major League umpires—twenty-eight in the AL and twenty-four in the NL.

"Umpires are a breed known only to themselves, their secrets many," Thomas Boswell wrote in September. But Luciano was different, loud and outgoing and known to everyone who followed the sport. So why choose him? The new element in the mixture was ire. "The arbiters are angry—mad enough to call a strike and take a walk during the regular season for the first time in history."[9] In their fury, the umps turned to Luciano.

He had a mixed reputation among his colleagues. Some, like Haller and Kaiser, loved him; others despised his showboating and disdain for umpiring traditions. "You have to live the life of a priest," retired NL umpire Ed Sudol declared. "You have to dedicate your whole life to it."[10] Luciano was clearly no priest, and not a few working umps were torn by the contradictions in his character. AL ump Joe Brinkman personally liked Luciano but thought he had turned umpiring into show business. "He could have been very good for umpires, because he was known to the press and the public," Brinkman later wrote. Luciano could have been an excellent pro-umpire leader, he added, but "went the other way and turned everything into a joke."[11]

But as spring training approached, Luciano knew why he now represented the umpires versus the leagues and club owners. Although many Major League umpires had been mad at him for years over how he umpired, he said, "they like the way I've always fought the administration. I refuse to be on the defense."[12] Even arbiters who couldn't stand him supported his presidency, he concluded, because he was always the last umpire to sign his contract. "I fight and battle with management," he said. "The other umpires want me to do for them what I do for myself."[13]

The umpires' one-day strike in August 1978 now seemed to many a tactical error that had accomplished nothing. *St. Louis Post-Dispatch* sports editor Bob Broeg wrote that as someone who felt for the daily abuse they took at the ballpark, "I wish the arbiters had thrown themselves on the mercy of management's understanding of inflation and asked only for a readjustment of their per diem."[14] But the fifty-two Major League umpires were in no mood to appeal to owners' better angels. In January all but one returned their 1979 contracts—not to the league offices but to lawyer Phillips. *New York Daily News* columnist Dick Young wrote that most had designated Phillips as their personal agent. "Now he is trying to negotiate for same points on individual basis . . . Tricky?"[15]

Inflation was a serious problem not only among umps but all across America. The annual rate rose to 8.5 percent during the fourth quarter of 1978. The Carter administration spoke of lowering that figure to about 7.5 percent during the coming year, only to see inflation tick up nearly another point during January. The *New York Times* said on its front page that if compounded over the full year that would equal a 12 percent annual inflation rate.

Many baseball fans thought the AL and NL umpires wanted to breach their existing five-year contract, but the situation was more nuanced. Sportswriter Red Smith explained to readers that the contract covered working conditions and established minimum wages, "but each umpire must negotiate his own salary in an individual contract and until he does, the union contract doesn't take effect."[16] The umpires weren't striking, in other words, but simply refusing to sign individual contracts until their demands were met. This simple and ingenious tactic offered about equal prospect for success or ruin for everyone involved.

Confrontation loomed as players, coaches, and managers prepared for spring training. Every Major League umpire received an identical February 2 letter from his league president, "a gesture of friendship brought on no doubt by Valentines Day," AP sportswriter Hal Bock wryly noted.[17] The letter stated that an ump could decline employment, "but if you do, the league will be compelled to hire a permanent replacement for you."[18] No umpire was permitted at spring training until he signed contract for the 1979 season. Luciano wasn't surprised by the leagues' move.

"Typical," he retorted. "I guess they figure we're all expendable and that they can walk into any bar, round up 52 guys and say, 'Hey, here's a blue suit. How about working our games?'"[19]

Phillips handled communications with the leagues while Luciano took care of communicating internally with the umpires and outreach to fans and writers. "Ronnie's high visibility should be a plus for us," Vic Voltaggio said. Luciano's main job was to keep the umps informed both of what was happening among themselves and with the leagues. "There's no doubt that as a communicator Ronnie can do the job."[20]

Baseball Bulletin later said that during his career, Luciano "probably drew more attention and had more written about him than any umpire in baseball's long history."[21] He'd been profiled over two dozen times by major papers, magazines, and wire services, including the *Kansas City Star*, *Los Angeles Times*, *Boston Globe*, *Minneapolis Star*, *Oakland Tribune*, *Toronto Globe and Mail*, *National Observer*, *People*, and *Sports Illustrated*. A pithy Luciano quote inevitably adorned pieces about big league umpires and their challenges. Photos of him making spirited calls were staples on sports pages across the country. He'd been profiled by NBC Sports and was featured in the 1974 World Series film. During late February the *New York Times Magazine* published a five-thousand-word profile plus pictures, headlining him as the "Likable Ump."[22] Scores of sports pages reprinted all or part of the article during the following weeks. The umpires wanted attention. Luciano delivered it by truckload.

His 1978 salary was $32,600, a decent wage for an American working man but a fraction of sums earned by such stars as Pete Rose and Jim Rice. Luciano and others were quick to point out the disparity. Attorney Phillips maintained that the umpires' individual contracts allowed for negotiations above the salary minimums. Other issues again included per diem and time off during the season. Luciano estimated that his daily expenses totaled $65, well above the daily allotment. Some colleagues said they spent five or six thousand dollars from their own pockets to make up the shortfall each season. "Common sense says, with inflation, how can you live on that?" NL ump Ed Vargo asked.[23] Luciano made the same argument in interview after interview.

An umpire working in the Big Apple had to pay for his hotel, laundry, meals, and cabs, all on fifty-two dollars a day. "About all that's left is a few bucks which, in New York, can't get you much more than a dill pickle," Luciano said.[24] John Cifelli, the association's former attorney, was sympathetic but felt he could have negotiated higher per diem pay without a holdout. "I'd have approached this whole thing on the basis of merit," he said. "There'd have been no strike."[25]

The umpires' pleas for days off during their long season also got a stony reception. Luciano told Thomas Boswell that he'd once gone four months without seeing his now former wife and complained that when an ump asked for a day off, "they try to make you feel three inches tall." Boswell added, "Naturally, baseball's brass called this a 'vacation,' rather than a 'sanity break,' and the press and public swallowed that description."[26]

Spring training games began March 7 without the umps, as collegiate and a few former Major and Minor League umpires took over the officiating. Both leagues sent telegrams the next day telling umpires to sign their contracts by March 15 and report for duty. McPhail and National League president Charles "Chub" Feeney added that refusal to do so "will compel the leagues to take appropriate action to protect their rights," although they didn't spell out what those actions might be.[27]

Some sportswriters called the confrontation Strike 3, the third umpire stoppage since 1970. Others considered it a lockout. Richie Phillips defined it as "an individual action on the part of 51 individuals who are unhappy."[28] The association excepted umpire Ted Hendry, who had signed his contract before the dispute began. Although officially a rookie, Hendry had worked 195 games as a fill-in over two seasons, including five with Luciano following Nestor Chylak's illness. Phillips said his clients welcomed the temporary use of amateur arbiters, since the contrast would emphasize the quality of their work.

The fill-ins got forty dollars per game, mileage, and workmen's compensation. The professionals would have received the same plus forty-nine dollars per diem. Luciano said to hell with spring training. "We lose money, anyway."[29] AL umpire supervisor Dick Butler, however, was sanguine about the lack of experience in blue. He foresaw no problem, because every town in the Citrus and Cactus Leagues had plenty of umps available. "So much college baseball is played down here and in Arizona."[30]

The association held fast as the amateurs worked the spring training games. The same federal judge who had ordered the umpires back to work during the fall held hearings in Philadelphia after the leagues charged that the umpires were violating his earlier injunction. *Sporting News* reported that baseball wanted to fine the arbiters $10,000 apiece each day they remained off the job. An attorney asked Bill Haller whether he would return to the field if satisfied with his own contract. Probably not, Haller replied. "I'd have to wait and see that every umpire went to work. As my dad said, 'Don't be a fink.'"[31]

The judge elated the balking arbiters with a March 27 ruling that they weren't employees because they hadn't signed contracts. He informed the leagues their motion was denied. "I have no authority to order them back to work," he said. "I have no authority to find them in violation of my injunction because the circumstances are not the same."[32]

Phillips urged baseball's leaders to descend from their lofty heights and deal with his clients. The AL and NL presidents responded with Western Union mailgrams to umpires the following morning. The message that reached Luciano said that since he wasn't an employee, the AL was withdrawing its contract offer, "so that we may be free to make other permanent arrangements for umpiring services."[33] He could reapply by March 30, Lee McPhail added, but his medical, hospital, and other insurance benefits would end April 30. The clear implication was that baseball was ready to hire permanent replacements.

Luciano's mother grew tearful over the threat, but the ump laughed at what he considered scare tactics. From their Badger Avenue home, he said he couldn't believe baseball would be so stupid. "But, having seen baseball men operate, you never know!"[34]

National League umpire Paul Pryor broke ranks by signing a two-year contract for various personal reasons, which he later said included severe financial troubles. "It is my hope," he added, "that the others will quickly make their own settlements and we can begin a new season."[35] The association granted Ted Hendry approval to work, but during a raucous March 30 session at Chicago the other fifty members held fast and refused to sign. A wire service said it might easily have been a scene involving Teamsters, airline machinists, or angry coal miners,

THE LABOR FACEOFF grew grimmer as the regular season began. The amateurs were now working games that counted in the standings. The leagues also launched an emergency plan to promote experienced Minor League umps to the bigs as crew chiefs. The AL plan included six class AAA arbiters plus Hendry, and the NL five plus Pryor. The Umpires Association quickly lobbied against this effort with considerable success.

The standard Major League umpire contract was for a year. *Sporting News* reported that eight of the first dozen AAA umpires offered crew-chief assignments had rejected what the paper called unprecedented two- and three-year deals. The fifty regulars were furious with any who chose to take their places and considered them scabs, labor's derogatory term for strikebreakers. "It just might be that we'll be working next to each other some day, and I won't forget," said Luciano, who was back home working in his sporting goods store. He added that he wanted a job but all he knew how to do was umpire. "I wonder if there's an opening in Japan."[36]

The strikebreakers knew they were in for a bad time from the older umps, whom they often liked and respected. Many made a purely economic decision to place the well-being of wives and kids above their own reputations. Dallas Parks, for one, signed a three-year AL contract for six times his International League salary. He tearfully ruffled the hair of his five-year-old son as he tried explaining his dilemma to Thomas Boswell, who then wrote a scathing, widely reprinted commentary in the *Washington Post* in which he said forcing low paid AAA umpires to choose between their families and their conscience was "typical of baseball's amoral, century-old attitude toward labor relations."[37]

The season began with the sprinkling of scabs leading the amateurs in calling balls and strikes. Fans and some sportswriters wondered why regular umps clung to their profession. A Fort Worth scribe wrote that if umpiring had any rewards, they weren't obvious. It certainly wasn't money, "else we wouldn't have the dilemma we're now facing, that of opening the season with Harvey Klutz, principal of Rasputin Junior High, bellowing 'Play Ball!' instead of Ron Luciano."[38] The ump himself told a news conference in New York it was conceivable he wouldn't work the diamond again. Luciano said he had applied for six other jobs, "and if I get one of them, I may quit."[39]

Luciano also announced a series of special sales at his Binghamton store, to regain his sense of humor and help make ends meet. First came a Strike Sale of baseball merchandise, followed by a Lee MacPhail Sale of unwanted items, then a Chub Feeney Sale of heavy items such as weights. The bargains concluded with a Commissioner Sale of "all light things, stuff like ping pong balls."[40]

Opening day on April 4 began with Reds-Giants at Cincinnati followed by Angels-Mariners at Seattle. Twenty-two uniformed umpires picketed outside Riverfront Stadium. They refrained from criticizing the amateur arbiters but said nothing good about Pryor behind the plate. Pryor later said he hoped they understood. "If they come back," he said, "I'll wish them well."[41] Hendry was the crew chief and plate umpire in Seattle, which saw no picketing. He said he worked with the full support of the other fifty.

Picketing arbiters wore chest-protector shaped signs that said BASEBALL UNFAIR TO UMPIRES. Several fans picked up extras, draped them around their necks, and joined the line. The sports press was growing more sympathetic too, one out-of-town scribe writing that the umpires weren't asking Bowie Kuhn to name a candy bar after them. He further noted that a day in Cincinnati cost his paper exactly $60.68—well above an ump's per diem yet still below costs in New York or Los Angeles. "What we're asking would cost each team in the major leagues about $20,000 a year," umpire Dave Phillips said.[42] Another ump said the clubs spent that much on a cocktail party.

The umpires set up a schedule to picket at ballparks in Detroit, Pittsburgh, and other Major League cities. They often got support from local labor organizations, sometimes from the NBA referees Phillips had represented earlier. Luciano led a dozen uniformed colleagues on April 7 outside Yankee Stadium. He mugged for photographers, wore a sign that read BASEBALL IS KILLING THE UMPIRES, and handed out flyers. One showed Lee MacPhail flicking ashes onto an umpire studying a contract, the caption reading, "It's fair because I say it's fair."[43]

Pryor joined a picket line that same day outside Busch Stadium in St. Louis. After four sleepless nights, the mental pressure had affected him. "I think now I will have some peace of mind," he said.[44] Most colleagues welcomed Pryor back, only to see him temporarily return to the diamond when Richie Phillips advised him to abide by a ten-day termination period that was called for in the contract. Hendry also gave notice nine days later, although Phillips urged him to stay. "I want to be with my brothers," Hendry said.[45] He added that the amateurs he worked with were incompetent and often intimidated by the job.

Phillips and Luciano now had all fifty-two Major League umps aligned. Luciano walked a picket line again April 15 outside a Red Sox game at Boston. An area sportswriter watched him enjoying himself on Van Ness Street, leaning against a van and chatting with anyone around—"a few writers, a few photographers and perhaps 20 to 30 members of the early-arriving crowd at Fenway Park."[46] Local labor groups later announced support for the umps and urged their six hundred thousand members throughout Massachusetts to boycott games at Fenway. Luciano said the umps hadn't expected that kind of support.

"I'm simply elated by it all," he said. "It has to reflect in the attitude the owners will be forced to take." Lawyer Phillips called his clients "52 lonely men who until now have had no one to turn to."[47] But he thought growing support would bring the leagues to the bargaining table.

Negotiations between the Umpires Association and the leagues resumed before Luciano picketed again outside Fenway with about thirty colleagues on April 21. They marched beside Boston police officers, letter carriers, and striking librarians from Boston University. Luciano said he didn't know where they had all come from, "but I love them for supporting us."[48] The picketing had little effect on Major League attendance, but writers sensed sentiment swinging behind the arbiters. Luciano said the fans had been great. "Those same people who yell 'Kill the umpire!' and make you sleep with your light on, are behind us now."[49] But he didn't know how much longer the umps could hold out.

Luciano said he was running out of money. "I'm a 300-pound guy and I need a lot of food."[50] He added that he had received a couple of outside job offers. A national sporting goods company, for one, wanted him to take a public relations slot at twice his baseball salary. And settlement or no settlement, he might still need a new job because his relations with the American League were tanking. "He's apparently tried to get himself fired, but how can we do it?" an unnamed AL official said. "He runs the union."[51]

A Southern California newspaper later reported a rumor that during the off-and-on negotiations, baseball wanted his job, along with National

League umpire Bruce Froemming's. Luciano acknowledged that it might've been true. "I have a big mouth and I'm always putting my foot in it," he said. "I made some horrendous statements about Baltimore, which I'm sorry for."[52] He added that the speculation might have begun because he and Froemming were both officers in the Umpires Association.

Luciano next picketed on April 23 outside Philadelphia's Veterans Stadium. Several dozen supporting members of a local teamsters union caused a traffic jam that delayed fans reaching the Dodgers-Phillies game. The press coverage was brutal, one newspaper calling the snarl "ugly and reprehensible."[53] Another said the teamsters put several thousand unsuspecting fans through "a gantlet of verbiage punctuated with the word 'scab.'"[54] Two candidates for mayor switched fundraising events from the stadium to other venues.

A biology professor recalled a much less confrontational encounter that evening, however. David Smith remembered decades later that Luciano wasn't picketing but providing information to fans entering the game. He also recalled telling the ump that he supported the umpires' position but wanted to see the game. "He graciously said he had no problem with my going in," Smith wrote. "He just wanted to be sure we knew what their issues were."[55]

Luciano believed that support from organized labor in Philadelphia and elsewhere was helpful. Unions *were* America, he declared. "Without union members, they don't have anybody in the stands," he said outside the stadium. "Sure, we may get some adverse reaction from this, but what the fans should be upset about is the poor umpiring they're getting now."[56]

After stops and starts, threats and counter-threats, and increasing unhappiness with the overall quality of umpiring, the two sides finally reached an agreement early May 18 in New York after a fourteen-hour bargaining session. Luciano attended the early-morning signing with umps Paul Runge and Rich Garcia. The returning umpires got salary increases averaging $7,000, a bump in per diem to $67 with increases each of the following two seasons, and two weeks off during the season for most. Neither side claimed victory.

"Two not happies," Luciano called the resolution. "A typical negotiation. We're not happy and they're not happy."[57] Many observers shook their heads over the absence of baseball commissioner Bowie Kuhn, so removed throughout the dispute that umpires mocked him on their picket signs as Bowie Whom. Luciano said he'd never understand why Bowie Whom had done almost nothing. Or why the league presidents had let the dispute drag on for months only to settle "for the basic $20,000 per club that we were asking for from the beginning."[58]

The fifty-two umps had stuck together and kept their jobs, but at a price. AL ump Dave Phillips later wrote that many were "absolutely devastated financially by the strike" because they didn't make much money in the first place.[59] But decades afterward he still applauded Luciano for doing a great job as association president. "He participated. He was there. He was a spokesman. He was out front," said Phillips. "He was able to garner the press and get them to listen to him."[60]

The agreement called for hiring eight of the Minor League umps who had crossed the picket lines. The leagues needed them to maintain full crews when the regulars took their new breaks during the season. The provision was so contentious it took a four hour meeting and some lively dialogue before the association approved the deal later that day. "Sure, we're not happy with some points," Luciano said, "but it is an agreement and we have to live up to it. I've been chomping at the bit to get back."[61]

Luciano noted that he and his colleagues had been out of work for a month and a half of the regular season. "We've been hurt, and baseball has been hurt," he said. "We're sorry it happened, but we're happy for the rapport that has developed as a result between the umpires and baseball."[62] He added that attorney Phillips had won his clients greater respect and made them stronger.

THE MAJOR LEAGUE umpires returned to work May 19 along with new hires Dallas Parks, John Shulock, Derryl Cousins, and Fred Spenn in the AL and Dave Pallone, Fred Brocklander, Lanny Harris, and Steve Fields in the NL. The newcomers worked as "swing" umps to cover when umpires went on vacation. The regulars despised them as strikebreakers, shunned them, and refused to let them join the association. A Montreal sportswriter later dubbed the group the "Exiled Eight."[63]

Luciano and most others never forgave them. Every barricade held until 1983, when Bill Kunkel accepted a ride from Shulock and the two became friends. Bob Engel and Paul Runge likewise later grew close to Pallone.

More than a decade after the labor dispute, Shulock said it had been handled wrongly from the beginning. "They should have never called on the umpires in Triple-A," he said, "and asked them to work while there was a strike going on."[64] By 1990 only he, Cousins, and Brocklander were still Major League umpires.

The regulars returning to duty in 1979 had no time to prepare after missing all of spring training and half a dozen weeks of the regular season. Bill Haller knew they'd all be rusty at first, but Luciano struggled throughout the season. He weighed three hundred pounds, was slower than he liked, and was never happy with his performance on the field.

It was "hard to move blubber around like that," Luciano recalled.[65] He hadn't been moving well during the last few seasons and increasingly missed plays because he didn't have the right angle. He believed that he'd once been a decent umpire but would confess that over recent seasons, "I wasn't concerned about being right every time."[66] AL ump Joe Brinkman later said players had loved Luciano early on because of his willingness to reverse a bad call. "He was the best umpire in their eyes," Brinkman said. "But three years later, he was the worst because he seemed to be saying 'I missed one' so often."[67]

Luciano jetted across the country to begin his delayed season working a White Sox-Angels game at Anaheim Stadium. He joked that the crew probably would receive a standing ovation when they walked onto the field but hear "Kill the umpire!" after the first close play. The *Los Angeles Times* said that he, Haller, Kaiser, and Russ Goetz "actually did get a little applause."[68] A news photographer captured them standing solemnly side by side behind the plate with their caps over their hearts during the national anthem.

The Haller crew got another warm reception two days later at a Twins-Rangers game at Arlington Stadium. A sportswriter noted that the umps received loud ovations, especially Luciano. "Imagine, fans CHEERING umpires!" Kaiser wandered into the Texas dugout to shake hands with players and coaches. "Ty Cobb would have laughed," the scribe wrote.[69] Although dissatisfied with the outcome of the labor dispute, Luciano was pleasantly surprised by the fan reaction and favorable press. "We all were excited and elated," he said. "I think that was one of the things that got them [owners] to sit down and talk with us."[70]

The returning umpires were unhappy, however, over the prospect of working with the Exiled Eight, who reported petty vandalism and anonymous harassment. The first two months following the strike were "really bad," Luciano said. "We weren't helping them at all."[71] After a conference call by the crew chiefs, the umps decided to work with the new men for the good of the game. Still, Luciano conceded, treatment of the eight was atrocious. His first encounter came when Shulock replaced Goetz for three games in Seattle at the end of May.

"I'm a rat," Luciano said, laughingly recalling that after a rhubarb Shulock had asked whether the pitcher had really balked. "There isn't a-n-y doubt in my mind," Luciano told him. When Haller asked Luciano later if he was crazy, he added, "Look, what I told him was there isn't any doubt in my mind, and there isn't—that it wasn't a balk."[72]

The crew worked with Parks for two weeks during June. Luciano said he wouldn't eat, socialize, or drive to a game with him and would speak to him on the field only when necessary. A sportswriter noticed the three veteran umps chatting between innings during a Twins–White Sox game before Kaiser finally spoke with Parks. It had taken them six innings to decide to have dinner that night in Evanston, the scribe said. "Then Kaiser was sent to tell Parks to meet them at a restaurant in Gary."[73]

MOST OF THE SEASON was calm for Haller's crew after the storm and stress of the start. Luciano had what proved to be his final confrontation with Earl Weaver during an Orioles–White Sox Sunday doubleheader August 26 at Chicago. These were the first and last Oriole games he worked all season, an earlier series at Baltimore falling during his new midseason vacation (likely due to careful scheduling by the league office). Luciano ejected the skipper during the fifth inning of the first game for arguing a called third strike on Oriole third baseman Doug DeCinces.

DeCinces said at the time that the ball was at least six inches outside and low; decades later he remembered it as a 3-2 pitch in the dirt. DeCinces was about to head to first base when he heard Luciano call strike three. Weaver somehow kept his temper in check; David Israel of the *Chicago Tribune* wrote that the Oriole skipper merely stood in front of the dugout with arms crossed, not saying a word. "Luciano must have known what

Weaver was thinking," Israel added, "because he tossed him out of the game, anyway."[74]

Weaver ran out now to have his say. Several years later he and Luciano chronicled what happened next in dueling memoirs. "It was then he invented the strangest protest I'd ever heard," Luciano wrote. "'I'm protesting the game on account of the umpire's integrity. . . . And I want it announced over the loudspeaker.'"[75] Weaver remembered it the same way but said he protested to crew chief Goetz. He made sure the White Sox announcer broadcast his reason to the twenty-five thousand people sitting in the stands. "Lee MacPhail happened to be one of them," Weaver wrote, "and I felt it was about time he took Luciano off our case permanently."[76]

The Oriole skipper had played a similar card in 1972, questioning whether Luciano's friend Bill Haller should officiate games involving his brother, Tiger backup catch Tom Haller. Weaver said he wasn't questioning ump Haller's integrity or accusing him of anything except missing pitches. "I'm not saying that he is dishonest. I am not saying he would lean one way or another. But there is a chance. Maybe he does it subconsciously."[77] Weaver's remarks had infuriated AL umps, and Haller asked to be shifted off Tigers games.

DeCinces was puzzled now by the explosion his manager had ignited in Chicago. The next time he came to the plate he asked Luciano what it was all about. "I owe you one Doug," the ump answered. "Too damn hot out here and I'm not gonna sit here and listen to that little guy scream at me all game!"[78] He and Weaver carefully tiptoed around further confrontation during the day's second game.

Integrity was a hot-button word for every umpire. Luciano had written a widely reprinted piece for the *New York Times* following the labor dispute in which he'd said that integrity was an elusive quality on a big league diamond. "Watching the action, you just assume it is there, but if you stop to look, you will be hard-pressed to find it."[79] A *Baltimore Sun* sportswriter wondered why Weaver had been so provocative now. With the Orioles commanding the first game from the start, the writer observed, "all he had to do was sit there, go along for the ride, and not give Luciano the satisfaction of even knowing he was alive. But he couldn't do it and it cost him."[80]

Lee MacPhail was often at odds with Luciano, but the AL president had seen and heard the incident himself and had no choice but to back his ump.

He promptly slapped Weaver with a three-day suspension, saying he simply couldn't tolerate a public announcement about an umpire's integrity. Weaver briefly extended his absence from the dugout, claiming he was too nervous and upset to return. "I've been submitted to undue humiliation by Ron Luciano," he said. "My health has become impaired and I'm better off not in the dugout." Not everyone believed him. The AP cited an anonymous Baltimore writer who thought Luciano might have cause to sue Weaver, who was "simply preparing his own defense."[81]

The suspension punctuated the end of the Weaver-Luciano feud. Their years-long spat hadn't resulted in nearly as many ejections as fans and sportswriters now remember. Luciano worked 228 Baltimore games during eleven seasons, fifty-six behind the plate.[82] He issued only seven of Weaver's ninety-seven career ejections, including both ends of the 1975 doubleheader, which amounted to slightly more than 3 percent of all the Orioles games he'd worked. Luciano thus ended tied with Marty Springstead atop what the AP had dubbed the "Make Weaver a Leaver" club.[83]

Luciano closed his season the last day of September with a Sunday afternoon Red Sox-Tigers game at Detroit. Jack Morris beat Boston 5–1 to finish with a season record of 17-7, top among AL righthanders. Luciano did nothing to warrant mention by the Boston or Detroit papers while working second base during the last Major League game he ever umpired. He didn't know but perhaps suspected that he had already auditioned for a new career in television.

12 Analyst

During the 1979 season, NBC Sports had asked Luciano to announce the lineups for its September 1 game from Yankee Stadium. Scheduled to work second base and happy to oblige, Luciano quipped his way through the Kansas City and New York starters.

He informed viewers that he and Yankee slugger Reggie Jackson always told each other how great they were. That New York second baseman Willie Randolph had played in the league for three years but had never spoken to him; couldn't the kid talk? That he hated to see KC leadoff hitter Willie Wilson get a hit, because Wilson would steal second and he'd have to make a close call. Luciano added that he liked working with short ballplayers because it was easy to see over them and call balls and strikes. Luciano's schtick was a hit. An NBC spokesperson said later he was naturally very glib, "sometimes serious, sometimes humorous, making a pertinent point here and there."[1] Gary Deeb applauded him in the *Chicago Tribune*. "His remarks were pithy and slightly controversial," the TV critic wrote. "It played almost like a Johnny Carson monologue."[2]

Luciano accumulated more air time later during the month with an appearance on the ABC news program *20/20*, which also included segments on disco queen Donna Summer and Vietnam refugees making new lives in Texas. "I don't think they'd ever give another Ron Luciano a chance," the ump told viewers. "No, they'd rather have 100 Bill Hallers and Doug Harveys than another me. I think they'd make it very tough on him. They gave me a job and figured I'd grow up. They tried to change me."[3]

As the postseason neared, NBC remembered Luciano's Yankee Stadium performance and approached him about covering the 1979 AL playoffs with sportscaster Dick Enberg and former Dodger Wes Parker. Luciano's agent and friend, Triple Cities advertising executive Ralph Fabrizio, later said they'd been working on a deal since the previous year. Luciano seemed a good fit, but MLB objected. An upstate New York sportswriter reported that the network had asked permission to add Luciano to its roster but that the request was rejected by the commissioner's office. "They didn't want Luciano criticizing other umpires," an NBC spokesman said.[4] But it was the AL president who blocked the deal like a fastball in the dirt.

Lee MacPhail said the league didn't think the two jobs went together, especially if the networks were looking for controversial people. "It's not harmonious with an umpire being neutral," MacPhail said. "He works for the league as an umpire for the entire season. Our policy is that umpires shall be umpires."[5] MacPhail conceded the prohibition wasn't a written rule, but he said it made sense. He told Fabrizio he couldn't legally stop the network from signing his client but doubted NBC would do so knowing the league was opposed.

Luciano kept umpiring as the season wound down, saying that NBC was trying to decide whether to use him and not let baseball dictate terms. MacPhail suggested that he work the National League playoffs instead, and NBC briefly considered it. Luciano thought the AL's position was legal foolishness. He owned a store in Endicott, he said. "Are they going to tell me I can't work there when the season ends?"[6]

Don Ohlmeyer was the executive producer of NBC Sports. He backpedaled by saying that Luciano was only one of the people under consideration and that the network wouldn't get involved in a policy squabble. "Baseball's taken a position that Ron is a baseball employee," Ohlmeyer said, "and they have a right to make that policy."[7] The network hired Detroit manager George "Sparky" Anderson for the spot before the month was out, despite what Fabrizio and Luciano said was their verbal agreement with NBC. The agent told John Fox they both were very upset.

"NBC said possibly next year they can use Ron in some capacity—we told them, forget it!" Fabrizio added that they could do business elsewhere. But Luciano managed to joke, saying he'd share his AL expertise with Anderson, completing his first season in the AL after nine years managing in the NL. "Or, I can throw him out of the game."[8]

Anderson was a safe bet for TV. The Tiger skipper was smart and inoffensive, a sports editor wrote, a "guaranteed mediocrity" who wouldn't clutter the airwaves with controversy or meaningless observations.[9] Anderson was a diplomat, Luciano a showman. Gary Deeb called NBC Sports the year's "most obedient puppy-dog" for letting baseball bar the umpire.[10]

MacPhail assistant Bob Fishel defended the league. Umpires seeing Luciano on TV, he said, might conclude that "they can get additional income by acting the same way." Luciano acknowledged he'd aggravated the league for years but saw no conflict of interest in working the playoffs for NBC. He thought the objections were far-fetched. Besides, he added, the network wanted him to tell stories and talk about umpires "to give the games a new dimension."[11] But he backed away from legal action. "How can Ron Luciano and my company sue baseball?" Fabrizio asked.[12] They were surprised, however, by how much control baseball had over the network.

Bad feelings lingered beyond the playoffs and World Series. *Boston Globe* sportswriter Peter Gammons noted in late December that after the labor dispute, his remarks about Weaver, and the NBC controversy, Luciano was no favorite with the league office. Nor was the ump admired by colleagues, he added, "because his showboating and mouth violate their unwritten 'never a star or personality' credo." Dick Butler added that Luciano had gotten out of hand. "The league doesn't know exactly what to do with him," the AL director of umpires said,[13]

An unsigned sidebar article tabbed Luciano as one of the half dozen worst Major League umpires. He was a personality who players and managers felt had become "a third-rate umpire. Fans pay to see players, not umpires."[14] John Fox responded that Butler was "a don't-rock-the-boat-type at odds from Day 1" and dismissed the *Globe's* poor rating as a bum rap.[15]

LUCIANO ALWAYS CLAIMED later that he had fully intended to work the 1980 season. The league expected to see him. So did Earl Weaver, who wanted the league to schedule his crew into Baltimore sooner rather than later. The manager said in February that he'd already asked MacPhail to assign Luciano the first game of the season. "But I already know what's going to happen." Weaver said. "I'll get suspended. Well, might as well get it out of the way."[16]

The AL umps shed their distinctive maroon coats this season to adopt the blue blazers, gray trousers, and dark blue caps of their NL counterparts. The only difference were the initials on the caps. *Sporting News* said the spiffy attire reflected baseball's shift toward uniformity in every aspect of umpiring, "procedure, position, hand signals, rules interpretation and dress."[17]

When he reported to Arizona for his first spring training in two seasons, Luciano didn't seem overly concerned about pleasing his employers. He blew a call during a Cubs-Brewers game in mid-March that went against the Cubs, "then doffed his cap and bowed to the pro-Brewer fans along the first base line who applauded him wildly," the *Chicago Tribune* said.[18] Fishel saw it all from the stands. He called the ump's action shameful and planned to file a report on both that game and another earlier in the week when Luciano had worked the plate wearing a pair of white sneakers. Gammons said in the *Globe* that the actions further infuriated the league office.

By now, however, the moods of the various parties might not have mattered anymore. The same day the *Tribune* story appeared, *Globe* TV-sports critic Jack Craig noted that Luciano was again flirting with television, NBC wanting him as an analyst for the coming season. He added in *Sporting News* that the network planned to give him an in-house audition shortly before the season began. "If he displays the spirit behind the microphone that he does behind home plate," Craig wrote, "Luciano may walk away from his umpiring career."[19] He said that if the ump did jump the fence, audiences for the first time might hear real insights into umpiring.

Luciano said later he had hoped to stay in professional sports after stepping away from umpiring but was thinking more along the lines of a job as team publicist or traveling secretary. He was already busy outside of baseball in other ways. Besides operating his store in Endicott, he'd made a telephone commercial and launched a fifteen-minute syndicated radio program called *Strike Zone* from Binghamton.

NBC's interest in him was heightened because the network expected to cover the 1980 Summer Olympic Games from Moscow. The United States, however, was threatening to boycott the games because of the Soviet Union's recent invasion of Afghanistan. Luciano said afterward the situation depended on timing more than anything. "They had all their big boys primed for the Olympics and they needed someone to do some baseball."[20] He kept mum about a possible new job but sister Dee Jester chipped in during late March by saying her brother and Fabrizio were meeting with network officials in New York.

Dee told the *Binghamton Press* it would have to be an attractive offer, not a one-year experiment. Her brother was excited by the possibilities, she said, "but has too good medical benefits, insurance plan, pension plan and so forth to switch unless it's super-good."[21] Joe Garagiola for one thought Luciano would make a good commentator because he wasn't afraid to speak out.

NBC officially auditioned Luciano in New York on Wednesday April 9 using a videotape of an Orioles-Angels playoff game from October. He supplied color commentary while sportscaster Merle Harmon sat beside him doing the play-by-play. Luciano thought it was about the worst thing he'd ever done. "A fat, ugly guy who can't speak more than a seven-letter word in with a good looking announcer with a voice that could shatter glass?"[22] He told critic Craig he'd been scared to death. "I pointed out all the things I had done wrong but they said I was fine," he said. "They told me they want me to tell stories."[23]

He still had no intention of going on TV. Luciano was scheduled to umpire in Anaheim on Friday, but Ohlmeyer offered him a contract on Thursday. He accepted a two-year deal with an option for a third, at a salary substantially higher than the $43,000 he made as an umpire. They didn't disclose his new pay scale, but journalists thought they knew. Dick Young of the *New York Daily News* predicted that he'd get $50,000 the first season and $75,000 the second. "If he clicks and they pick up the option, there's a promise of big bucks."[24] The columnist also quipped, "You had to figure Ron Luciano would wind up in show biz or on rye, ham that he is."[25]

As congratulations poured in, Luciano said he felt like a new bride. He often joked later about hearing champagne corks popping in the background when he phoned MacPhail with the news. He also claimed he'd sent a telegram to Earl Weaver saying the good news was that he was retiring, the bad news that "I'll be second-guessing you from the broadcast booth."[26] (Weaver correctly predicted he'd probably see more of Luciano now than during the previous two seasons.) The AL waived its requirement for prior notice before releasing the umpire to start his new gig. Luciano said he had a new lease on life but admitted to being scared because he'd never done a broadcast in his life. Colleague Durwood Merrill watched him go with mixed feelings.

Merrill's flamboyance on the field was sometimes compared with Luciano's, probably to his detriment. He later described Luciano as not only a great showman but possibly the biggest pain in the ass ever to wear the mask, and he believed that Luciano had been unhappy the past few seasons. "I really felt that Ronnie got run out of major league baseball by the American League office, and I'm not so sure that it was fair," Merrill wrote. "He still had some skills, and I thought he was a good umpire. But let's be realistic about Ronnie and his style. It didn't work, even for him."[27]

Luciano acknowledged that he'd lost some enthusiasm after eleven seasons in the big leagues. But until the last inning of his last game, he wrote, "I never lost the thrill of standing on a major league baseball diamond. It was every bit as good as the fantasy of it."[28] But at least now he could speak freely about anything. He'd been opening his mouth since the beginning of time, he said, "and now they're gonna pay me for it."[29]

Most critics applauded his move to the airways. The *Miami Herald* said Luciano had been spectacularly unsuited to being an umpire anyway. "He is gregarious, garrulous, amusing, emotional, theatrical and flamboyant—all qualities frowned upon in the sober, somber, blue-suit, black-shoes fraternity of umpires."[30] But now the supposed flaws were assets. A *Charlotte Observer* columnist dubbed his leap to NBC "'The Liberation of Luciano,' a play in nine innings."[31] Naturally not everyone applauded.

Washington Star columnist William Taaffe said Luciano could cause even more PR trouble for the lords of baseball as an analyst than he had as an umpire. "As long as they could control him, he was relatively harmless," Taaffe wrote. "Now he has access to the air waves, which is like putting a kid in charge of a candy shop."[32]

GARAGIOLA AND EX-YANKEE SHORTSTOP Tony Kubek handled NBC's primary *Game of the Week*. The network assigned the former ump to work the backup game with Harmon. Sportswriters often noted Luciano's resemblance to craggy, gap-toothed actor Earnest Borgnine, and the contrast now with Harmon amused him. "Poor Merle," Luciano said. "They hired me to make Merle look good. He's got steel gray hair, beautiful blue eyes, chiseled features and a great big deep voice. I've got a high voice, I talk too fast and I've got a face made for radio."[33] Luciano called their partnership Beauty and the Beast.

NBC's new color man had little time to reflect. He signed his contract on Thursday and was in Texas the next day, scheduled to work in front of a microphone Saturday, April 12. He later wished that he'd had a couple of months to get ready. A writer watched him mingle with the Yankee and Ranger players at the Arlington Stadium batting cage Friday evening. The ex-ump wore loose-fitting slacks and a wrinkled white shirt. "The tail hung out in the back; his tie was loosened; and his shoes ('Space shoes') defied description. 'I can wear a $300 suit and look like 50 cents,' he admitted."[34]

When rain began falling early Saturday afternoon, producers told the neophyte to take a mic down to the dugouts. "Alone?" Luciano asked.[35] He could only shake his head in wonder once the game was postponed. For fifteen years, he said, he'd done rain dances, hoping to miss the makeup double-header or catch a plane out of town. "Now, I'm praying for sunshine."[36]

Although the backup game was a washout, Luciano appeared during a quick cut-in to the national broadcast. Harmon asked about Ranger pitcher Gaylord Perry's alleged spitball. "Everybody in baseball knows that man throws a spitter," Luciano answered. ("I can't help it if the ball sinks," the hurler replied in a pre-taped rebuttal.) The newcomer also made news off the air by saying AL umps didn't eject Perry for tossing wet ones, because the league office didn't want them to call it. Sportswriter Murray Chass wrote in *Sporting News* that Luciano's brief performance was a "glimpse of things that are perhaps to come."[37]

The same day as the rainout, the U.S. Olympic Committee voted to support President Carter's call for a boycott of the summer Olympic games in Moscow. NBC hadn't needed to boost its baseball staff after all. And even with an extra week to prepare, Luciano still was nowhere near being technically proficient for TV. He later said he didn't even know how to keep score. "I actually had to ask them just what it is a baseball color man does," he recalled. "When I was umpiring, I never had time to watch a game."[38]

The ump-turned-analyst didn't know the right moments to talk; or that a so-called cough button kept a ticklish throat from interrupting the broadcast; or that a hero wasn't a sandwich but a graphic under a player's photo. The earphone that producers used to communicate from the truck to the booth also confounded Luciano. He could talk or listen, he said. "So far anyway I can't do both."[39] The device's inventor was one of two people who wouldn't go to heaven, he added, the second being any stadium organist who played "Three Blind Mice."

At least he was familiar with his partner. Harmon was an acquaintance of a dozen years, and besides working as a broadcaster, he owned a chain of fan shops. Luciano later wrote that he had consulted him before opening his own store in Binghamton. Harmon was an ideal TV companion whose professionalism and generosity Luciano always praised. The pair called their first game together the following Saturday, April 19, Rangers versus Red Sox at Boston. Luciano said he was so nervous that he'd started biting his nails for the first time since he'd played football. "Then the game started, and Merle's voice boomed, 'This is NBC's Game of the Week,'" he said. "God, I almost jumped out of the booth."[40]

The Rangers scored three runs in the first inning on their way to an 8–0 romp. NBC had no replay equipment at Fenway Park to help the crew fill airtime. Producer Mike Weisman said afterward that Luciano couldn't have started with a tougher game but still offered terrific insight into the players instead of second-guessing umpires as skeptics had expected. Luciano was ebullient, having discovered a whole new world during the past two weeks. "I could probably even get married again," he exclaimed. He added, however, "There is no way I'm qualified to be a big league announcer."[41]

The partners covered the Red Sox against the Tigers April 26 at Detroit. Luciano's knowledge of the AL was evident in his work. The ex-ump said Earl Weaver had won 102 games last season, "so he's got to know something about baseball, and he says enclosed parks are the best to play in." He called Jim Rice of Boston Mr. Strong, "the only man who ever scared me as an umpire." He noted that Red Sox catcher Carlton Fisk had been awake all night battling a virus and that Detroit backstop Lance Parrish had once worked as a bodyguard for singer Tina Turner. Luciano almost cheered when Carl Yastrzemski smacked an upper-deck homer but caught himself and said hastily, "It doesn't matter who the team is as long as it's exciting."[42]

NBC briefly feared that having lost the Olympics, it might also lose Major League baseball to a threatened players strike. The union had forced cancellation of the last eight days of spring training and set May 23 as the date for reaching a new agreement. The Saturday before the deadline, Harmon and Luciano called a fourteen-inning game in Toronto. Luciano would have hated working such a long contest as an umpire but admitted, "I maybe miss being on the field just a little bit."[43] NBC prepared to fill the hole in its schedule the following week by re-airing Game Six of the 1975 World Series. Garagiola, Kubek, and Luciano were to provide a live studio voiceover to keep the event topical. But the players reached a last minute deal to avert a strike for another year and the live commentary wasn't needed.

The good news was dimmed for Luciano, however, by the death following surgery of his brother-in-law Clifford Walton, his sister Bobbie's husband. The color man worked that Saturday's Indians–Red Sox game in Boston and somehow was in good form. "That's not tobacco he's chewing, that's raw nails!" Luciano quipped about Cleveland's rookie phenom "Super Joe" Charboneau. He said his teammate Mike Hargrove (also known to fans as the human rain delay) was so slow getting ready to bat "they have to call 'Time!' if the ball hits the catcher's mitt."[44]

Luciano was still president of the Umpires Association, although vice president and NL ump Paul Runge actually ran things until an election to choose a successor. Luciano showed at the end of May that he retained strong ties with his old colleagues. At issue was Pittsburgh Pirate third baseman Bill Madlock, hit with a fifteen-day suspension and $5,000 fine by NL president Chub Feeney for slapping plate umpire Gerry Crawford in the nose with his glove during a May 1 argument at Three Rivers Stadium. Arbiters were unhappy about the long delay in enforcing the penalties, caused by Madlock's appeal to commissioner Bowie Kuhn.

Union lawyer Richie Phillips sent a May 31 telegram informing the Pirates that NL umpires had "suspended Madlock indefinitely." The suspension would begin Friday, June 6, Phillips said, and would take the form of repeated ejections for what he called aberrant behavior. "Said ejections will all be within the official rules of baseball." In effect, Madlock would get the boot continuously for any little thing at all. The *New York Daily News* noted that the telegram "was conveniently given to Luciano to read over TV."[45]

Garagiola and Kubek discussed the telegram during their *Game of the Week* broadcast from Boston. Ex-catcher Garagiola said Madlock would be kicked out "just for having bad breath."[46] NBC then cut to Detroit, where Luciano and Harmon were working. "They'll do it, you wait till Friday," Luciano said of the threat to bounce the Pirate. AL umps had considered similar actions against managers and players during his day, he added, including versus Earl Weaver and journeyman outfielder Alex Johnson, much despised by umpires. Harmon asked whether such threats were fair. "Is it fair that Chub Feeney has suspended him for 15 days and weeks later the man is still playing?" Luciano replied.[47]

Phillips's telegram outraged Feeney, who declared that no umpire would eject a manager, coach, or player from any game without just cause—including Madlock from any game in which he was eligible to play. The threat of a major confrontation dissolved, however, when Pirate owner and chairman John Galbreath convinced Madlock to drop his appeal for the good of the game and the team. Luciano said no more about the controversy.

NBC AIRED THE BACKUP *Game of the Week* in areas only where the primary game was blacked out or when it was rained out. Luciano likened his job to "hosting a telethon for hiccups. Nobody cared. Nobody even knew we were on."[48] The network even cut away from its May 10 backup game after six innings to begin coverage of a golf tournament. (The Royals were leading the Red Sox 12–8 at Fenway Park, where Luciano and Harmon said no lead was safe.) Still, the rookie sportscaster's work got noticed and attracted both cheers and catcalls.

A Minneapolis sportswriter wrote that Luciano seemed to be the rarest of human beings, "totally happy and without pretentions."[49] White Sox broadcaster Jimmy Piersall emphatically disagreed. The acerbic ex-Major Leaguer called Luciano terrible. "He knows nothing about the game, and the players really hate him."[50] Luciano ignored it all and enjoyed his new position, saying he never figured umpiring was all that important anyway. "But hey, Ron Luciano, NBC Sports. Wow! That's something."[51]

Luciano nonetheless knew he had a lot yet to learn, his booth time amounting to on-the-job training. He was not only learning the TV business, he said, but also more about baseball itself. Luciano joked later about mangling the pronunciation of Hispanic or uncommon names such as Joaquín Andújar and Garth Iorg. Facts sometimes eluded him, and more than once, he firmly inserted his size 15-D shoes into his mouth. *Sports Illustrated* said that his overbearing on-air personality stemmed from "an intense desire to please, and from nervousness; he squeezes Harmon's arms in moments of fright, and both arms are now black and blue." Harmon didn't manage to block his partner's quip during a Texas-Boston game that batter Rusty

Staub "looks like a girl, he runs like a girl, he swings like a girl, but he hits like a man."[52]

Staub took offense and later confronted him. A Texas paper said Luciano told the Ranger that he was kidding, but Staub wasn't laughing. Luciano hadn't meant to insult the player or women but mistakenly thought the remark was "a super thing to say about him."[53]

Luciano also covered a serious news story involving illegally prescribed amphetamines that swirled around the Philadelphia Phillies. NBC touched on the case during a pregame show in July. The *Kansas City Star* said the network assigned Luciano to be its investigative reporter. The doctor involved refused to speak with him, "but this did not prevent Luciano from doing a report from the steps of [his] home."[54] Authorities filed criminal charges (later dismissed) against the physician but none against any player mentioned. Lighthearted banter was more Luciano's specialty anyway.

Knight-Ridder television reporter Ron Miller considered Luciano "one of the brightest additions to sports coverage within recent memory." Miller presciently noted that the color man had a devilish sense of humor, "and my guess is if he wrote an autobiography right now the title probably would be 'The Umpire Strikes Back.'"[55]

LUCIANO CAUGHT UP with Earl Weaver and his Orioles late that summer during a series with Billy Martin's A's at Oakland. Weaver wanted to avoid talking with Luciano in front of cameras. "I can't think of any reason to do it," he said, "but if somebody can give me a reason, then we'll see."[56] Surprisingly, the person who convinced Weaver was Luciano, who approached him in the Baltimore dugout before Friday's night game. Anyone expecting an explosion was disappointed.

"Hi, Earl, how ya doing," Luciano said. They exchanged mutual congratulations—for Luciano's new career and for the Orioles' being in the thick of the AL East divisional race. A Baltimore beat writer said the conversation got so congenial it was almost sickening to anyone who remembered years gone by. The odd couple briefly discussed what Weaver was and wasn't willing to chat about on TV Saturday afternoon. "Okay Earl, whatever you want to do is okay with us," Luciano agreed.[57]

The pair met on-air before the August 23 game. The Baltimore skipper danced around a question about appealing a three-day suspension for accidentally poking umpire Rich Garcia in the eye with the bill of his cap. He spoke instead about his club's chances of passing the division-leading Yankees. "Okay, the altercations with the umpire," Luciano said. "Are they going to continue as well as the winning?" Weaver answered with a slight smile that he doubted it. "I've only been ejected two times this year since you quit."[58] Luciano laughed, the hatchet perhaps not buried but at least not embedded in either man's head.

NBC seemed to like the job Luciano was doing and gave him some of the credit for the *Game of the Week*'s improved ratings. "And Luciano himself appears to be having a grand time," a Milwaukee columnist wrote, "although he said the adjustment was a big one."[59] The big man had the gift of gab necessary for television, and according to critic Gary Deeb, he was scrupulously candid about the umps whenever there was a controversial play. As the 1980 postseason began, although Luciano didn't yet consider himself a true broadcaster, he did appreciate his job. "Listen, I'm still doing baseball but now I have time off," he said. "I was married to baseball before."[60] Now he had three days off each week and was having much more fun.

Luciano joined the NBC team covering the Philadelphia-Kansas City World Series to comment on umpires or controversial calls. Cincinnati pitcher Tom Seaver joined Garagiola and Kubek as a color analyst. "NBC, hamming things up a bit, also plans to dress up Luciano like Darth Vader tomorrow night for a pregame spoof entitled, 'The Umpire Strikes Back,'" the *Philadelphia Inquirer* said before Game Two.[61] The spoof was corny but entertaining. Luciano didn't have much else to do, but he did comment on Kansas City first sacker Willie Aiken's batting stance, back foot planted out of the box. "Luciano played it straight by stating the rule instead of truth," the *Miami Herald* said, which was that umps traditionally ignored the infraction, just as they did a shortstop taking a double-play relay with his shoe a foot past the bag.[62]

The Phillies won the series in six games. The *Cincinnati Enquirer* said Luciano, in the booth to explain technical aspects, and Harmon, in the stands as a roving reporter, were largely left out of the network's coverage. NBC took a few other knocks but overall got good marks. "When ex-jocks Garagiola and Kubek got still-active jock Seaver and ex-umpire Luciano winging it on a disputed play," the *Los Angeles Times* said, "it sounded like a rap session around a country store cracker barrel. All are chatterboxes."[63]

Luciano's working year ended at the same time as it had when he was an umpire. NBC had no plans to keep him on to cover football, he said, since it might detract from his being a baseball expert. He kept busy during the offseason by working on his radio program, checking on his sporting goods store, and making a guest appearance on Reds catcher Johnny Bench's TV show in Cincinnati. He also hit the lucrative banquet circuit and trained a new birddog, named Billy after Bill Haller. John Fox wrote in Binghamton as Christmas neared, "Ron Luciano is a hard man to catch up with these days."[64]

THE 1981 SEASON was approaching when Luciano canceled a February banquet appearance in Edmonton, Alberta. A Canadian newspaper said he'd suffered a severe reaction to a bug bite while vacationing in Florida and was resting in a New York hospital. He recovered without complication but learned that during the new season, he would call a handful of games with Dick Enberg instead of Harmon. Spring training then began under a cloud as players again threatened to strike during the summer. It wasn't an altogether auspicious start to his sophomore season with NBC.

Luciano first worked with Enberg on a Phillies-Cardinals game April 11 at St. Louis. Enberg provided play-by-play and Luciano the color. If the former ump resented this pairing he didn't say so later, nor did anyone especially comment on their performance together. TV critic Jack Craig wrote during early May that it remained to be seen whether Luciano would advance from being an anachronism—"an ex-umpire who smiles and laughs—to an analyst who delivers little nuggets that only someone who has been so close to the game would know."[65]

Luciano did himself no favors when he got into trouble only a month later, and not even on his own broadcast. Not surprisingly, it happened in Baltimore, during early June as local Channel 2 was about to switch its network affiliation from CBS to NBC. Luciano made a promotional appearance on the station's Orioles broadcast and promptly offended many listeners with a joke about *Game of the Week* colleague Tony Kubek. "He's not the brightest Polack, you know," Luciano said.

The network's switchboard lit up and *Washington Star* television, and radio critic William Taaffe called out Luciano for obnoxious announcing and bad taste. "He means well, but he comes across as the guy on the bus you do not want to sit next to."[66] Luciano apologized (again) for having a big mouth, saying Kubek knew he meant no harm. "But yeah," he added, "I've really got to watch what I say on the air."[67]

He had little time to make amends to his audience before the players struck eight days later. The issue was the murky one involving what a Major League club losing a quality player to free agency would receive in return. Owners and players were far apart, as they had been since the narrowly averted strike the previous season. Thomas Boswell had written earlier that neither side had any significant new ideas on the issue of partial compensation. "Instead, each is focusing its efforts on a bluff-and-bluster battle of rhetoric." After many months of public posturing, Boswell added, "the old game has shown its all-too-familiar face—with age-old animosities and swollen egos butting in."[68]

Nothing changed before the players walked out after their games on June 11, after which nobody played again for two months. Luciano spent what should have been the middle of the season back home with his mother in Endicott. Taaffe reported that unlike the players, Garagiola, Kubek, and Luciano all received their pay during the strike but Harmon worked on a per diem basis and lost income.

NBC filled some of the broadcasting gap with Japanese baseball. The *Los Angeles Times* regretted that the network didn't use Luciano and former player and announcer Bob Uecker instead of Lindsay Nelson and Jerry Coleman. The color that the pair could have generated, the paper said, would have been worthy of Cinemascope. "Imagine the time they'd have had comparing Japanese and American baseball, the stories that would come to mind triggered by some play action."[69] Luciano did join Garagiola in Toronto during late July to tape *Home Run Classic*, a contest that saw striking American and National League sluggers competing for individual and team honors.

Once owners and players finally reached a settlement, Major League Baseball resumed with the postponed All-Star Game on August 9. NBC stuck with Garagiola and Kubek for the Sunday telecast from Cleveland. Luciano got back on the air the following Saturday, calling the Royals-Indians game with Harmon also from Cleveland. He got off one of his trademark wisecracks when a camera panned to the Kansas City manager. If it was true that we learn by our mistakes, Luciano said, "then Jim Frey will be the best manager ever."[70]

The results of the long strike were "really, really messy," as *Sporting News* said long afterward.[71] Clubs finished the season after playing only 102 to 111 games instead of the normal 162. For the first time in big league history, first- and second-half standings determined which teams continued to the postseason. The messiness also produced what Buffalo sportswriter Erik Brady called a lethal loophole that made it possible (if extremely unlikely) for a team to make the playoffs by tanking a game at the end of the truncated season. Luciano and Harmon backed baseball's contention that such a scenario would never happen. "These guys are professionals," the color man said. "I can't believe they would ever go out and lose a game intentionally." Brady scoffed that Luciano must be blind, "something many an American League umpire accused him of when he was a hot-dogging umpire."[72]

NBC continued to experiment with its booth alignment during the rest of the season. During early September it paired Enberg with Phillies broadcaster and former Cardinal catcher Tim McCarver for a Friday night game at Veterans Stadium. The *Philadelphia Daily News* said it was no secret that NBC was less than thrilled with Luciano's performance and suggested that McCarver's appearance on the Cincinnati-Philadelphia national telecast meant the network was "testing the waters of public opinion."[73]

As the ragged season ended, NBC again announced Seaver as a member of its playoff team. The *Cincinnati Enquirer* said the assignment showed that the Harmon-Luciano backup team hasn't worked well together; "in fact, rumblings are that Luciano will not be asked to return as the brutally frank No. 2 color man."[74] One such rumbler said Luciano would be wise to look around for another job. The *Washington Post* added that he likely wouldn't play any sort of role during the playoffs and might even get the thumb once his contract expired, "proving once again that umpires should be seen, not heard."[75]

Losing two months of work experience might have harmed Luciano's prospects. The dire predictions proved accurate; after he completed his second contracted season, NBC didn't exercise its option for a third. The network also parted ways with Harmon (who signed with the Texas Rangers as a broadcaster) and replaced him with young Bob Costas. Hints that

Luciano might catch on with ESPN as a college football analyst didn't pan out. When the backup team disappeared from the air, Jack Craig wrote in the *Boston Globe* that Luciano was deemed "too hot for the cool medium."[76] But the reality wasn't quite so simple.

An unnamed NBC executive said a few years afterward that he loved Luciano and thought he could have succeeded. "But I said to him 'Ron, it would be nice if you knew the names. Ron, it would be nice if you knew the teams. Ron, it would be nice if you studied the statistics.'"[77] A New England sports editor observed much later, "Unfortunately, his schtick was a sight gag. Mouthing platitudes into a microphone submerged Luciano in that wide, bland sea of color analysts, and he quickly faded to obscurity, as cruel a fate as could meet any man who so clearly loved the spotlight."[78]

Although out of television, Luciano was hardly headed into obscurity. He went home to prepare Ron Luciano's Sports World for the Christmas rush, planned to participate in Endicott's annual holiday parade, and surely expected to grow his usual offseason beard for winter hunting trips. But the best indication of his plans came the first of December when he spoke to a Sports in Literature class for advanced senior English students at Vestal High School.

"Why would a former jock who talks non-stop about sports be lecturing to a high school literature class?" the *Binghamton Press* asked. "One reason may be to promote his new book, *The Umpire Strikes Back*."[79]

13 Author

David Fisher began his career writing for *That Show with Joan Rivers* on daytime TV. He first noticed Luciano on television too, chatting with Yankees broadcasters during a rain delay one unknown Saturday afternoon. Fisher recalled decades later that Luciano was in the booth to help fill air time. "He was very funny and I thought, you know, I could write a book with that guy and it would be terrific."[1]

Luciano had considered writing a memoir or autobiography for some time. Earlier he'd cooperated with a New Jersey-based writer who had grown up near Endicott and interned for the *Binghamton Press* before graduating from Princeton University. Their work resulted in a 1977 profile for *People* magazine—"The biggest thing Luciano has is a great sense of humor," Joe Garagiola said—but not in a contract between them.[2] Three years later Fisher asked his agent to get in touch with Luciano rep Ralph Fabrizio. By December 1980, following Luciano's first season with NBC, John Fox reported that the ex-ump was near a deal with Bantam Books for what Fox called an autobiography. "Ron's got so much to say, it naturally takes two to write it—himself and David Fischer [*sic*], whose previous works include *Joey*, about a hit-man for the Mafia."[3]

Both Syracuse graduates, the wannabe and the professional penman became the Yogi Berra and Whitey Ford of baseball authors. Their pitch to Bantam was funny, outrageous, and entertaining, the literary version of Luciano shooting Amos Otis out-out-out-out-out-OUT! at first base. Fisher had a dollar figure in mind once they'd finished the proposal. "I thought, 'This is what they'll pay for,'" he recalled. "They offered double."[4]

The duo went to the Mount Airy Lodge in the Pocono Mountains during the middle of winter to assemble the manuscript. Years later the *New York Times* recalled its floor-to-ceiling mirrors, velvet-swagged canopy beds, and shag carpeting so deep and blue "it successfully hid several generations of dirt."[5] Fisher thought everything about that place was funny. "We would sit in the room for hours and I would interview him about everything, about baseball, about players," he said.[6] He then went off and wrote, adding his own touch to the text.

The book Luciano and Fisher produced was the first of five. Given the earlier suggestions, the 1980 World Series Darth Vader segment, and the continuing popularity of *Star Wars* movies, Bantam almost inevitably called it *The Umpire Strikes Back*. Luciano disliked the title, however, fearing it implied some unintended criticism of baseball. Propelled by serious marketing muscle, copies hit the bookstores on April 1, 1982.

Luciano said the initial print run was sixty thousand copies with an ad budget of $70,000, which was perhaps an exaggeration but still within the ballpark. *Sports Illustrated* ran two ten-thousand-word pre-publication excerpts that helped boost sales enormously. Newspapers ranging from small country dailies to the *New York Daily News* likewise began running excerpts the first week of May. Bantam also bought an ad in *Sporting News* in which fourteen big league players and managers praised the book.

Sal Bando said Luciano was even funnier as a writer than he'd been as an umpire. "And he was a very, very funny umpire."[7] Bando added that the book was terrific. Even sour Earl Weaver contributed, if only to say that Luciano was one of very few umpires people would pay their way into a park to see. The Baltimore skipper had a memoir due out during the summer called *It's What You Learn after You Know It All That Counts*. With their on-field competition over, Luciano said later, they argued now about their respective book sales. Weaver, he added, "couldn't stand it when he found out my book sold more than his did."[8]

Reviewers weren't ecstatic over *The Umpire Strikes Back*, but many agreed with Bando's critique. Noting that sales of a sports book rarely hit ten thousand copies, the *Cleveland Plain Dealer* said, "This one is big because it's light and bright."[9] The *Cincinnati Enquirer* wasn't as enthused but thought the book had a place on sports bookshelves because Luciano was an engaging personality "and baseball really doesn't need *all* umpires to be conformist clones."[10] Once it became a blockbuster, the *Indianapolis Star* said the book might better be titled *The Umpire Strikes It Rich*. The author whose name appeared first and largest on the cover reacted with unusual modesty. "It's just nice little funny stories about baseball," Luciano said. "And I think that's what sold it."[11]

A media blitz began before publication April 1. Luciano appeared with Bryant Gumble on the *Today Show* one morning in late March then hours later showed up with writer Gloria Steinem and evangelist Reverend Ike on *Late Night with David Letterman*. During mid-May he landed any author's dream spot, chatting with Johnny Carson on the *Tonight Show*. For several frantic weeks Luciano seemed to be everywhere, both on the air and geographically. The *San Diego Union* said he careened through his book tour with bewildered PR people holding on behind "like so many dinghies being towed by a minesweeper in giant seas."[12]

He also received new interest from television reps, although not this time from the sports division. During April he had a screen test for a TV sitcom called *Cheers*, "produced by the same outfit as 'Taxi,'" Dick Young reported in his telegraph style. "Role calls for bartender who used to be a football coach."[13]

Luciano seemed a natural to play Ernie Pantusso. But rewritten as an ex-baseball coach, the role went instead to Nicholas Colasanto, an experienced actor who earned three Emmy nominations on the NBC megahit. Luciano's resemblance to George Wendt, cast to play barfly Norm Peterson, might have worked against him. The ex-tackle told *People* magazine that during the summer, he was reading for a part in another show that featured a talking orangutan. "I've got a perfect voice for an orangutan," he said.[14]

The publishing juggernaut that was *The Umpire Strikes Back* meanwhile rumbled on. John Fox said later it outsold every hardcover sports book in nearly a decade, "unless *Jane Fonda's Exercise Book* is sports."[15] *Library Journal* found the memoir jocular and self-deprecating, "good, light baseball fair."[16] The *Binghamton Press* said the ex-ump "cannily places himself in the role of victim the way Jack Benny used to do it."[17] The *Sacramento Bee* said the book was often hilarious but noted, "Noel Coward, Luciano is not," his approach to comedy being only slightly more sophisticated than Abbott and Costello's.[18] The *Philadelphia Inquirer* placed Luciano higher, though, calling him the "Woody Allen of the baseball diamond."[19]

Luciano dedicated the book to his mother, "who taught me the difference between safe and out."[20] When their copies arrived, his sister Dee Jester told their mom to turn to the dedication page. "How nice!" Josephine burbled. "And how did he word the dedication in your copy?"[21]

THE UMPIRE STRIKES BACK appeared on the *New York Times* bestseller list at the end of September 1982, with some readers perhaps bemused to find it listed under nonfiction. It remained there for eighteenth consecutive weeks, a mass-market paperback soon to follow. Luciano said he couldn't believe how well the book was selling. "Baseball players can't read or write so I thought, 'Who's going to buy it?'"[22] He wanted Robert Redford for the lead if Hollywood ever bought the movie rights but thought they'd probably choose Orson Welles instead. "He's got the weight."[23]

The outlandish persona Luciano had developed as an umpire and sportscaster got even larger and louder. He portrayed himself as a big lovable galoot, someone who could "tell of his travails in the manner of Job," the *Binghamton Press* later said.[24] He inscribed one review copy of *The Umpire Strikes Back* to a reporter, "Sorry I can't write as well as you but remember my level is a 10 yr old. . . . mentaly!! [*sic*]."[25] His Emmy-worthy performance as himself surely equaled anything he might have done on *Cheers*. During eleven seasons as a big league umpire, Luciano had been "establishing a character and doing a very good job," said Fisher, who helped him polish the character in print.[26] Give the pair of them two or three inches—past, present, real, or fictional—"and what they'll write will be a yard wide," John Fox observed.[27]

Luciano had resurrected tales for the book that he'd used to entertain sportswriters for years and told them again now to interviewers. It surprised no one who knew him that he embroidered so often and or that writers gladly played along. Atlanta sports editor Furman Bisher called the book a riot but added drily, "I don't know that I'm thoroughly convinced it's all true."[28] A *Baltimore Evening Sun* columnist later wrote that Luciano was as imaginative an author as he'd sometimes been as an umpire, "altering situations to fit his style."[29] Triple Cities friends knew he also took liberties in describing his boyhood, the Italian-American community in Endicott, and his friendship with the infamous Barbara brothers. "Well, when Ron does anything, he does it *enthusiastically*—let's leave it at that," one said.[30]

No one seriously objected, however. Luciano clearly was a jokester and entertainer, a complex man posing as a simple one, and one of nature's great storytellers. His tales shifted or expanded during telling, and under scrutiny, some (such as his encounter with Big Daddy Lipscomb) evaporated altogether. Occasionally, he made up detailed tales on the spot. No one, though, considered him a liar or a con man. "Oh, such stories he would tell," Fisher remembered in the *New York Daily News*. "Ronnie simply wanted to make people happy, and sometimes that required embellishing a story a bit. Actually, a lot. I mean, he told some whoppers."[31]

Fisher was amazed that so many people believed them. He related a chat between Luciano and Yankee coach Jeff Torborg, who once asked what the former ump had done over the winter. Luciano said he'd made some small investments; in fact, he'd spent the winter hunting and ice fishing. Then, bit by bit under friendly questioning, he concocted an entire narrative about buying a diner off the New Jersey Turnpike. Fisher didn't recall this anecdote decades later but said, "Somebody told me that I told that story."[32] Here then was the ultimate expression of the charm and wackiness of Luciano Lore. Even a tale about the unreliability of his tales was unreliable.

The Umpire Strikes Back offered scores of stories. Many were pure inventions, some were at least inspired by fact, and a few were delightfully true. Did pitcher Tommy John really drop the ball during a windup, continue his motion, and collapse in laughter when Luciano called the phantom pitch a strike? "Absolutely false," John said. "That whole story is a figment of Ron Luciano's imagination."[33] Did he trade places with infielder Buddy Bell during spring training and play a half inning at third base? Years later Bell said it never happened. Did Luciano once cause future Hall of Famer Harmon Killebrew to be picked off second base when "Killer" politely stepped away from the bag to reply to the ump's chatter? This one seems likely, a respected baseball database revealing a game in which thirty-nine-year-old Killebrew, three days before playing his final game, was "picked off and caught stealing third (pitcher to shortstop)."[34]

Many fans recalled stories about Luciano eating or drinking on the diamond during play. Did it ever actually happen? Yes, at least once, in July 1978, while he worked third base during a Mariners-Blue Jays game at Toronto. Luciano hadn't finished his Coca-Cola between innings before a Seattle batter lofted a fly ball to center. As second base umpire Hank Soar ran back to see whether the outfielder had made a catch, Luciano rushed to cover the vacated bag—and took his refreshment with him. He explained that he was thirsty and wanted to finish his drink. "I tried to keep it under control and I only spilled a couple of drops."[35] He probably would have finished it earlier, he said, had the ball girl come to him before the third-base coach.

In addition to his blurb for the Bantam ad, Earl Weaver read his own name dozens of times between the covers of *The Umpire Strikes Back*. The tales there didn't always match his recollections, and he said the book was interesting if you weren't expecting to learn what really happened. The skipper even tried to set Luciano straight. "You know what he says?" Weaver demanded. "He says it's literary license."[36] Luciano gleefully replied to his old sparring partner's claim that his memoir was half fiction. "I agreed, and told him the fiction part was where I said he was a shoo-in for the Hall of Fame and is a genius in motivating players."[37]

A few traditionalists who had never understood Luciano were almost apoplectic over his book. NL umpire Bruce Froemming sputtered that Luciano was a disgrace to the profession. "He's a nice guy, but he's just a clown," he said. "To put that stuff in a book, like how he let catchers call balls and strikes, was a disgrace."[38] Luciano had been a brutal umpire, he added, as any good ballplayer who'd seen him would agree. Luciano said later that Froemming wouldn't say hello if they passed on the street. Sportswriter Scott Ostler injected some objectivity while writing for the *Los Angeles Times*. If baseball people voted to determine the most popular and least popular ump over the past ten seasons or so, Ostler wrote as summer began, "the top vote getter in both categories would probably be Ron Luciano."[39]

LUCIANO RODE HIGH on the success of *The Umpire Strikes Back*. Newspapers later pegged sales at 150,000 copies in hardcover plus half a million in paperback. Some articles said Luciano was rich, but he made no extravagant claims. "I'm in great shape," he said simply. "I can hunt and fish whenever I want."[40]

His second book with Fisher was *Strike Two*, which hit bookstores in 1984, exactly two years after the first. "RON LUCIANO'S NEW BOOK IS OUT! OUT! OUT!" Bantam Books proclaimed in newspaper ads.[41] Luciano laughingly told John Fox it was the story of his life: "no sex, no violence."[42]

It actually was about men who made their livings on big league diamonds. He told *Chicago Tribune* sportswriter Jerome Holtzman that sequels were never any good. "I couldn't keep writing about myself," he said. "So I went around and talked to the umpires."[43]

Luciano said during one interview that he and Fisher had talked with about 150 ballplayers, coaches, and managers, plus forty or so umpires. He later told John Fox they'd taped "more than 130 hours, with about 30 umpires and 100 players."[44] If flexible with his figures and employing a broad definition of research, the pair put considerable time and effort into their second collaboration. Luciano described for National Public Radio (NPR) host Terry Gross a laborious process of interviewing, reviewing and categorizing transcripts, and finally outlining the 326-page book. But the writing itself took less than a month, and Luciano felt deflated once they had a finished manuscript. "Those three weeks that we did that book," he said, "I was just the happiest person in the whole world."[45]

Strike Two also cracked the *New York Times* bestseller list, debuting at number twelve the first of July. This was nine places below *Balls*, San Diego Padre Graig Nettles's memoir about his eleven seasons playing in pinstripes with the Yankees. The third baseman's book fell to number 11 the following week, while Luciano's dropped off altogether, never to reappear. Reviews for *Strike Two* were generally good but more mixed than for *The Umpire Strikes Back*.

The *Orange County (CA) Register* found the book even funnier than the first and said it "leaves you waiting at the plate for a strike three."[46] Jerome Holtzman didn't know if it would sell a million copies but called it "a wonderfully humorous romp through the majors."[47] The *Dayton (OH) Daily News* said its combination of straight narration with tongue-in-cheek exaggeration "keeps the book moving considerably faster than most baseball games."[48] Back in the Triple Cities, a reviewer admitted that it might not win the Nobel Prize but asked "what Nobel Prize book ever made me laugh as hard as *Strike Two* has?"[49] A Binghamton bookseller added that the area's favorite author was "crazy, but wonderful."[50]

Naturally, not everyone agreed. A *Toronto Globe and Mail* reviewer said Luciano was the sort of author who had one good book in him. "He wrote it, which is where he should have quit."[51] The *Arizona Daily Star* said *Strike*

Two was no *Gone with the Wind* and added, "Unfortunately, it's not 'The Umpire Strikes Back,' either."[52] And the *Philadelphia Daily News* dismissed *Strike Two* as one long banquet speech, calling it an anthology of anything funny that had ever happened to umpires Luciano knew. "It has the rancid aroma of a ripoff."[53]

Dedicated fans still snapped up the book, which like *The Umpire Strikes Back* soon appeared in a paperback edition. Luciano appreciated the compliments, ignored his critics, and looked ahead to his next project. He said that in ten years, he could have *Strike*, *Strike Four*, or *Strike Eighty-Five*. Umpires, ballplayers, and managers, he added, shared stories with him all the time. "I ran into [pitcher] Phil Niekro the other day and as soon as he saw me, he ran over and said, 'I've got a new one for you.'"[54]

Luciano wrote that after two popular books, Bantam wanted the "third half of my autobiography."[55] He confessed, however, to having exhausted material from his own life. He didn't have any stories left to tell and couldn't even make anything up. The solution was *The Fall of the Roman Umpire*, a book containing mini biographies of fifteen current or former players Luciano considered good guys overlooked by fans and scribes alike. The approach let him accomplish two goals: "first, give some recognition to deserving players and, second, complete this book without working very hard."[56]

This third Luciano-Fisher collaboration featured a cover photo of the ex-ump clutching an umpire's mask, reclining in a white toga, and wearing a grin and a crown of laurel leaves. Inside were individual chapters on baseball journeymen—Ranger outfielder Tom Paciorek, who broke into the Majors a year after Luciano and was still playing (for his sixth team); Giant righthanded reliever Greg "Moonie" Minton, who grew up dreaming of becoming a surfer rather than a big league pitcher; former catcher Steve Nicosia, noted by an Alberta newspaper for having the "undignified distinction" of being cut by both Canadian baseball teams during the same season; and a dozen others.[57]

The Fall of the Roman Umpire hit bookstores in April 1986 but got lukewarm reviews and didn't make the *New York Times* bestseller list. The *San Francisco Examiner* said it made for good reading but that there was something wrong with Luciano's getting the credit. The reviewer urged readers not to plunk down $15.95 for the book. "Just wait for it to show up at a garage sale. It won't be long."[58] *Publishers Weekly* admired Luciano's "delightful" first chapter ("Didn't I Used to Be Me?") and his "telling and humorous observations" but found most of the players' stories tedious.[59]

Luciano and Fisher regained some of their lost luster two years later with *Remembrance of Swings Past*, punning on the title of Marcel Proust's famous early twentieth-century novel. Luciano joshed that he was proud of this fourth book because it was so literary. "I have multi-syllable words in it!"[60] It was a funny, thoughtful reflection on baseball's continual change and evolution. Luciano wrote that he had umpired his first game in 1964; about the only thing that hadn't changed since was a ball park hot dog, "just as stale today as it was then."[61] His chapters included "The Cast of Characters," "Baseball Is a Money Game," and "The Electric Glove and Other Shocking Developments." Luciano said *Remembrance* involved much more research into the sport's long history than his earlier works. "Baseball has changed so dramatically," he told *People*, "and I didn't think it had."[62]

Reviewers gave the book an approving nod. *Library Journal* called it good fun, with anecdotes on everything from artificial turf to relievers to night baseball to the ever-changing strike zone to the lively ball, all delivered with "the rapid-fire delivery familiar to readers of his earlier books."[63] *Publishers Weekly* deemed it a very successful effort, "featuring the hyperbolic humor so beloved of sports figures."[64] Red Barber had never seen Luciano work from his catbird seat but wrote in the *New York Times Book Review* that *Remembrance* was a pleasant read. "You'll learn much about umpires and umpiring from it," Barber wrote. "In fact, after reading it, you might ask yourself why anyone would want to become an umpire."[65]

While not another *New York Times* bestseller, *Remembrance of Swings Past* found a waiting audience. Like the three previous Luciano-Fisher books it later went into a paperback edition. Luciano quipped to an Endicott TV interviewer that the first book made him a writer, the second an author, and the third a rich man. "The fourth one, now I'm literary," he said. "Now, I command respect."[66] Some critics, however, thought he had overstayed his welcome. "One, two, three books and you're out—of fresh material," a reviewer in Atlanta wrote. "Four books and you deserve to be tossed out of the game."[67]

Luciano refused to abandon the literary game. By 1989 spring training, he and Fisher were working on a fifth book. Fisher said everything else now consisted of statistical analysis. "This will be just the opposite," he said. "Anything funny."[68] Luciano joked that he hardly ever saw his coauthor anymore, since Fisher was collaborating on other celebrity memoirs that were climbing the bestseller lists. He had worked with George Burns on *Gracie: A Love Story* and was tackling a second project with the comedian. "Pres. Reagan called him to say how much he liked the book," Luciano said laughing. "He couldn't get rid of him."[69]

The fifth and final Luciano-Fisher collaboration was *Baseball Lite: The Funniest Moments of the 1989 Season*. Bantam claimed that the only statistic a reader would find inside was a list of players who hadn't hit their weight that year. "In over 300 stories and anecdotes," the back cover said, "Ron Luciano will tell you about the most enjoyable moments of the '89 season."[70]

But 1989 was a particularly unfunny season, jinxed by multiple scandals. These included former Los Angeles and San Diego first baseman Steve Garvey's paternity problems, Boston third baseman Wade Boggs taking his mistress on the team plane, commissioner A. Bartlett Giamatti dying of a heart attack soon after banning Reds manager Pete Rose from the Major Leagues for betting on baseball, a devastating earthquake during the Giants-A's World Series, and Billy Martin then dying too, on Christmas Day, in an alcohol-related traffic accident outside the Triple Cities. Luciano suggested an alternative title: "Baseball, Bimbos, Booze and Betting."[71]

The book went straight to paperback in April 1990 and drew very little attention. Luciano called it a first annual edition and supplied a post office box at Endicott's Union Station, where readers could send stories for future editions. He ended the text, however, with a quotation from Toronto outfielder Lloyd Moseby: "Don't ask me about baseball anymore. It's over, and I'm going home."[72] *Baseball Lite* was the last volume in his unlikely literary career.

Luciano never again worked with Fisher, who by now had also collaborated with Dodgers manager Tommy Lasorda on *The Artful Dodger*. Fisher went out to work with former star reliever Sparky Lyle (*The Year I Owned the Yankees*), Pittsburgh Steelers quarterback Terry Bradshaw (*It's Only a*

Game), umpire Ken Kaiser (*Planet of the Umps*), and various figures outside sports, including David L. Wolper (*Producer*), Jackie Cochran (*A Lawyer's Life*), and actors Leslie Nielsen (*The Naked Truth*) and William Shatner (*Up till Now*, *Leonard*, and *Live Long and . . .*).

Fisher's former writing partner appreciated everything they had accomplished and created together. "He took my character, molded and polished me a little," Luciano said. "He really created me."[73]

14 Homebody

Luciano made Endicott his full-time home after leaving umpiring but was often busy elsewhere. During spring 1982 he missed the busiest season for his sporting goods store at Northgate Plaza—which surprisingly wasn't Christmas—while promoting *The Umpire Strikes Back*. Binghamton's city softball leagues fielded four hundred teams, and every April they all bought uniforms and equipment for the coming season. Ron Luciano's Sports World held a city contract to issue certificates entitling each team to a new ball for every home game, which prompted an annual sale. The general manager whom Luciano now employed said the week amounted to Christmas. "In fact, this week makes up for two Decembers."[1]

The boss meanwhile was occupied promoting his book. Earl Weaver's name cropped up often as the months sped past filled with interviews, appearances, and signings. In September a Connecticut newspaper reviewed both their books at once and likened the manager's ejections by Luciano to Wile E. Coyote's inevitable fate versus the Roadrunner. Winter then seemed to arrive quickly. Luciano's store held a fifth-anniversary sale the week before Christmas. Following the holiday a sign on the door said the business was closed and would reopen January 2, but it never did. No one in the family ever explained the abrupt failure.

Luciano later wrote a funny, exaggerated account of his travails as a businessman. He claimed, for instance, that his employees wouldn't come to work after a python escaped from the pet shop next door. The tale sparked an angry rebuttal from the shop's owner. "I do not and have never sold snakes in my store," he wrote to the *Binghamton Press*. "So it would be very hard for one to escape as Luciano claims."[2] Auctioneers liquidated all of Luciano's remaining stock and fixtures the last weekend of February 1983. This was arguably the most successful sale in the store's history.

The people who lined up halfway around the business were all bargain hunters. "I guess this is not a good location for a sporting goods store," said one customer making his first visit.[3] Afterward, a Triple Cities jewelry and sports shop snapped up the $25,000 in merchandise left over.

A dozen years later the *New York Daily News* said Luciano's sisters oversaw operations but "unscrupulous employes [*sic*] whom Luciano trusted ran the business into bankruptcy."[4] He worked to repay his creditors and never spoke publicly about the debacle, even to John Fox. "That guy will bounce back every time," predicted Luciano's old Lions teammate turned sportscaster Wayne Walker, who wondered what would come next.[5]

Luciano soon hit the road to promote the paperback edition of *The Umpire Strikes Back*. He was inexhaustible. One day at St. Petersburg, Florida, during early March, he gave interviews to local radio, television, and newspaper outlets before flying on to Miami for a TV talk show that night. A sports editor wrote that Luciano's schedule called for stops in thirty cities over the coming month, "putting the hit on every level of interviewer, from the $3-million-a-year Johnny Carson to $3-an-hour part-timers at 100-watt radio stations."[6] He added that the author was headed everywhere except Battle Creek, Butte, and Tombstone.

The ex-ump missed the many characters who'd once surrounded him on the diamond. While in Florida he swooped into Citrus League spring training sites to gather material for his second book. Luciano said he'd aged a decade over the last year because he was no longer around "all those idiots I used to have to deal with. They kept me young."[7] But he wasn't considering a return to umpiring, and he said any Minor League ump who acted the way he had would never make it to the Majors. "They don't want any more of my kind," Luciano said. "That's why I have no chance of making a comeback."[8]

He looked instead toward Hollywood. Former Lion Alex Karras was a success out there, known for playing the behemoth horse-punching cowboy Mongo in the 1974 hit movie *Blazing Saddles*. Karras was now about to costar with wife, Susan Clark, and young Emmanuel Lewis in an ABC family sitcom debuting in the fall. *Webster* would be a hit and run four seasons on the network and another two in syndication.

Luciano hosted a thirty-minute pilot of his own in June for a lighthearted show on CBS. *Ron Luciano's Lighter Side of Sports*, he said, was "a cross between Saturday Night Live and Benny Hill."[9] Working before a studio audience, he taped segments with tennis star Martina Navratilova, champion boxer Gerry Cooney, Phillies ace pitcher Tug McGraw, hockey star Wayne Gretsky, supermodel Christie Brinkley, and a Yankee Stadium chef. Luciano told one interviewer he'd asked Navratilova about the first thing to learn in tennis. "How to throw a tantrum," she said.[10] Luciano thought his would be the first funny sports program.

The show aired nationwide, but CBS didn't pick it up for a series. Luciano bounced back as a popular guest on talk shows, like Buddy Hackett and Charles Nelson Reilly rolled into one big body. He said the key was simply to take over and tell his own stories. "On the Tonight Show, I just out-talked Carson," Luciano said. "I had my lines rehearsed, and I just took off. I feel like I've been wearing a mask all my life."[11]

He appeared on top talk and interview shows on television and radio throughout the mid-1980s, chatting with Johnny Carson, David Letterman, Arsenio Hall, David Brenner, Larry King, and Pat Sajak, sharing sofas with such fellow guest as *Murder, She Wrote* star Angela Lansbury, feminist and author Gloria Steinem, jazz pianist Chick Corea, and Alex Karras. One guest spot he somehow missed was on the children's program *Sesame Street*. A TV critic once described Luciano as "an incredible bulk of a man with the spirit of a little elf."[12] Big Loosh would have blended perfectly with the show's assorted cast of fuzzy birds, frogs, grouches, and cookie monsters.

Luciano made a brief return to baseball August 1 by umpiring a New York–Pennsylvania League game at Oneonta, New York, an hour's drive from Endicott. He joined the two regular umpires as the Oneonta Yankees hosted the Erie Cardinals in a Class A contest. The former AL ump hoped to gather new book material at Damaschke Field, only twenty-four miles from the National Baseball Hall of Fame. He joked that Oneonta was the closest he'd ever come to Cooperstown. Luciano said he would work the bases where he couldn't screw up too badly, but like a little kid, "I want to see if it's still fun and whether I made a mistake getting out."[13]

The *Binghamton Press* said it might have been the first time umpires ever got applause during their "almost reluctant walk to home plate for the exchange of lineup cards." Luciano worried about his timing but thought afterward he'd done okay. He felt no desire to resume umpiring. "The difference is, I can go home," he said, nodding toward his partners. "But those poor SOBs have to go out and do it again tomorrow."[14] He never again returned to a pro diamond, working only a few charity games here and there.

Luciano made another national TV appearance that December on *Saturday Night Live* with guest hosts the Smothers Brothers. He played himself, wearing an umpire's uniform and wandering silently about the set during the cold open as Tom Seaver commented on a unique rain delay. "There's umpire Ron Luciano, he's checking the stage. He doesn't look very happy—of course not," the Met star said. "He's the guy who's gonna have the final decision on whether or not to cancel the show tonight. Boy, this is really a shame." Once the indoor rain relented Luciano began the show by bellowing its signature line: "Live, from New York, it's Saturday Night!"[15] The big man later said he'd never had as much fun as on *SNL*.

The following spring Luciano attended the 1984 baseball season opener at Memorial Stadium in Baltimore while awaiting reviews and reaction to *Strike Two*. Earl Weaver had retired after the 1982 season and wasn't there to bedevil him. (The Earl of Baltimore later returned as skipper during the 1985 season and stayed through 1986.) President Ronald Reagan helicoptered in from Washington, DC, to throw out the first pitch. The crowd's chant of "Ronnie, Ronnie" was directed toward the commander in chief, not the ex-umpire.[16] Reagan stood along the third base line and popped an easy overhand toss into the mitt of Oriole catcher Rick Dempsey. "Good thing *he's* not pitching today, we'd lose 80 to 1!" the ex-ump cracked.[17]

Luciano finally seemed to get a break in Hollywood that spring, signing to play an umpire in a 20th Century Fox movie called *Bases Loaded*. The storyline involved a Japanese automaker sending a softball team to America to challenge a squad from Detroit. Luciano was excited about being cast along with Ruth Gordon and Jonathan Winters and athletes-turned actors and former NFL star players Lyle Alzado and Charles "Bubba" Smith. But the film hit roadblocks and delays and was never made.

A project that Luciano vaguely alluded to starring Chevy Chase didn't become reality either. Nor was he among several MLB umpires who made uncredited cameos in the baseball sequences of the 1988 comedy *The Naked Gun: From the Files of Police Squad!* NL ump Joe West, however, not only appeared in the movie but had a line—"You can't throw an umpire out of the game!"—for which "Country Joe" received residuals that he said over the decades totaled $250,000.[18]

Despite the movie disappointments, Luciano did carve out a profitable niche as an advertising spokesperson for print and TV. Over the next several years he appeared in commercials for telephone, airline, automaker, and soda companies. He likewise appeared in newspaper ads for a muffler firm, a Canadian betting company, and various small businesses around the Triple Cities.

All the while he lived with his mother and sister Bobbie in the modest Badger Avenue home in Endicott. The working-class neighborhood was less than two miles from where he'd grown up above Perry's Grill on North Street. Within three years he would buy the house from his mother and live there the rest of his life. Josephine was now eighty-three, he said in March 1985, and needed someone living with her. "I don't want her in a nursing home or something like that," he said. "Besides, this is home."[19]

Luciano had aspirations for yet another career, this one in politics. He had campaigned earlier for the region's New York state assemblyman, a Democrat whose retirement led to the election of a Republican. Luciano hoped to oust the incumbent in 1986. He said he would begin campaigning in June, work hard through the fall, and be in office in January 1987. "That I'm sure of," he asserted.[20] He'd even mentioned his plans at the end of *The Fall of the Roman Umpire*.

"I'm going to run for the New York State Assembly for the 123rd District," he wrote. He somehow refrained from adding any smart-aleck remarks about the nature of politics, fearing that they might be used against him. Would he win? There was one good omen—the general election was held in the fall. "This old Roman umpire's time of year."[21]

Pro sports offered several encouraging examples. Former New York Knicks and Basketball Hall of Famer Bill Bradley was a United States senator from New Jersey. Former pitcher and future Hall of Famer Jim Bunning had been a Kentucky state senator, run unsuccessfully for governor, and was aiming now for Congress, where he would serve twenty-four years in the House and Senate. Former NFL quarterback Jack Kemp represented an upstate New York district in the House of Representatives and dreamed of higher office.

Luciano believed he had the makings of a legislator because of his experience as an umpire and broadcaster. He'd been around and seen how different communities operated. Serving as the Umpires Association president during the 1979 labor dispute required political skills too. He met with aides to Democratic New York governor Mario Cuomo in May 1986 to talk about running. Luciano said they suggested several offices. He was most interested in the assembly, but state Democratic leaders wanted him instead to challenge state senate majority leader Warren M. Anderson.

Another candidate named Luciano had opposed the powerful senator eight years earlier. "I'm sure glad it isn't Ron," Anderson joked.[22] According to Luciano, Cuomo now wanted him to oppose the Republican. The would-be pol said only half-jokingly that nobody else wanted in. "They want somebody with a name," he said. "It doesn't have to be a good name." Luciano claimed that nobody had asked if he was qualified or could make a good speech. "The guy's been there for 24 years," he said. "I even voted for him. Now I have to run against him."[23]

Luciano soon abandoned his political aspirations. Support for a senate run eroded, he said, because Anderson put pressure on Democratic leaders not to back him. He didn't point to specifics, "but said Anderson's power to prevent bills from reaching the Senate floor could have been a factor." (Anderson responded that he hadn't even discussed Luciano's senate bid in Albany except in "jocular conversation.")[24] Nor did Luciano care to oppose a qualified Democrat for an assembly seat. "Nothing good can come out of a primary," he said.[25] He added that such a run was bound to cause bad feelings within the party and he didn't want that kind of conflict.

Newspapers ran short articles under headlines about a big league ump striking out in politics. Luciano told the Associated Press he'd thought Yankees owner George Steinbrenner was tough but politics was tougher. The *New York Times* said he planned to spend two years studying issues and might return to politics afterward. A fan in Binghamton hoped he wouldn't. "He seems to be an affable fellow," the sympathizer wrote to the Binghamton paper, "and I hope he never allows himself to become embroiled in the (sometimes) sordid game of politics."[26] The correspondent got his wish. Luciano vaguely mentioned running before the next election cycle but didn't pursue it and never publicly spoke about politics again.

IF LUCIANO THOUGHT he would avoid controversy by steering clear of politics, he was wrong. He sparked a furor over women umpires while promoting *Remembrance of Swings Past* in April 1988 and had only his big mouth to blame.

An interviewer for *People* magazine asked if baseball should hire female umpires. Luciano mentioned Pam Postema, working in the AAA Pacific Coast League (the highest level any female ump had yet reached) with hopes of making the Majors. She had spent seven years at the AAA level—three was the norm—and was getting lots of press. Maybe Postema could be a superstar, Luciano said, maybe not. The question was why the Major Leagues might hire her. Was it because they saw something in her that they didn't see in other Minor League umps?

"No. They're hiring her because she's a woman," Luciano said. "And actually, they're exploiting her."[27]

He said he'd seen Postema work in the Minors, which she later disputed. According to Luciano, she was adequate behind the plate but needed work on the bases. He also mentioned the cursing she would hear on a big league diamond, as if Postema hadn't already heard anything a player or manager might hurl at her. Perhaps he imagined one of his sisters trying to break into the big leagues, although his mother surely could handle the likes of Billy Martin or Earl Weaver. Luciano might easily have backed away or softened his comments afterward. But reporters kept asking, and he kept bashing Postema, comparing her to Emmett Ashford, who had reached the Majors only after long years in the minors.

Luciano said Ashford had confided to him that he'd held back other Black umpires. "I was too old. I couldn't umpire as well anymore," Ashford said. "A lot of people said he can't umpire because he's black." Luciano believed the first woman umpire, like the first African American, had to be the best. If a Major League hired Postema, he added, she wouldn't work out, "and they're never going to hire another woman for 30 years."[28]

He reiterated several times during his book tour that Postema wasn't the best person for the job. Good umpires had to make players believe in them, he observed, no matter whether they were right or wrong. He said Postema wasn't that type of person and added that she didn't handle the media well. Luciano joked that a league would do better to hire a New York

City cabbie who yelled at her passengers. "A woman like that would make a great umpire."[29] He believed the first woman ump to break into the majors had to be a female Jackie Robinson. "She has to be the ultimate umpire," he said. "And Pam is not that."[30]

Postema fought back. She later wrote that she didn't have a clue how someone who'd never seen her call a pitch could pop off that way. "But that was Luciano for you: talk first, think later."[31]

Writers and fans across North America jumped to her defense. A *Pittsburgh Press* columnist said Luciano was "desperate to make any kind of controversial statement just to keep his name in the media."[32] A Southern California fan wrote that Luciano made it sound as if the first female ump had to be Wonder Woman. "That's like saying a person has to be a race-car driver in order to qualify for a driver's license."[33]

Despite his reservations, Luciano predicted that Postema would reach the Major Leagues the following season. He was wrong. The Minors instead released her without explanation, along with a handful of male umps. She responded bitterly that if she couldn't make the Majors, "I don't see how any woman can."[34] *Oakland Tribune* columnist Dave Newhouse called her ejection emphatic and cruel. If baseball felt it was the national pastime after so callous a banishment, he wrote, "the pastime must be chauvinism."[35]

But Luciano was right about one thing. Thirty years would pass without the majors hiring a female umpire, and the seasons kept rolling by without one.

THE FORMER UMP often responded to questions without thinking while promoting *Remembrance of Swings Past*. His reply when someone asked about Cincinnati manager Pete Rose's thirty-day suspension and $10,000 fine for shoving umpire Dave Pallone caused another dispute, this one about officials.

Luciano had always spoken scathingly about Pallone and other "scabs" who remained in the Major Leagues following the 1979 labor dispute. But now he said Pallone had acted correctly in an ugly April 30 dispute at Cincinnati. Rose claimed he pushed the ump only after Pallone first poked him in the face. Critics said the ump should simply have walked away.

"Walk away from Pete Rose? From Charlie Hustle?" Luciano scoffed.[36] He said Rose would've been back in front of Pallone before the ump even turned around. But Luciano disagreed with umpires and baseball officials over the severity of the penalties leveled by Commissioner Giamatti. He recalled his own altercation and shove from Yankee Johnny Ellis at Oakland and how it had blown over after former AL president Joe Cronin bawled out the hotheaded first sacker. Luciano thought Rose's thirty days were excessive.

"I agree that he should probably be suspended, and I agree that he should be fined, but Jesus . . . ," Luciano said.[37] He should have stopped there, but instead repeatedly commented on the ruckus. The problem with baseball was the wrong people running it, he claimed, meaning the commissioner who "just doesn't have a baseball mind."[38] He added that Giamatti looked at the issue from a Yale point of view: "Thou shalt not touch the umpire."[39] If the commissioner didn't want any bumping, Luciano said, he'd have to chain managers in their dugouts.

This was too much for one of his old umpiring heroes. Augie Donatelli snapped in rebuttal that Luciano "wasn't that good an umpire to be criticizing anybody else." Now assistant supervisor of NL umpires, Donatelli added that the outspoken author seemed to have forgotten how much he had once resented rhubarbs himself. "I think he did this to improve his book sales," he concluded.[40]

The Pallone and Postema brouhahas certainly did keep Luciano's name on the sports pages for days on end as he promoted *Remembrance of Swings Past*. If he regretted opening his yap about either one, he never said so.

LUCIANO STILL OCCASIONALLY SPOKE wistfully about the silver screen but Hollywood never beckoned. As his writing career began winding down he kept himself busy elsewhere. He appeared in July on comedian Robert Klein's syndicated TV special "Baseball's All-Star Comedy Classics '88," an hour-long program filmed at an amusement park and baseball facility near Orlando. The show starred ex-ballplayers Jay Johnstone, Sparky Lyle, and Bill "Spaceman" Lee, sportscaster Marv Albert, Morganna "the Kissing Bandit" Roberts, and others—"a collection of what we call characters of the game," according to Klein.[41] Luciano later guested on the first episode of *The Bob Huckabone Show*, a local Triple Cities television talk and variety program. The old softie appeared again in December with an animated reading of "A Visit from St. Nicholas."

The following spring, Luciano joined celebrity athletes Ernie Banks, Billy Williams, Joe Theismann, Boomer Esiason, Mary Lou Retton, and Billie Jean King in promoting an indoor sport called flyball at a new facility at Schaumburg, Illinois. The *Chicago Tribune* described it as "sort of like softball from inside a net . . . patterned after a successful Australian indoor version of cricket."[42] A newspaper ran a photo of Cincinnati Bengals quarterback Boomer Esiason questioning a call by Luciano. The ex-ump was so intrigued by flyball that he mulled opening a facility near home in Vestal, but the game never took hold like pickleball decades later.

In September 1989 Luciano was the national spokesperson and presiding judge for an annual contest sponsored by Fisher Nuts to name the Sports Nut of the Year. He said he'd run into every sports nut imaginable while umpiring. "It's great that the loyal, diehard fans can get the recognition they deserve," Luciano said.[43] Ex-Yankee Goose Gossage, boxing commentator Ferdie Pacheco, sports talk show host Pete Franklin, baseball clown Max Patkin, and ESPN anchorman Charley Steiner formed his panel of judges. They chose as their winner a basketball fan who attended every Providence College basketball game costumed as the Phantom Friar, whom he described as a combination of Dom DeLuise and Darth Vader. *Sporting News* and various metro newspapers ran features on the nutty contest.

Luciano's public appearances then began to dwindle during the early 1990s. He shot a commercial in Los Angeles with Joe Garagiola, Johnny Bench, and Joe Morgan that was observed by actor Kevin Costner, who stopped by to watch. He spoke at a few banquets and signed books that were no longer found on the bestseller lists. No doubt he was thrilled when nephew Brian Jester, Dee's son, starred for the University of Georgia Bulldogs during the 1990 College World Series.

The following winter Luciano worked at a Red Sox fantasy camp in Florida. He still attended spring training every year but didn't have new books in the works. During July 1991, looking thinner and with his salt-and-pepper hair gone white, he entertained residents of a Vestal nursing facility with stories about Billy Martin, Nolan Ryan, Don Mattingly, and others. He revealed to the old folks an umpire's key to success: "It's all what you say, not what it looks like you're saying."[44]

During the summer of 1992 he umpired an All-Star Game for the Reviving Baseball in the Inner Cities youth program in Harlem. His uncle Nick

DiNunzio passed away at Binghamton the following January, breaking one of his last links to boyhood. At spring training in Florida two months later, Luciano shared a story from his own days in the Cactus League. An elderly woman fan, he claimed, was exasperated by a pitcher dawdling on the mound. "Mr. Pitcher," she yelled, "would you please hurry up, some of us don't have that much time left."[45]

Luciano spoke to a high school assembly in April 1993 at tiny Canton, Pennsylvania, doing a favor for the parents of a student. He guffawed when the principal presented him with a team sweatshirt emblazoned with the words "Earl I'm Back."[46] That November he worked a Make-A-Wish Foundation charity benefit ballgame starring Harmon Killebrew and several other ex-big leaguers at Fort Myers, Florida, then stayed on for a fantasy camp. He again worked the Red Sox fantasy camp in January 1994. Following an April gala in upstate New York for the Special Olympics, he then disappeared from public view. He later startled a friend in Endicott by saying that he'd admitted himself to a hospital suffering from depression. His writing partner David Fisher was among the few people who knew.

"He admitted to me it was really bad," Fisher recalled. The writer urged him to visit New York or Los Angeles.[47] "He was a terrific entertainer. But it was hard for him, because Ronnie was actually very shy. . . . He never got out of Endicott. And he should have; he needed to."[48] Luciano eventually stopped returning Fisher's calls. For most friends and relatives in the Triple Cities, however, Luciano seemed his usual self.

Rick Stefano was a landscaper and handyman who had gone to school with Luciano's nephews and become a hunting and fishing buddy. Decades later Stefano remembered excursions into the outdoors at all hours, during all seasons, in all weathers, fueled by enormous ham sandwiches. They chatted about baseball, football, and wrestling. Together they also trapped pigeons (which they always kept alive) that Luciano used to train bird dogs to recognize scents.

The former umpire and author made a point of talking with everyone who approached him, Stefano recalled, unwilling to disappoint anyone. He would remember Luciano later as the most generous man he'd ever met, one who let him pay for nothing and was equally generous with charities. He didn't realize the full extent of Luciano's fame, however, until glimpsing him on a TV commercial for pickup trucks in Canada. But despite his seemingly outgoing personality, Luciano was also intensely private. He shared little of his internal struggles and allowed his young pal no glimpse of them at all. Instead, Stefano said, "he was like a father to me."[49]

ENDICOTT SURELY SEEMED gray and depressing when Luciano returned to Badger Avenue following his hospitalization. It wasn't the vibrant place he remembered from his boyhood living above Perry's Grill. The homely old building still stood, as did the handsome IBM lab up the block. But most factories on North Street were closed or gone, lost to globalization and the decline of American manufacturing. Vacant lots gaped everywhere. Sidewalks and storefronts along Washington Avenue downtown were largely empty as well.

If not a ghost town, Endicott certainly looked gaunt and ill. Its population had fallen from over twenty thousand in 1950 to a plateau of about thirteen thousand in 1990.[50] Any line charting its decline paralleled the one showing the steady weakening of the Endicott-Johnson Corporation. Sales by the mighty shoemaker peaked in 1951 before dramatic reversals the following decade. Factories and tanneries began closing in 1968, followed by warehouses and distribution centers. E-J stopped making shoes and became mainly a merchandiser. A syndicate based in London bought the remnants of the company in 1981.

The area's other big employer was nearly gone too. The *New York Times* recalled that IBM began slashing operations and closing factories during the 1980s. "Indeed, the entire region was once sort of an extended company town for the tech giant, which started there and spurred much of its housing and retail growth. When Big Blue left, economic pain ensued."[51] The giant's departure left Endicott coping with leftover industrial pollution, the first glimmers of an economic rebound and reinvention still thirty years in the future.

Watching the nightly news was depressing too. Luciano surely noted coverage of Dr. Jack Kevorkian, a controversial physician known as Dr. Death for helping terminally ill people end their own lives. A Detroit jury acquitted Kevorkian in May 1994 of assisting a suicide after he supplied a canister of carbon monoxide to a landscape architect suffering from amyotrophic lateral sclerosis, also known as Lou Gehrig's disease. The ailing man willingly breathed in the tasteless, odorless, and colorless gas through a mask and died in the back of a van. Perhaps Luciano read a piece by syndicated columnist Ellen Goodman that ran in the Binghamton newspaper, one passage of which read, "Now this renegade—have carbon monoxide, will travel—has issued a new challenge: Stop me before I kill again."[52]

Luciano at least had baseball to distract and entertain him, but only until late summer. Major League players went on strike after their games on August 11. In a front-page story the next day, the *New York Times* reported that the dispute, which centered on the owners' demand to control costs by limiting player payrolls, was so severe that negotiators "didn't even bother to meet and barely spoke to each other."[53] The strike was arguably the most traumatic and damaging event in baseball history. Fans didn't see another game all season.

Twenty years later *USA Today* remembered the '94 strike for ending Michael Jordan's try for a baseball career, killing the Montreal Expos franchise, and ending Tony Gwynn's splendid effort to become the first man to hit .400 since Ted Williams in 1941. Players ranging from Goose Gossage to Bo Jackson to Sid Bream to Lloyd McClendon never suited up again. Future Hall of Famer Gossage refused to announce his retirement then or ever. "The strike got me, man," he said.[54] No war had ever caused cancellation of a World Series, but October 1994 passed without one.

Luciano said nothing publicly about baseball's continuing woes. To the contrary, he all but vanished from public view. Friends outside the Triple Cities seemed to have a clearer sense of his flagging morale than many who saw him every day and who perhaps were fooled by his unchanged facade. Joe Garagiola later commented that Luciano was lonely and much more sensitive than most people knew. They mistakenly thought that each day was like New Year's Eve for the big man, he said, "but I can attest to the fact that he had a lot of August the twenty-thirds and October the fifths."[55]

Like Pagliacci, Garagiola added, Luciano had simply run out of funny stories. During the last six months of 1994, his name appeared only on sports pages noting the anniversary of his ejection of Earl Weaver from both ends of a doubleheader nineteen years earlier.

15 Yorick

Luciano's final weeks are unfathomable. Perhaps as a lifelong lover of Shakespeare, he felt a kinship with both Hamlet and Yorick, a melancholy prince clutching the skull of the fellow of infinite jest, pondering whether to take arms against a sea of troubles. He shared the Badger Avenue house with his widowed sister Bobbie Walton, but their mother lived now in a care facility, enveloped in the mists of Alzheimer's disease.

Josephine no longer recognized her son even though he visited her every day. A Syracuse sportswriter wondered later whether his visits still served any purpose. "Ronnie was her baby," recalled Dave Phillips, one of many umpiring crewmates who had known and liked her. "And by God, she let everyone know that she was very proud of him."[1] His mother's absence created a gigantic void in Luciano's life. "And of course typically Ronnie, he did not let anybody know what was going on," David Fisher said. "He didn't look or ask for any help because he didn't want to bother people."[2]

Wednesday, January 18, was gray and chilly in the Triple Cities. The temperature hovered in the forties, warmer than usual. Luciano was alone in the pale green house that he hadn't left much recently. Bobbie was away visiting relatives in Denver, and his dog, Billy, was off in a kennel, the bill already paid. Neighbors who saw Luciano that morning later told his other sister, Dee Jester, that he had appeared cheerful and normal. At some time during the day, he laid out a note for Bobbie and Dee along with his insurance policies, tax receipts, financial paperwork, will, and funeral instructions. Luciano then stepped out into the attached garage barely big enough to house his brown Cadillac. He attached a long black hose to the tailpipe and ran it through the window. Then he got in the Caddy and started the engine.

"The garage was set up," Dee said. "It was carefully orchestrated."[3]

Luciano had asked Rick Stefano to come by later to help around the garage. Stefano had seen his friend the night before and sensed nothing amiss. He arrived about 3:45 that afternoon to find the garage door shut but the front door standing open. Stefano went through the house into the garage and found Luciano dead in his car. He called 911 and was emotional when other people arrived. Stefano later learned Luciano had left him an apology, explaining that he wanted to spare family members from making the discovery. A few days afterward Stefano missed his pal but wasn't angry. "It's just hard to figure," he said. "Ronnie's Ronnie. I'm very surprised."[4]

The news rocketed around Endicott. The *New York Daily News* said shock and sadness darkened the town. The family was devastated, and friends couldn't understand what had happened. Fisher said suicide was the only selfish thing Luciano had ever done. The notes he'd left expressed a wish for a small private funeral but gave no indication why he ended his life.

"As outgoing as Ronnie was, he wanted all of this to remain private," Dee said.[5] She added that the one thing Luciano had wanted the public to know was that his death wasn't related to drugs or alcohol.

The loss confounded his cousin Nick DiNunzio Jr., an Endicott police detective who'd last seen Luciano two weeks earlier. He chose not to be involved in the case. But it was a small community, and the lieutenant who took charge of the investigation remembered Luciano as one of his substitute teachers back in school. There'd been no indication the big man was suicidal.

"He was Ronnie right up to the end—he was always the outgoing, nice guy," DiNunzio told the press. "Whatever was going on was something he was wrestling with. He took the answer with him."[6] Stefano agreed, and time would deliver no fuller understanding of his friend's passing. "When I'm gone," he said nearly thirty years later, "I'll see him and we'll be back to normal."[7]

Authorities took the body to Our Lady of Lourdes Hospital, where Luciano had entered the world in 1937. An autopsy showed he had been in good health for a middle-aged man. Lacking any indication of foul play, police soon concluded his death was suicide by carbon monoxide poisoning.

Men usually resort to more violent means for suicide than carbon monoxide poisoning. A hunter like Luciano might more easily have picked up a firearm or steered his car into a tree or road abutment. He probably knew about the gas's effectiveness from the recent Kevorkian coverage. Succumbing to carbon monoxide from car exhaust was tidy, nonviolent, and aside for its brutal finality almost courteous to the victim's family.

A few dozen relatives attended a private memorial service at a local funeral home followed by the burial in the family plot at Calvary Cemetery in Johnson City. Several days later a sportswriter in California wrote that he couldn't get over the shocking suicide, "a classic case of an unhappy man cloaking his misery with a smile and a joke."[8]

IT'S OFTEN DIFFICULT or impossible to determine why someone ends their own life, especially thirty years afterward. The Endicott police retain no record of the Luciano investigation, and surviving relatives politely decline to discuss either his life or his passing. But several possibilities might help to explain his suicide.

The deaths of several former NFL stars have fueled speculation about chronic traumatic encephalopathy (CTE), a degenerative brain disease linked to head trauma in football players, combat soldiers, and others liable to take repeated blows to the head. Ex-All-Pro defensive end and actor Bubba Smith, for example, suffered from the disease when he died from an overdose of a weight-loss drug in 2011.

CTE's numerous overlapping symptoms include depression, anxiety, impaired judgment, risk of suicide, and progressive dementia. A top concussion and traumatic encephalopathy expert has said that footballers who begin playing at a young age have a greater chance of experiencing cognitive, behavioral, and mood issues as adults—"and if they get CTE, it'll be worse."[9] Luciano had played football for a dozen seasons as a teenager and young man at the high school, collegiate, professional, and semipro levels. He'd lined up both offensively and defensively, and although often sidelined by illness or injury, he'd driven himself hard to become an All-American before joining the Detroit Lions.

It's not yet possible, however, to predict the chance of anyone's developing long-term cognitive problems. Doctors can't look at players and get a good idea of their comparative head impact exposure, a researcher has said, "because there's this huge difference person to person that we can't quite account for."[10] There's also no way to determine today if Luciano suffered from CTE long ago, or if so, whether it contributed to his death.

CTE can be definitively diagnosed only after death, and no coroner in 1995 looked for indications of the disease.

A different set of questions arose during the weeks and months after Luciano's suicide, with baseball men and sportswriters quietly wondering if he might have been gay. This wasn't surprising or particularly judgmental, since homosexuality in baseball and other pro sports had been in the news during recent years. The facts of Luciano's history, background, and largely unattached lifestyle can lead to similar conjecture today.

Former NL umpire Dave Pallone, one of the Exiled Eight in 1979, was the first (and still rare) Major League umpire to step out of the closet. Pallone told the story of his ten contentious seasons in a 1990 memoir and said afterward there were at least a half dozen gay Major Leagues players plus a general manager. During the fall of 1994, fans had also learned that former Dodgers and A's outfielder Glenn Burke (inventor of the exuberant high-five with LA teammate Dusty Baker) was dying of AIDS. The disease that would end his life in the spring had killed tennis star Arthur Ashe, and infection by HIV, the virus that is its cause, had forced Los Angeles Laker great Earvin "Magic" Johnson out of basketball.

Luciano had worked eleven of Burke's games in the AL, including the player's last in the Majors. The ump hadn't worked in the same circuit as Pallone, but life in the American League no doubt mirrored conditions in the National. The stereotypes of 1995 seemed to suggest the possibility that Luciano too was gay. He also was an inveterate gossip who knew quite a bit about what was happening in players' lives. "I know who's gay on the field," Luciano once gleefully told interviewer Terry Gross. "That's a heck of a thing, I know who's gay!"[11]

Such comments surely helped to fuel speculation about his own preferences, although no mention of a specific relationship or liaison ever surfaced. Dee Jester said her brother had girlfriends following his divorce from Polly Dixon but added that romance hadn't seemed important to him. Despite his criticism of Pam Postema, Luciano had displayed a ham-fisted courtliness toward other women while on his book tours. Decades later, Rick Stefano firmly rejected any suggestion Luciano had been gay. "No. Absolutely not," he said.[12] Former AL umpiring crewmate Dave Phillips likewise had never seen any indication it was true.

Soon after Luciano's death, David Fisher commented that he'd always felt his friend had been "born into the wrong kind of body. But he tried hard to be what others wanted him to be."[13] He later said he'd meant only that Luciano had been physically larger than most other people but didn't have the natural disposition to match. "That was not his big boisterous personality," Fisher said. "But he would be that person because he knew people expected it." He also doubted that Luciano had been gay. "If anything he was asexual," Fisher said. "And I think it might have had to do with his feeling of inferiority. I don't think he felt he was a particularly physically attractive person."[14]

Luciano's own comments during his lifetime tend to support Fisher's view. "I'll be ugly and fat the rest of my life," he once said.[15] For years he made light of his bulk, his clumsiness, his face made for radio. He once even told Terry Gross it was embarrassing for a 6-foot-4 umpire ordering a new athletic supporter to ask for an extra small.

What then had gone so terribly wrong at the end? Perhaps only that his burdens had accumulated slowly, like snowfall. There were many. The regrets and consequences of a punishing football career. The realization that a network salary and hefty book royalties were years in the past. The fading of attention and fame. The loss of his mother, who yet still lived. The lack of a romantic partner. The fears or desires that kept an aging man awake at three in the morning. The depression that inexorably darkened everything. Perhaps finally some deep secret he never shared. Together, they overwhelmed him.

Luciano had always made personal decisions alone. In his last message to his family, he said there was no one to blame, it was "just time for me to leave." His sister Dee struggled to understand. "I think he felt his work was done," she said. "He'd given us everything we could ask for emotionally, spiritually and financially."[16]

GRAYING BASEBALL FANS often remember Luciano fondly. "As a teenage baseball fan completely obsessed with the game, he was the only 'celebrity' umpire and easily the most recognizable to me," recalls baseball and travel writer Charlie Vascellaro, who once corralled the smiling ump for a photo during Cactus League spring training. "He seemed to be just as happy to pose for that picture as I was, and he signed a ball for me as well."[17] Many fans still keep Luciano's hardcover and paperback books on their shelves. A small press reissued *The Umpire Strikes Back* in 2022. In popular memory the umpire remains loud, contrary, and endearing.

Will the big leagues ever see another like him? Luciano always said no, and as organized baseball edges toward robotic arbiters, it does seem increasingly unlikely. Joe West was perhaps the most colorful and best known Major League ump to follow him. West's career overlapped Luciano's during four seasons, after which he continued working the diamonds until 2021. But Country Joe is recognized more for his music career and colorful quotes than for outrageous on-field behavior or butting heads with MLB officialdom.

AL umpire Durwood Merrill wrote following Luciano's death that baseball's bosses "never could control Ronnie, and they sure as heck didn't want another Luciano cavorting around their ballparks."[18] Dave Phillips later agreed it would never happen. "Baseball is too changed," Luciano's old crewmate said. "The personalities of the umpires are non-existent anymore. There's no pageantry in the game."[19]

Phillips enjoyed working with Luciano, but in hindsight he thought his pal probably had been wrong in how he umpired. "His reputation as an entertainer was not the kind of image an umpire should portray," Phillips wrote.[20] Umpiring with Big Loosh in the American League during the 1970s, however, was unforgettable. "There would be tears in my eyes in the field watching him," Phillips said half a century later. "He'd just do things I couldn't imagine. Ronnie was a special person."[21]

Acknowledgments

Thank you to former colleagues at the old *Peninsula Times Tribune* for assigning me to interview author Ron Luciano at the St. Francis Hotel in San Francisco in 1982. My thanks as well to David Fisher, Dave Phillips, and Rick Stefano for sharing memories of their late friend, and to Charlie Vascellaro for his anecdote and photo. Special appreciation to Jan Finkel, Rick Huhn, and Chris Welsh for advice and encouragement.

Notes

1. ALL-STAR

1. "College All-Star Squad Opens Drills for Colt Date," *Denver Post*, July 23, 1959.
2. Luciano and Fisher, *The Umpire Strikes Back*, 10.
3. Tex Maul, "Nice Boys, but No Match," *Sports Illustrated*, August 24, 1959.
4. Paul Hornung, "It Wasn't All-Starry Night," *Columbus (OH) Dispatch*, August 15, 1959.
5. William Nack, "The Ballad of Big Daddy," *Sports Illustrated*, January 11, 1999.
6. Nack, "The Ballad of Big Daddy."
7. Luciano and Fisher, *The Umpire Strikes Back*, 11.
8. Charles Chamberlain, "Halfback Fights Life-Death Battle," *Newburgh (NY) Beacon News*, August 15, 1959.
9. Paul Hornung, "Buckeyes Battered; Brown Beats Death," *Columbus Dispatch*, August 15, 1959.
10. George Strickler, "Unitas Passes Colts to 29–0 Victory," *Chicago Tribune*, August 15, 1959.
11. Maul, "Nice Boys."
12. Maul, "Nice Boys."
13. Luciano and Fisher, *The Umpire Strikes Back*, 11.
14. Alan Goldstein, "Luciano: An Earl of Laughs," *Baltimore Sun*, April 19, 1983.
15. Jack Horrigan, "Luciano Joins Bills in Camp," *Buffalo News*, July 25, 1961.
16. David Condon, In the Wake of the News, *Chicago Tribune*, August 15, 1959.

2. TIGER

1. "Capt. Millard's Cook School," *Oneonta (NY) Star*, November 17, 1917.
2. "Building Mechanical Bakery," *Oneonta Star*, August 26, 1918.
3. "Perry's Grill Is Remodeled," *Endicott (NY) Daily Bulletin*, December 6, 1940.
4. Aswad and Meredith, *Images of America: Endicott-Johnson*, 13.

5. "IBM's Christmas Gift," editorial, *Endicott Bulletin*, December 24, 1936. The weekly newspaper later became a daily publication.
6. "Endicott Business Increases," editorial, *Endicott Bulletin*, December 24, 1936.
7. "More Than 3,000,000 Pass IBM Plant Here Annually," *Endicott Bulletin*, July 20, 1937.
8. "An Umpire Strikes Back," *Fresh Air with Terry Gross*, April 23, 1982, https://freshairarchive.org/segments/umpire-strikes-back.
9. Russ Worman, "Luciano, 267, a Skinny Kid in '49," *Binghamton Press*, October 20, 1954.
10. "The Winnah! Luciano!," *Binghamton Press*, December 28, 1958.
11. "U-E Outlook Rosy with Weight, 7 Lettermen, Veteran Backfield," *Endicott Daily Bulletin*, September 9, 1953.
12. Tim Schum, "Your Turn: The Story of Union-Endicott's Ty Cobb," *Binghamton Press & Sun-Bulletin*, December 7, 2017.
13. Donald C. Johnson, "Teammates Took Varied Paths," *Somerville (NJ) Courier-News*, September 15, 1975.
14. Emanuel Perlmutter, "Apalachin Story Still Unresolved Mystery," *New York Times*, December 22, 1957.
15. David Cooper. "The Mafia: How Little Joe Got a Big Name," *Detroit Free Press*, November 20, 1968.
16. Andrew Tully, "Undercover Men Bare Secrets of the Mafia," *Detroit Free Press*, October 4, 1958.
17. Tom Cawley, "Barbara Fete Put Apalachin on Map," *Binghamton Press*, November 17, 1957.
18. John A. Cavanaugh, "Ailing Croswell Calm in Tough Quiz," *Binghamton Press*, December 21, 1959.
19. Bernie Shellum and Low Montgomery, "Mob Has History in Area Trash Contracts," *Detroit Free Press*, July 6, 1993.
20. John W. Fox, "U-E Line May Average over 200 Pounds, Backs Present Biggest Problem to Cobb," *Binghamton Press*, September 18, 1954.
21. Worman, "Luciano, 267."
22. Worman, "Luciano, 267."
23. "Determined Ron Luciano."
24. "Vestal Humbles U-E 13-0," *Endicott Daily Bulletin*, October 16, 1954.
25. John W. Fox, "Oh, What a Beautiful Morning for Vestal," *Binghamton Press*, October 17, 1954.

26. David Rossie, "Show Ends on Sad Note," *Binghamton Press & Sun-Bulletin*, January 20, 1995.
27. John Kelly, "U-E 'Zephyr' Geared to April Fool Theme," *Binghamton Press*, April 10, 1955.
28. Worman, "Luciano, 267."
29. Ed Casey, "Family Anxiously Awaits Decision," *Endicott Daily Bulletin*, November 19, 1958.
30. John W. Fox, "Can Bowls Ignore Bill Orange Now?," *Binghamton Press*, November 16, 1958.

3. ORANGEMAN

1. John W. Fox, "'Big Luce' Shrinks, Wrecks Equipment in Orange Practice," *Binghamton Press*, October 9, 1955.
2. Bun Kuhl, Yours in Sports, *Endicott Daily Bulletin*, November 18, 1955.
3. John W. Fox, "Orange Cruder with Brown, Cuter with Tricks," *Binghamton Press*, September 18, 1956.
4. Sean Kirst, "Old Syracuse Buddies Remember Luciano," *Syracuse Post-Standard*, January 20, 1995.
5. Scott Pitoniak, "Luciano Made Us Laugh Often," *Rochester (NY) Chronicle and Democrat*, January 20, 1995.
6. William Kates, "Former Umpire Luciano Remembered," *Potsdam (NY) Clarkson University Integrator*, January 23, 1995.
7. Harry Cronin, "He Turns On the Orange Juice," *New York Daily News*, October 21, 1956.
8. Paul F. Kagan, Time Out, *Endicott Daily Bulletin*, January 6, 1960.
9. Fox, "Orange Cruder with Brown."
10. John W. Fox, "'Twas Big Bay for TC Gridders," *Binghamton Press*, September 25, 1956.
11. John W. Fox, "Syracuse's Brown Rips West Virginia," *Binghamton Press*, October 14, 1956.
12. Bun Kuhl, Yours in Sports, *Endicott Daily Bulletin*, November 30, 1956.
13. George Beahon, "A Masked Orangeman: Luciano's the Name," *Rochester Democrat and Chronicle*, May 22, 1966.
14. Frank Woolever, "Luciano Wearing No Man's Collar," *Syracuse Herald-Journal*, December 16, 1957.
15. John W. Fox, "Sin Doesn't Pay, .992 Average Does," *Binghamton Press*, September 7, 1958.

16. "Hazzard out for Cornell, Syracuse Tilt," *Binghamton Press*, October 7, 1958.
17. "Line on Luciano—Rough Road, Detour," *Binghamton Press*, October 21, 1958.
18. "Fashion Note: Tigers' Sachs Shaping Up," *Binghamton Press*, October 23, 1958.
19. Arnie Burdick, "Orange Halts Dying Panther Thrust for 16 to 13 Triumph," *Syracuse Herald-American*, November 2, 1958.
20. Bill Reddy, "SU Grabs Thriller from Pitt," *Syracuse Post-Standard*, November 2, 1958.
21. "Foes and Pros Scouting, Chasing Luciano," *Binghamton Press*, November 3, 1958.
22. Ed Casey, "Luciano All over Field: All America?," *Endicott Daily Bulletin*, November 3, 1958.
23. John W. Fox, "'Loosh' Is Ready to Go 'All' the Way," *Binghamton Press*, November 2, 1958.
24. "Orange Coach Lauds Tackle Ron Luciano," *Schenectady (NY) Gazette*, November 14, 1958.
25. "Talk of Bowl Games Taboo at Syracuse," *Elmira (NY) Advertiser*, November 5, 1958.
26. Bill Reddy, Keeping Posted, *Syracuse Post Standard*, November 17, 1958.
27. John W. Fox, "But None as Sweet as Yuny's Tune," *Binghamton Press*, November 2, 1964.
28. "Union District's Luciano Makes All-America Teams," *Endicott Daily Bulletin*, December 8, 1958.
29. "'4 Strangers' Beat Luciano," *Binghamton Press*, December 2, 1958.
30. Dick Evans, "Gee, It's Warm Here, Syracuse Discovers," *Miami Herald*, December 29, 1958.
31. "Sooners, Syracuse Duel in Orange Bowl," *Shawnee (OK) News-Star*, January 1, 1959.
32. Phil Parrish, "Oklahoma's Bowl Win Fails to Impress Miami," *Norman (OK) Transcript*, January 2, 1959.
33. Bill Reddy, Keeping Posted, *Syracuse Post-Standard*, January 2, 1959.
34. John Cronley, Once over Lightly, *Oklahoma City Daily Oklahoman*, January 3, 1959.
35. Edwin Pope, "Perils of Syracusers Just Kept Right On," *Miami Herald*, January 2, 1959.
36. Sid Hartman, Hartman's Roundup, *Minneapolis Tribune*, January 2, 1959.

37. Bill Connors, "Syracuse Better Than Duke, Says OU's Line Coach," *Tulsa Daily World*, January 3, 1959.
38. Bob Whittemore, "Parking Problems? We've Sure Got 'Em," *Endicott Daily Bulletin*, January 12, 1959.

4. LION

1. John W. Fox, "Colt Overtimes a Deadly Thing," *Binghamton Press*, March 5, 1959.
2. John W. Fox, "One All-Star Honor Loosh Didn't Want," *Binghamton Press*, June 18, 1959.
3. "Luciano All-Star Whether or Not He Wants to Be," *Binghamton Press*, July 8, 1959.
4. George E. Van, "Star Game Balking Lion," *Detroit Times*, July 12, 1959.
5. Ed Casey, Casey's Corner, *Endicott Daily Bulletin*, July 9, 1959.
6. Ed Casey, Casey's Corner, *Endicott Daily Bulletin*, July 23, 1959.
7. "Luciano out 6 Weeks," *Binghamton Press*, July 29, 1959.
8. Ed Casey, Casey's Corner, *Endicott Daily Bulletin*, October 13, 1959.
9. Paul F. Kagan, "Luciano Sat All Season, and Learned," *Endicott Daily Bulletin*, December 31, 1959.
10. Casey, Casey's Corner, October 13, 1959.
11. Art Rosenbaum, "The Tackle Who Became an Umpire," *San Francisco Chronicle*, March 31, 1983.
12. John W. Fox, "TV, Poor Site, Weather Cut Wilt's Crowd to 700," *Binghamton Press*, April 23, 1960.
13. "Orange Spring Look May Be 'Off Color,'" *Binghamton Press*, April 29, 1960.
14. Butch Clegg, "Luciano Reflects on Umpires' Absence," *Vestal (NY) News*, March 29, 1979.
15. Watson Spoelstra, *Detroit News*, reprinted in "How Detroiter Saw Loosh's Latest Injury," *Binghamton Press*, August 1, 1960.
16. George Puscas, "Morrall Seen as Holdout," *Detroit Free Press*, July 31, 1960.
17. Doc Greene, *Detroit News*, reprinted in "If Loosh Calls 'Em as He Sees 'Em," *Binghamton Press*, April 5, 1964.
18. "Greene Awaits Green Light, But Luciano's on the Fence," *Binghamton Press*, July 16, 1961.
19. "Is 'Loosh' Fit? Bills Try Him," *Binghamton Press*, July 25, 1961.

20. Jack Horrigan, "Even with the All-Stars Back, Bills Resemble the Spirit of '76," *Buffalo News*, August 5, 1961.
21. Jack Horrigan, "No More Experimenting by Bills; O'Connell Is Regular Quarterback," *Buffalo News*, August 26, 1961.
22. Miller, *Rockin' the Rockpile*, 125.
23. "'Taxi' May Call for Luciano," *Binghamton Press*, September 7, 1961.
24. Randy Galloway, "Ump Strikes Funny Bone," *Dallas Morning News*, July 2, 1972.
25. "City Joins Pro Ranks with Team in UFL," *Indianapolis Star*, September 22, 1961.
26. "Saturday Last Chance to See Indianapolis Warriors in Action on Home Field," *Elwood (IN) Call-Leader*, November 13, 1961.
27. Luciano and Fisher, *Strike Two*, 4.
28. Don Skwarr, "Luciano: Never a Dull Moment," *Morristown (NJ) Daily Record*, August 3, 1975.
29. Ron Luciano, "An Umpire's Motivation: Preserve Integrity," *New York Times*, June 3, 1979.
30. Lewis Freedman, "A Former Umpire is the Woody Allen of the Diamond," *Philadelphia Inquirer*, April 25, 1982.
31. Bob Shryock, "Falcons on Turkey Day?," *Binghamton Press*, October 30, 1962.
32. Robert Lipsyte, "Football Has Minor Leagues, Too," *New York Times*, September 22, 1963.
33. John Fox, eponymous column, *Binghamton Press*, September 24, 1963.
34. Scott Pitoniak, "Luciano Has Them Roaring in the Aisles," *Utica Observer-Dispatch*, August 10, 1984.
35. Zimmerman, *The New Thinking Man's Guide to Pro Football*, 370.
36. Fox column.

5. ARBITER

1. Barry Meisel, "There Are 51 Umpires—and Ron Luciano," *Susquehanna Magazine, Binghamton Sunday Press & Sun-Bulletin*, April 9, 1978.
2. John Smyntek, "Umpire Forgets to Touch Base with the Facts," *Detroit Free Press*, April 4, 1982.
3. Bernard Kahn, "Ron Luciano Is Big Man in Florida State League," *Daytona Beach Evening News*, April 1, 1964.
4. "'Loosh' and Danny One Step from Top," *Binghamton Press*, November 12, 1964.

5. John W. Fox, "Luciano 'Weaver? He's Unbelievable!'," *Binghamton Press*, October 16, 1969.
6. Al Mallette, "He'll Be Back," *Elmira (NY) Star-Gazette*, June 22, 1965.
7. George Beahon, "A Masked Orangeman: Luciano's the Name," *Rochester Democrat and Chronicle*, May 22, 1966.
8. Bob McNally, Hoop Chatter, *Utica (NY) Observer Dispatch*, February 3, 1973.
9. Paul Henniger, "Batter up for Monday Night," *Los Angeles Times*, May 31, 1980.
10. Stan Hochman, "He Umpired by His Own Rules," *Philadelphia Daily News*, May 30, 1984.
11. Ian Hamilton, "The Clown Prince of Baseball," *Brandon (MB) Sun*, May 29, 1989.
12. Steve Geimann, "Blocked from TV Booth, Luciano May Try Radio," *Binghamton Press & Sun-Bulletin*, October 20, 1979.
13. Greene, "If Loosh Calls 'Em."
14. Rich Tosches, "A Light Look at Baseball with Ex-Ump Ron Luciano," *Buffalo News*, May 23, 1982.
15. Sid Bordman, "Umpiring Is Fun for Ron Luciano," *Kansas City Star*, August 4, 1971.
16. Bill Reddy, Keeping Posted, *Syracuse Post-Standard*, May 13, 1969.
17. Rick Pezdirtz, "Two Former Sports Stars Start on Road Back as FSL Umps," *Miami News*, May 10, 1964.
18. "Danny Reads the Mirror," *Binghamton Press*, March 24, 1964.
19. Jim Selman, "The 'Umping' of 2 Men in Blue," *Tampa Tribune*, April 22, 1964.
20. Del Ossino, "Saints Win 'Sennett Comedy' 8-7," *Tampa Tribune*, June 6, 1964.
21. Tom McEwen, The Morning After, *Tampa Times*, June 7, 1964.
22. Bob Bassine, Top O the Morn, *Orlando Sentinel*, July 12, 1964.
23. McEwen, The Morning After.
24. Chico Genovese, "'Kill the Umpire' Rings out at Lopez," *Tampa Times*, June 30, 1964.
25. Russ Worman, "Ernie's Golf News a Wetter Report; Pat on Ron's Back," *Binghamton Press*, August 16, 1964.
26. John Fox, "Loosh a Riot in Literary Offering," *Binghamton Press*, March 24, 1982.
27. "'Loosh' and Danny."
28. Jerry Crowe, "The Last Pitch at Ebbets Means More to Him Now," *Los Angeles Times*, September 25, 2007.

29. Weaver and Stainback. *It's What You Learn after You Know It All That Counts*, 35.
30. Jim Elliott, "Old Friends Sees Weaver," *Baltimore Sun*, June 23, 1968.
31. "Fined Weaver Bounces Back—and Out," *Elmira Star-Gazette*, June 29, 1962.
32. A. L. Hardman, "Pioneers Still in Thick of Fight," *Charleston Gazette*, August 26, 1963.
33. "Eastern League," *Sporting News*, May 29, 1965.
34. Al Mallette, "Smorgasbord," *Elmira Star-Gazette*, April 15, 1965.
35. Gene Levy, "Earl Turns Philosophical at End of 17th Year," *Elmira Telegram*, September 6, 1964.
36. Sandy Padwe, "Umpires Keep Managers List," *Newsday*, August 19, 1973.
37. Edwin Pope, "Luciano, Earl Trade Bouquets, Not Barbs," *Miami Herald*, March 27, 1982.
38. "Springfield's Kasheta 4-Hits Pioneers, 7-2," *Elmira Sunday Telegram*, May 2, 1965.
39. Paul Lukas, "Weaver Ejected but Pioneers Triumph, 3-1," *Reading Eagle*, May 14, 1965.
40. Ray Fitzgerald, "When Serving Loosh Beef, Short Orders Are Best," *Binghamton Press*, May 16, 1965.
41. Roger O'Gara, Fair or Foul, *Pittsfield (MA) Berkshire Eagle*, September 29, 1965.
42. Roger O'Gara, Fair or Foul, *Pittsfield Berkshire Eagle*, April 8, 1966.
43. Al Mallette, "Nichols Tough in Pinch for Pioneers," *Elmira Star-Gazette*, August 28, 1965.
44. Scott Ostler, "To Him, Baseball Was Just a Game," *Los Angeles Times*, June 22, 1982. Belanger was ejected only once during eighteen seasons in the Major Leagues, by Jerry Neudecker.
45. Fox, "Luciano 'Weaver? He's Unbelievable!'"
46. Brian Sullivan, "MacLeod: That Magic 18–0 Season," *Pittsfield Berkshire Eagle*, September 2, 1990.
47. John Fox, column, *Binghamton Press*, September 18, 1965.
48. John Fox, column, *Binghamton Press*, February 6, 1966.
49. Bill Reddy, Keeping Posted, *Syracuse Post-Standard*, March 4, 1966.
50. Eddie Fisher, "Shep Can Expect Tough Competition for 1966's Award," *Columbus Dispatch*, July 31, 1966. Weaver's middle name was Sidney.
51. Shelley Rolfe, "It's IL 'Award' Time Again," *Richmond (VA) Times-Dispatch*, August 28, 1966.

52. Bill Reddy, Keeping Posted, *Syracuse Post-Standard*, June 14, 1966.
53. Bruce Conley, "Schirmer Gives Up Struggle to Become Major League Umpire," *Sioux Falls (SD) Argus-Leader*, March 28, 1977.
54. Geoff Fraser, "Former Ump Ron Luciano Striking Back at Baseball," *Ottawa (ONT) Citizen*, June 16, 1982.
55. Hubert Mizell, "Ron Luciano: Basepath Pizazz," *St. Petersburg (FL) Times*, August 31, 1975.
56. John Egan, "Luciano Brings Humor to Big Leagues," *Sioux Falls (SD) Argus-Leader*, January 10, 1979.
57. George Beahon, "Avon Vet Likes U.S. Chances," *Rochester Democrat and Chronicle*, September 23, 1968.
58. "Big Loosh an AL Ump," *Binghamton Press*, July 26, 1968.

6. GUNFIGHTER

1. Merrell Whittlesey, "Big, New Umpire Recalls Manners," *Washington Star*, March 27, 1969.
2. "Loosh Our Man in Washington," *Binghamton Press*, March 28, 1969.
3. "No Cartwheels for Ted, Clyde," *Binghamton Press*, April 8, 1969.
4. "Cronin Liked Luciano's Wardrobe," *Binghamton Press*, April 8, 1969.
5. Ron Berman, "Giant Nat Ejected in A's Victory," *Oakland Tribune*, May 8, 1969.
6. George Minot Jr., "Frank Howard about Umpire's Shortcomings," *Washington Post*, May 9, 1969.
7. Merrell Whittlesey, "Ump's Call Gets to Gentle Giant," *Washington Star*, May 8, 1969.
8. "Loosh Takes THE Big One for First Bounce," *Binghamton Press*, May 20, 1969.
9. "A First for Hondo—Given Boot by Ump," *Sporting News*, May 24, 1969.
10. "Loosh Takes THE Big One."
11. Bob Addie, "White Sox Approve," *Washington Post*, May 11, 1969.
12. Fred Ciampa, "Sox Split on 8-Run Rally," *Boston Sunday Advertiser*, July 6, 1969.
13. Bill Liston, "Fisticuffs as Sox Divide," *Boston Herald Traveler*, July 6, 1969.
14. Merrell Whittlesey, "Hondo Blasts Two as Senators Split," *Washington Star*, July 6, 1969.
15. Luciano and Fisher, *Strike Two*, reproduced as an illustration between pages 166 and 167.

16. George Cantor, "Tight Pitches Stir Up Fuss and Cries of Headhunting," *Detroit Free Press*, July 9, 1969.
17. Jack McCarthy, "Five HT Kings Still on Game," *Boston Herald Traveler*, July 10, 1969.
18. John Fox, "Nobody See Red Rose, Greengrass Lately?," *Binghamton Press*, July 20, 1969.
19. Bob Kurland, "Men on the Moon Give Aker Assist," *Hackensack Record*, July 21, 1969.
20. John Wiebusch, "May Stops Tigers; Egan Beaned after Slugging Home Run," *Los Angeles Times*, August 12, 1969.
21. Richard L. Shook, "Tiger Streak Broken, 3-1," *Lansing (MI) State Journal*, August 12, 1969.
22. Fox, "Luciano 'Weaver? He's Unbelievable!'"
23. Galloway, "Ump Strikes Funny Bone."
24. Bill Gleason, "Ron's O-U-T of This World," *Binghamton Press*, May 25, 1970.
25. "Umpire at Work," *Los Angeles Times*, July 11, 1970.
26. "Cheer the Ump!," *Chicago Tribune*, July 20, 1970.
27. Bacchia, *Augie*, 187.
28. Gerlach, "Augie Donatelli," in Gerlach and Nowlin, *The SABR Book of Umpires and Umpiring*, 92.
29. Luciano and David, *Remembrance of Swings Past*, 38.
30. Sushant Sagar, "Baseball as Seen through the Mask of the Umpire," *Memphis Press-Scimitar*, May 29, 1982.
31. Luciano and Fisher, *The Umpire Strikes Back*, 122.
32. Red Foley, "Indians, 2-1; Yankees, 5-4," *New York Daily News*, April 13, 1970.
33. Foley, "Indians, 2-1; Yankees, 5-4."
34. Russell Schneider, "Fosse Charges Fan," *Cleveland Plain Dealer*, June 25, 1970.
35. Joe Trimble, "Murcer Belts 4 in Row; Yanks Split," *New York Daily News*, June 25, 1970.
36. "Cherry-Bomb Misses 'Loosh' by Inches," *Binghamton Press*, June 25, 1970.
37. Max Nichols, "Labor in Pro Sports Boosted," *Minneapolis Star*, October 10, 1970.
38. Edwin Pope, "Overworked, Underpaid Umps Getting Ready for Strike 3," *San Francisco Examiner*, February 21, 1979.
39. William Barry Furlong, "At Last, a Likable Ump," *New York Times Magazine*, February 25, 1979.

40. John Bell, "Larry Napp: An Umpire Who Gets Lots of Respect," *Fort Lauderdale News*, November 13, 1973.
41. Dave Kaye, "Those Men in Blue Lead a Lonely Existence," *Greenfield (MA) Recorder*, July 19, 1977.
42. Robert Cross, "The Fine Art of Umping," *Chicago Tribune Magazine*, July 18, 1976.
43. Diane K. Shah, *National Observer*, reprinted in "An Umpire Never Has to Say He's Sorry," *Miami Herald*, August 26, 1973.
44. Charlie Jaworski, "Don't Tell, but Loosh Prefers Orioles and Cardinals," *Binghamton Press*, January 14, 1973.
45. Bob Verdi, "Ron Luciano Still Talking a Good Game," *Chicago Tribune*, June 26, 1980.
46. Bob Peel, "Baltimore Not Only Oriole, Ump Says," *Syracuse Herald American*, May 7, 1989.
47. Sandy Padwe, "Umpires Turn the Tables, Call a Few on Themselves," *Newsday*, August 19, 1973.
48. "First Comes Joe Garagiola," *Franklin-Greenwood (IN) Daily Journal*, July 7, 1973.
49. Seymour S. Smith, "Umpire Keeps Wary Eye on Birds," *Baltimore Sun*, July 25, 1973.
50. Robert Lipsyte, Sports of The Times, *New York Times*, October 8, 1970.
51. Leonard Koppett, "30,052 See Blue Defeat Yanks on Six-Hitter at Stadium, 5–2," *New York Times*, June 2, 1971.
52. "Umpire's Accidental Punch Flattens Yankees' Michael," *Sporting News*, June 26, 1971.
53. Joe Trimble, "Blue, 20 Hits, Too; Yankees Overkilled, 13–3," *New York Daily News*, June 13, 1971.
54. Joe Trimble, "Ellis' Woes," *New York Daily News*, June 14, 1971.
55. Jim Ogle, "Blue's 13th Stifles Yanks, 13–3; Mets Lose," *Newark Star-Ledger*, June 13, 1971.
56. "Yank Notes," *Jersey City (NJ) Journal*, June 14, 1971.
57. Weber, *As They See 'Em*, 14.
58. Jim Hawkins, "Here's What Striking Umps Want—and Why," *Detroit Free Press*, April 20, 1979.
59. "Luciano Likes Life as Ump—He's 6-4, 270," *Newark (NY) Star-Ledger*, August 7, 1971.

60. Richard Dozer, "Strike Ends; Season Opens Tomorrow," *Chicago Tribune*, April 14, 1972.
61. Ron Berman, "A's Promise Vida Tonight," *Oakland Tribune*, May 24, 1972.
62. Glenn Schwarz, "Not-So-Blue Story for A's," *San Francisco Examiner*, May 24, 1972.
63. "Blue Still Idle; A's Still Winning," *Escondido (CA) Times-Advocate*, May 24, 1972.
64. Dick O'Connor, "Blue to Make Debut with A's Tonight," *Palo Alto (CA) Times*, May 24, 1972.
65. "Shoot 'Em Up," *Mansfield (OH) News Journal*, September 13, 1971.
66. Mark Goldberg, "Personality, Enthusiasm Make Luciano Top Umpire," *Ithaca (NY) Journal*, August 8, 1979. Luciano also said elsewhere that he'd once "shot" Otis in the International League.
67. Dick Schneider, "Former Umpire Luciano's Shots Still Keep Royals' Otis Laughing," *Fort Myers (FL) News-Press*, February 24, 1982.
68. Volney Meece, "Luciano Has Answer No Manager Can Question," *Oklahoma City Oklahoman*, March 13, 1983.
69. Eric Levin, "Meet Baseball's Wackiest Ump," *US*, July 11, 1978, reprinted in *Binghamton Sunday Press & Sun-Bulletin*, June 25, 1978.
70. Conlan and Creamer, *Jocko*, 15.
71. Kaye, "Those Men in Blue."
72. Luciano and Fisher, *Remembrance of Swings Past*, 212.
73. "Old Ulcer Knockout for Loosh," *Binghamton Press*, September 14, 1972.
74. Bill Hart, "A Yelling Series . . . Happy Hollerday for Ron," *Binghamton Press*, October 10, 1972.
75. Bill Hart, "Rudi Catch Not Bad for Outfield Reject," *Binghamton Press*, November 12, 1972.
76. "Ump Luciano to Be Cited," *Quincy (MA) Patriot Ledger*, December 30, 1972.
77. Jaworski, "Don't Tell."
78. Ray Fitzgerald, "Ump Luciano Set to Get Back Behind the Plate," *Boston Globe*, December 31, 1972.

7. SHOWMAN

1. John W. Fox, "Locked Out of Spring Training? Luciano'd Love It," *Binghamton Sunday Press & Sun-Bulletin*, February 18, 1979.

2. Ray Fitzgerald, "What's Next? Bermuda Shorts?," *Boston Globe*, April 8, 1973.
3. Jim O'Hara, "DPH: Views from Ump and Hurler," *Elmira Star-Gazette*, February 6, 1973.
4. Phillips and Rains, *Center Field on Fire*, 39.
5. Author interview, June 27, 2023.
6. Sid Bordman, "Kirkpatrick—Designated Player," *Kansas City Star*, May 3, 1973.
7. Jim Trinkle, "A Choice of Abuses," *Fort Worth Star-Telegram*, May 25, 1973.
8. Shropshire, *Seasons in Hell*, 67.
9. Galyn Wilkins, "Slow Crowd, Fast Arms Clyde's Big Night," *Fort Worth Star-Telegram*, June 28, 1973.
10. Kirk Bohls, "Rangers Reveal 35,698 Reasons for Picking Clyde," *Austin American-Statesman*, June 30, 1973.
11. Howard Green, "Memorable Moments," *Irving (TX) Daily News*, August 20, 1975.
12. Luciano and Fisher, *The Umpire Strikes Back*, 61.
13. Dan Stoneking, "'Aw, You Wait until We Meet Him Again,'" *Minneapolis Star*, June 28, 1973.
14. Bob Nold, "Kusnyer Caught Ryan by Sound," *Akron Beacon Journal*, March 28, 1974.
15. Ryan and Frommer. *Throwing Heat*, 93.
16. Nold, "Kusnyer Caught Ryan by Sound."
17. Steve Wulf, "Heaven for Seven: The Men behind Nolan Ryan's No-Hitters," *Sports Illustrated*, May 13, 1991.
18. Dick Miller, "Ryan's Smoke Sends Tigers into No-Hit Blind," *Sporting News*, July 28, 1973.
19. Gib Twyman, "N. L. Had Bench . . . And Not Just Johnny," *Kansas City Star*, July 24, 1973.
20. Harold McKinney, "Able Umps Rare in American League," *Fort Worth Star-Telegram*, August 12, 1973.
21. Shah, "An Umpire Never Has to Say He's Sorry."
22. John Fox, column, *Binghamton Press*, August 22, 1973.
23. Padwe, "Umpires Keep Managers List."
24. Jim Elliot, "Birds End Season, Divide with Indians," *Baltimore Sun*, September 30, 1973.

25. Ray Recchi, "Umont Shocked by His 'Retirement,'" *Fort Lauderdale News*, November 14, 1973.
26. Ken Nigro, "AL Players Call Umpires Out," *Baltimore Sun*, September 29, 1974.
27. Chuck Heaton, "Injured Umpire: 'Like a Zoo,'" *Cleveland Plain Dealer*, June 5, 1974.
28. Mike O'Brien, "Umpire's Thumb Adds Spice to Twinbill," *Sheboygan (WI) Press*, July 15, 1974.
29. Conlan and Creamer, *Jocko*, 213.
30. O'Brien, "Umpire's Thumb Adds Spice."
31. Mike Shropshire, "Foucault Runs Salvage Job," *Fort Worth Star-Telegram*, July 15, 1974.
32. "Martin Receives Three-Game Ban," *Fort Worth Star-Telegram*, July 17, 1974.
33. "5 Rangers Tossed Out," *McAllen (TX) Monitor*, July 15, 1974.
34. Ron Berman, "Bando's Bat Sending Loud MVP Signal," *Oakland Tribune*, August 5, 1974.
35. Mark Mulvoy, "He Calls 'Em as He Feels 'Em," *Sports Illustrated*, August 19, 1974.
36. Sandra McKee, "Teacher of Umpires Has Much Distaste for Showoff Types," *Baltimore Evening Sun*, April 4, 1980.
37. Bill Gleason, "Two Men Brought Laughter," *South Bend (IN) Tribune*, January 24, 1995.
38. Bob Maisel, The Morning After, *Baltimore Sun*, September 12, 1974.
39. Ken Nigro, "Orioles Split with Yankees, Fail to Gain in Pennant Chase," *Baltimore Sun*, September 12, 1974.
40. Dan Coughlin, "Guess Who's Going to Root for Yanks?," *Cleveland Plain Dealer*, August 3, 1974.
41. H. A. Dorfman, "The Umpire Is Always Right, Except When He Is Proved Wrong," *New York Times*, October 20, 1974.
42. "Letters Flare Up over Umps' Ratings," *Sporting News*, October 12, 1974.
43. "Interview: Ron Luciano," *Referee*, September-October 1976.
44. Bob Snyder, "Luciano: Jumbo Soprano," *Syracuse Herald-Journal*, January 15, 1988.
45. Bob Roesler, "Luciano: No Grudges," *New Orleans Times-Picayune*, March 17, 1983.
46. Jack Lang, "'Tom and Ron Show' in Series Film," *Sporting News*, February 15, 1975.

47. Fallon, *Dodgerland*, 36.
48. Mulvoy, "He Calls 'Em as He Feels 'Em."

8. WINDMILL

1. "The Ump's Got the Jumps," *Kansas City Times*, May 1, 1975.
2. William Gildea, "Ashford Doesn't Miss Grind of Travel in Minor Leagues," *Washington Post*, May 4, 1966.
3. Bob Sudyk, "Emmett Ashford: Only His Suit Is Blue," *Sporting News*, April 23, 1966.
4. "Pioneer Ashford's Role Not Velvet, But It Beats Blue Serge of Minors," *Washington Post*, July 24, 1966.
5. Merrell Whittlesey, "Senators Notes," *Washington Star*, June 10, 1966.
6. Motley, *Ruling over Monarchs, Giants & Stars*, 201, 205.
7. Bob Ortman, "It's 'St-e-e-e-rike!' Now," *Tonawanda (NY) News*, April 3, 1975.
8. Terry Monahan, "The Color Line behind Home Plate," *Escondido (CA) Times-Advocate*, April 18, 1978.
9. Tom Briere, Baseball, *Minneapolis Tribune*, September 7, 1975.
10. Kent Ward, "A Book for Spring," *Bangor (ME) Daily News*, March 6, 1982.
11. Gorman, *Three and Two!*, 139.
12. Sam Blair, "Clean Joe and the Ratings Game," *Dallas Daily News*, April 13, 1975.
13. Dwight Chapin, "The Man in Black," *San Francisco Examiner*, March 31, 1983.
14. "Ump Please Speak into My Uniform," *Dallas Daily News*, April 13, 1975.
15. "Martin Has 'Noose' for Luciano's Neck," *Binghamton Press*, April 13, 1975.
16. Red Smith, Sports of the Times, *New York Times*, April 23, 1975.
17. Dick Young, Young Ideas, *New York Daily News*, April 16, 1975.
18. Young, Young Ideas, April 16, 1975.
19. Don Merry, "Luciano: An Umpire or an Entertainer?," *Long Beach Press-Telegram*, June 11, 1975.
20. "Martin Charges Bias, Wants Ruling by M'Phail," *Los Angeles Times*, June 27, 1975.
21. "A. L. Flashes," *Sporting News*, July 12, 1975.
22. Ira Berkow, Sports of the Times, *New York Times*, March 13, 1982. Luciano apparently refers here to Martin's 1974 double ejection at Milwaukee.
23. Marc Hansen, "Luciano Still on Hit Parade," *Des Moines Register*, September 26, 1982.

24. Ross Newhan, "It's Not Duncan's Kind of Offense but It Wins, 6–3," *Los Angeles Times*, May 18, 1975.
25. Don Merry, "Day of the Gnat: Angels Win 6–3," *Long Beach Independent Press-Telegram*, May 18, 1975.
26. Lou Hatter, "Orioles Drop 6–3 Decision," *Baltimore Sun*, May 18, 1975.
27. John Stellman, "Angels Lose Argument, Win Anyway," *Orange County Register*, May 18, 1975
28. Dick Miller, "Luciano Blows Call, Harper Loses HR," *Sporting News*, June 7, 1975.
29. Newhan, "It's Not Duncan's Kind of Offense."
30. Stellman, "Angels Lose Argument."
31. Neil Milbert, "Irate Robinson Ejected for Arguing as Sox Romp," *Chicago Tribune*, May 18, 1975.
32. "Suspension, Fine Facing Robinson," *Orlando Sentinel*, May 19, 1975.
33. "Good Night Frank," *Kansas City Times*, June 12, 1975.
34. Robinson and Anderson, *Frank: The First Year*, 124.
35. Hank Kozloski, "Robby Overstayed His Welcome," *Willoughby News-Herald*, June 12, 1975.
36. Gerald B Jordan, "Robby Gets Off-Field Hit," *Kansas City Times*, June 13, 1975.
37. "Sox Should Pretend Boston Part of Road Trip," *Quincy (MA) Patriot Ledger*, June 25, 1975.
38. Hank Kozloski, "Robby Umps' Natural Enemy," *Willoughby News-Herald*, July 7, 1975.
39. Russell Schneider, "Ump's Thumb Had Robby Sore," *Cleveland Plain Dealer*, July 9, 1975.
40. Russell Schneider, Schneider Around, *Cleveland Plain Dealer*, July 10, 1975.
41. Russell Schneider, Schneider Around, *Cleveland Plain Dealer*, July 12, 1975.
42. Angel Notes, *Los Angeles Times*, July 12, 1975.
43. Eliot Kaplan, "Ex-Ump Luciano Cries Foul," *Orange County Register Family Weekly*, April 18, 1982.
44. Michael Janofsky, "Birds Played 18 Innings; Weaver Saw Only Four," *Baltimore Evening Sun*, August 16, 1975.
45. "Same Old Story (Ax) for 'Being Billy,'" *Binghamton Press*, July 22, 1975.
46. Steve Hershey, "Weaver Fumes in Defeat," *Washington Star*, August 16, 1975.
47. Luciano and Fisher, *Strike Two*, 203.

48. Steve Hershey, "Weaver Fumes in Defeat."
49. "Earl's Exit a Big Hit," *Long Beach (CA) Independent Press-Telegram*, August 16, 1975.
50. "Bouton Loses But Keeps Faith in Knuckler," *Miami Herald*, August 17, 1975.
51. Bill Keating, Keats Kolumn, *Holyoke (MA) Transcript-Telegram*, September 23, 1975.
52. Peter Richmond, "Luciano's List of Liked, Loathed," *Miami Herald*, March 20, 1983.
53. Kaplan, "Ex-Ump Luciano Cries Foul."
54. Thomas Boswell, "Umps Return Venom on Weaver," *Washington Post*, May 20, 1981.
55. Bob Drzewiczewski, "From Fenway Park: Mr. Finley's Hopes Becoming Unbuttoned," *Rutland (VT) Herald*, October 6, 1975.
56. Dave Kaye, "Yerrrrr out!," *Austin American-Statesman*, July 3, 1977.
57. "Yaz Says Ump Missed Overslide at Third, Too," *Cincinnati Post*, October 15, 1975.
58. Merry, "Luciano: An Umpire or an Entertainer?"
59. Luciano and Fisher, *The Umpire Strikes Back*, 228.
60. Author interview, June 27, 2023.
61. Bob Fowler, "Loneliest Man in Town Is an Umpire," *Minneapolis Star*, July 2, 1976
62. Cross, "The Fine Art of Umping."
63. James Tuite, "For Six Months a Year, Umps Have No Homes nor Families," *Miami News*, August 27, 1978.
64. Hal Bock, "300-pound Ump Big on Working, Eating," *Wichita (KS) Beacon*, April 17, 1979.
65. James Timm, "Are Major League Umpires Justified in Staging a Strike?" *New York Times*, April 28, 1979.
66. Russell Schneider, "Umpires Are People Too. Honest," *Cleveland Plain Dealer Magazine*, June 1, 1980.

9. NEMESIS

1. Boswell, "Umps Return Venom on Weaver."
2. Mark Kram, "Umpire Strikes Back with Flamboyance," *Washington Times*, September 2, 1982.
3. Lou Hatter, "Indians Defeat Orioles," *Baltimore Sun*, May 26, 1976.

4. Hank Kozloski, "Wins over Orioles Helping Confidence," *Lorain (OH) Journal*, May 26, 1976.
5. Weaver and Stainback, *It's What You Learn after You Know It All That Counts*, 53.
6. Tom Fitzpatrick, "Ron Luciano: Confessions of an Umpire," *Chicago Sun-Times*, June 13, 1976.
7. Palmer and Dale, *Together We Were Eleven Foot Nine*, 69.
8. Phil Hersh, "Lucky Luciano to Get a Call," *Baltimore Sun*, June 22, 1976.
9. Eisenberg, *From 33rd Street to the Camden Yards*, 194.
10. Phil Hersh, "Meetings No Help to Birds," *Baltimore Evening Sun*, July 8, 1976.
11. "Earl Weaver," in Vincent, *It's What's Inside the Lines That Counts*, 109.
12. Ron Rapoport, "An Umpire and the Angels Surrender to the Orioles," *Los Angeles Times*, July 10, 1976.
13. Ken Nigro, "Umpire Ron Luciano Apologizes to Orioles," *Baltimore Sun*, July 10, 1976.
14. Rapoport, "An Umpire and the Angels Surrender."
15. Phil Hersh, "Luciano Is Sorry, But Earl Ousted Again," *Baltimore Sun*, July 10, 1976.
16. Kaiser and Fisher, *Planet of the Umps*, 125. Kaiser debuted in the American League the following season, in 1977.
17. Snyder, "Luciano: Jumbo Soprano."
18. *The Bob Huckabone Television Show*, September 1, 1988, accessed November 6, 2022, https://www.youtube.com/watch?v=hFqskznqJmQ.
19. Bruce Lowitt, "Donatelli Rebuts Luciano," *St. Petersburg Times*, May 11, 1988.
20. Ron Newhan, "Umpire with a Flair," *Los Angeles Times*, June 27, 1975.
21. "Baseball's Unwanted Fan," *Oakland Tribune*, July 7, 1976.
22. Sam Blair, "Echoes for an Umpire," *Dallas Daily News*, August 24, 1976.
23. Terry Price, "Baseball Umpire Ron Luciano Pumping Life into Profession," *Hartford Courant*, August 6, 1976.
24. Russ Worman, "'Loosh' Can Be More Fun than a Run," *Binghamton Sunday Press & Sun-Bulletin*, August 22, 1976.
25. Jim Fox, "Ron Luciano, Modern Ump," *Springfield (MA) Daily News*, July 24. 1976.
26. "Interview: Ron Luciano," *Referee*, September-October 1976.
27. Steve Daley, "Those Maligned Umpires: The Group Deserves Better," *Palo Alto (CA) Times*, March 21, 1979.

28. Mark Bausch, "Whitey Herzog Q and A," *St. Louis Sports Online*, March 12, 1995, www.stlsports.com/archives/files/03march1995.html.
29. Viv Bernstein, "Luciano's Sense of Humor Is Not in Retirement," *Binghamton Sunday Press & Sun-Bulletin*, July 27, 1986.
30. Dick Young, Young Ideas, *New York Daily News*, February 11, 1977.
31. "'Loosh': About Time We Gained on Players," *Binghamton Press*, February 11, 1977.
32. Gene O'Donnell, "Gregarious Luciano Brought Wit, Personality to Umpiring," *Springfield (MA) Republican*, January 22, 1995.
33. Bob Holt, "A Place to Play," *Ventura County (CA) Star-Free Press*, March 31, 1977.
34. Russell Schneider, "Welc Is Vocal Baseball Fan," *Cleveland Plain Dealer*, September 11, 1977.
35. Tom Weir, "The Call Drives 'Em Wild," *Oakland Tribune*, May 31, 1977.
36. Steve Jacobson, "Umpires Join the Real World," *Newsday*, April 1, 1979.
37. Keith Nichols, Sports Spotlight, *Vestal (NY) News*, April 12, 1984.
38. Peter Pascarelli, "The Scrimping Finally Ends," *Rochester (NY) Democrat and Chronicle*, May 26, 1977.
39. Luciano and Fisher, *The Fall of the Roman Umpire*, 8.
40. Mike Wyne, "Bases Were Loaded to See the Mariners," *Seattle Times*, April 7, 1977.
41. Ross Newhan, "Kaye Blacks Out Instant Replay," *Los Angeles Times*, April 8, 1977.
42. John Lawrence, "M's Lament: 'Yes, We Have No Tananas,'" *Tacoma News Tribune*, April 7, 1977.
43. Don Bradley, "Lights Go out on Angels," *Pomona (CA) Progress Bulletin*, April 22, 1977.
44. Richard Dozer, "White Sox, Angels Play 'Lights Out,'" *Chicago Tribune*, April 22, 1977.
45. John Stellman, "Lights Out! For Angels," *Orange County Register*, April 22, 1977.
46. Bradley, "Lights Go out on Angels."
47. Paul Oberjuerge, "Angels, Chisox Play 'Lights Out!' at Big A," *San Bernardino Sun-Telegram*, April 22, 1977.
48. Ross Newhan, "Angel Night Game Called on Account of Darkness," *Los Angeles Times*, April 22, 1977.
49. Stellman, "Lights out! For Angels."

50. Larry Whiteside, "Lynn: Nothing to It, 'I Had It All the Way,'" *Boston Globe*, June 5, 1977.
51. Luciano and Fisher, *The Umpire Strikes Back*, 176.
52. "Umpire Luciano Calls Them as He Sees Them," *Stamford (CT) Advocate*, October 2, 1978
53. Merrell Whittlesey, "The Telephone's Ring Cost McKeon His Job," *Washington Star*, June 12, 1977.
54. "Anybody Spying behind Yanks' CF Fence?," *Binghamton Press*, August 26, 1977.
55. Bob Fowler, "Twins Back on Tightrope," *Minneapolis Star*, August 26, 1977.
56. Dente, "Yanks' Steals Limited to Signs?"
57. "Angel Notes," *Los Angeles Times*, September 12, 1977.
58. "Tomorrow Is the Day," display ad, *Binghamton Press*, December 14, 1977.
59. Luciano and Fisher, *Strike Two*, 318.
60. Allan Levinsky, "Ron Luciano: Worth the Price of Admission," *Binghamton (NY) Chenango Courier*, January 12, 1978.
61. John W. Fox, "Ump Shift Riles Loosh," *Binghamton Sunday Press and Sun-Bulletin*, February 19, 1978.

10. HUCKLEBERRY

1. Herb Anastor, "Voltaggio 'Other Guy' in Veteran Ump Crew," *Vineland (NJ) Times Journal*, April 27, 1978.
2. Fox, "Ump Shift Riles Loosh."
3. Dave Philips, interview by author, June 27, 2023.
4. Jimmy Calpin, Lookin' 'Em Over, *Scranton Tribune*, March 28, 1978
5. Gerry Finn, "Only 99.3% Right," *Springfield Republican*, April 23, 1978.
6. "A's Run Catches Yanks Sleeping," *Nyack (NY) Journal-News*, June 14, 1978.
7. Frank Corkin, "Rizzuto's Antics," *Meriden (CT) Record and Journal*, July 5, 1978.
8. "A's Run Catches Yanks Sleeping."
9. "A's Run Catches Yanks Sleeping."
10. "Baseball Made to Face Up to Instant Replay Issue," *Pittsburgh Post-Gazette*, June 15, 1978.
11. Gar Kearney, "Fan Violence Concerns Chylak," *Scranton Times*, March 25, 1978.
12. Phil Jackman, "Nesting Chylak Is Itching to Umpire Again," *Baltimore Evening Sun*, August 9, 1978.

13. "Chylak: Just Need A Rest," *Scranton Tribune*, August 3, 1978.
14. "Chylak out for Season," *Scranton Tribune*, August 31, 1978.
15. Jack Seitzinger, "Chylak Gives Up Umpiring Chores to Take Supervisory Staff Post," *Scranton Tribune*, November 9, 1978.
16. John Fox, "Steve Can Use a Spa Elixir," *Binghamton Press*, August 1, 1978.
17. Richard Dozer, "Ex-Counsel Opposed Ump Strike," *Chicago Tribune*, April 27, 1979.
18. Kaiser and Fisher, *Planet of the Umps*, 252.
19. Red Smith, "Umpire Hendry Joins His Brothers," *New York Times*, April 17, 1979.
20. Jerome Holtzman, "Talk about Spitters," *Sporting News*, September 9, 1978.
21. Phillips and Rains, *Center Field on Fire*, 143.
22. "No Sympathy for NBA Refs' Strike," *Yonkers Herald Statesman*, April 11, 1977.
23. "League Presidents Plan to Meet with Umpires," *Newsday*, August 24, 1978.
24. Dick Young, "Umps Want a $-Replay," *Binghamton Press*, August 24, 1978.
25. "Umpires Close to Strike Call," *Binghamton Press*, August 25, 1978.
26. Jerome Holtzman, "Judge Calls Foul on Striking Umps," *Sporting News*, September 9, 1978.
27. Jim Hawkins, "Striking Umps Ordered Back to Work," *Detroit Free Press*, August 26, 1978.
28. "'It was a Dream Come True' for One-day Umpires," *Miami News*, August 27, 1978.
29. "Umpires Ordered Back to Work—Will Comply," *Spokane (WA) Spokesman-Review*, August 26, 1978.
30. "Quote 'Em," *Chapel Hill (NC) Newspaper*, August 27, 1978.
31. Herb Anastor, "Voltaggio Glad to Be Home after 2nd Year in Majors," *Vineland (NJ) Times Journal*, October 5, 1978.
32. Dave Philips, interview by author, June 27, 2023.
33. "'Incredible': Kuhn," *Indianapolis Star*, August 26, 1978.
34. Thomas Boswell, "Long-Suffering Umpires Want a Turn at Bat," *Washington Post*, September 3, 1978.
35. Grant Hall, "Umpires Added Spice to KC-Yanks Series," *Fayetteville Northwest Arkansas Times*, October 10, 1978.
36. Dick Brinster, "Luciano: Baseball's Most Unique Umpire," *Asbury Park (NJ) Press*, October 6, 1978
37. "The Play's the Thing," *Kansas City Star*, October 6, 1978.
38. Joe Gergen, "When No One Counted to 3," *Newsday*, October 4, 1978.

39. John Fox, "'Huckleberries' Can't Count 3," *Binghamton Press*, October 5, 1978.
40. Gergen, "When No One Counted."
41. Joe Gergen, "Luciano Turns on the Piniella Show," *Newsday*, October 7, 1978.
42. Elliott Denman, "'Ailing' Munson Inflicts Pain on Royals," *Asbury Park (NJ) Press*, October 7, 1978.
43. Bob LeNoir, "Playoffs Mean Pressure Too for the Men in Blue," *St. Petersburg Times*, October 8, 1978.
44. "1978 ALCS, Game 3 (Royals-Yankees) (ABC)," accessed May 23, 2023, https://www.youtube.com/watch?app=desktop&v=tObubfCrW-Y.
45. John W. Fox, "Magnetized by Guidry," *Binghamton Sunday Press & Sun-Bulletin*, October 15, 1978.
46. David Rossie, "A Good Call at the Plate; Bad Calls at Ron's Store," *Binghamton Press*, October 11, 1978.
47. John W. Fox, column, *Binghamton Press*, October 25, 1978.

11. ORGANIZER

1. Tom Fegely, "Outdoors: Bluebird Weather Compounds Goose Hunting Problems," *Allentown (PA) Morning Call*, November 2, 1978.
2. George Kimball, "For Ron Luciano the Gag Is off and Fun Is about to Begin," *Boston Herald American*, April 13, 1980.
3. Kaiser and Fisher, *Planet of the Umps*, 253.
4. Mark Winheld, "Obituary," *USA Today*, January 19, 1995.
5. "Luciano, Umpires' Head, Begins Study of Baseball," *New York Times*, November 7, 1978.
6. Steve Twomey, "Major League Umpires Withdraw Unfair Labor Charge," *Philadelphia Inquirer*, October 27, 1978.
7. "Bigger Series Lump for Umps," *Binghamton Press*, October 8, 1970.
8. Luciano and Fisher, *The Umpire Strikes Back*, 232.
9. Boswell, "Long-Suffering Umpires."
10. Jacobson, "Umpires Join the Real World."
11. O'Malley and O'Malley, *Game Day*, 235.
12. "Luciano Heads Umps: 'Reforms Overdue,'" *Binghamton Press*, November 7, 1978.
13. Larry Felser, "A 'Stylish' Ump," *Buffalo News*, February 18, 1979.
14. Bob Broeg, "Big League Umpires Made Tactical Error on Pay," *St. Louis Post-Dispatch*, November 5, 1978.
15. Dick Young, Young Ideas, *New York Daily News*, January 16, 1979.

16. Smith, "Umpire Hendry Joins His Brothers."
17. Hal Bock, "Baseball Starts with Verbal Showdowns," *Poughkeepsie Journal*, February 21, 1979.
18. Jonni Falk, "Kunkel Awaits Umps' Action," *Red Bank (NJ) Daily Register*, February 21, 1979.
19. "Report: Umpires Get Ultimatum," *Nyack Journal-News*, February 12, 1979.
20. Herb Anastor, "Voltaggio Heads for Florida after Short Off-Season Break," *Vineland Times Journal*, February 2, 1979.
21. "Bulletin Replay: Ron Luciano," *Baseball Bulletin*, June 1980.
22. Furlong, "At Last, a Likable Ump."
23. Bill Stieg, "Butler's Eddie Vargo: Will He Be Calling Strikes or Strike?," *Pittsburgh Post-Gazette*, February 15, 1979.
24. Phil Ranallo, "What's New Harry?," *Buffalo Courier-Express*, March 7, 1979.
25. Dozer, "Ex-Counsel Opposed Ump Strike."
26. Thomas Boswell, "Umpires Just Ask Justice," *Washington Post*, March 15, 1979.
27. Stan Isle, "New Report-or-Else Order Sent to Umps," *Sporting News*, February 24, 1979.
28. "Teams Spring into Play Minus Major League Umps," *Fort Myers News-Press*, March 7, 1979.
29. Ken Nigro, "Talks at Impasse, Umpires Barred from Exhibitions," *Baltimore Sun*, March 4, 1979.
30. "Teams Spring into Play."
31. Stan Hochman, "Umpires Rally behind Richie Phillips," *Philadelphia Daily News*, March 27, 1979.
32. Chris Roberts, "Umps Gain Favorable Ruling," *San Angelo (TX) Times*, March 28, 1979.
33. "The Letter," *Binghamton Press*, March 29, 1979.
34. John W. Fox, "Loosh 'Out': It's a Bluff," *Binghamton Press*, March 29, 1979.
35. "Umpire Asks Peers to Settle," *New York Times*, April 2, 1979.
36. Ross Newhan, "They're Called out on Strikes and Not Safe at All," *Los Angeles Times*, April 4, 1979.
37. Thomas Boswell, "Umpire's Hardest Decision—to Work," *Washington Post*, April 7, 1979.
38. Bob Lindley, "Downtrodden Umpires Deserve Some Favorable Calls," *Fort Worth Star-Telegram*, March 31, 1979.
39. "Kuhn Is Now Being Asked to Intervene in Umpires' Strike," *Pittsfield Berkshire Eagle*, April 17, 1979.

40. Hal Bock, "300-Pound Ump Big on Working, Eating," *Wichita (KS) Beacon*, April 17, 1979.
41. "Pryor Defies Strike," *Cincinnati Post*, April 5, 1979.
42. Dave Kindred, "Baseball's Treatment of Umpires Brings on Sad Days," *Washington Post*, April 8, 1979.
43. "Pryor Walks out to Join Umpires on Picket Line," *Louisville Courier Journal*, April 8, 1979.
44. "Pryor Joins Picket Line," *Pittsburgh Press*, April 8, 1979.
45. "Hendry Joins Striking Umpires," *Ithaca Journal*, April 17, 1979.
46. Mike Fine, "Umps Take Case to the Public," *Quincy (MA) Patriot Ledger*, April 16, 1979.
47. Neil Singelais, "Organized Labor to Join Fenway Picket," *Boston Globe*, April 20, 1979.
48. Larry Whiteside, "Contract Talks Resumed in Umpires' Dispute," *Boston Globe*, April 22, 1979.
49. "Fans Now Siding with Umps in Dispute," *Palm Beach (FL) Post*, April 24, 1979.
50. Garry Brown, "Umpires Feel Money Pinch," *Springfield Morning Union*, April 24, 1979.
51. "Eckersley: A Little Luck Goes Far," *Boston Globe*, May 16, 1979.
52. Jim Ruffalo, "Luciano Right about Reaction," *Orange County Register*, May 20, 1979.
53. Thom Greer, "Umpires Team Up," *Philadelphia Daily News*, April 24, 1979.
54. Martin Ralbovsky, "Teamsters Picket at Vet," *Philadelphia Inquirer*, April 24, 1979.
55. David W. Smith, email to author, June 7, 2023. Professor Smith later founded the Retrosheet baseball database, in 1989.
56. Greer, "Umpires Team Up."
57. Mark Heisler, "Angels Make It 5 in a Row before 41,941," *Los Angeles Times*, May 20, 1979.
58. Ken Sins, "Lack of Strike Action by 'Whom' Puzzles Luciano," *Fort Worth Star-Telegram*, May 22, 1979.
59. Phillips and Rains, *Center Field on Fire*, 143.
60. Dave Philips, interview by author, June 27, 2023.
61. "Umps Reach Settlement," *Nashville Tennessean*, May 19, 1979.
62. "At Last, It's Play Ball for Major League Umps," *Washington Star*, May 19, 1979.

63. Michael Faber, "One Strike the Umps Will Never Forget," *Montreal Gazette*, August 2, 1980.
64. Dave Dye, "Acceptance: A.L. Umpire Shulock Perseveres for Years Despite Peers' Sullenness," *Detroit Free Press*, July 29, 1990.
65. Gross, "An 'Umpire Strikes Back.'"
66. Jack Craig, "300-Pounder Finds His Niche at Last," *Sporting News*, May 3, 1980.
67. Steve Krasner, "Umpires Come under Attack for Their Aggressiveness," *Ottawa (ONT) Citizen*, June 30, 1991.
68. Heisler, "Angels Make It 5 in a Row."
69. Bob Fowler, "Enjoy It, Mr. Ump, It Won't Last," *Minneapolis Star*, May 22, 1979.
70. Mike Jones, "Regular Umps Return; But All Is Not Rosy," *Dallas Morning News*, May 22, 1979.
71. Michael Farber, "One Strike the Umps Will Never Forget," *Montreal Gazette*, August 2, 1980.
72. John W. Fox, "Billy Frowned on Flights—Luciano," *Binghamton Sunday Press & Sun-Bulletin*, August 5, 1979. Shulock later claimed that Haller, Luciano, and Kaiser once plotted to ship his equipment trunk to the wrong city, but he misdirected theirs instead. Shulock never traveled with Haller's crew, however.
73. Bob Fowler, "Umps' Attitude Is Bush League," *Minneapolis Star*, June 28, 1979.
74. David Israel, "Weaver's Act Earns Three-Game Layoff," *Chicago Tribune*, August 27, 1979.
75. Luciano and Fisher, *The Umpire Strikes Back*, 208.
76. Weaver and Stainback, *It's What You Learn after You Know It All That Counts*, 55.
77. Lou Hatter, "Weaver Wants Ump Out," *Baltimore Sun*, July 24, 1972.
78. "Spitballin': Doug DeCinces," *BallNine*, July 22, 2022, https://ballnine.com/2022/07/22/doug-decinces/.
79. Luciano: "An Umpire's Motivation."
80. Bob Maisel, "Weaver Fine or Suspension Appeared a Must," *Baltimore Sun*, August 27, 1979.
81. Scott Papillon, "Is Weaver Preparing His Case?," *Elmira Star-Gazette*, August 30, 1979.
82. Compiled from Retrosheet database, www.retrosheet.org/boxesetc/L/Plucir901.htm.

83. Herschel Nissenson, "Lemanczyk Bests Palmer; Umpire Ousts Weaver," *Nyack Republican-Times*, July 7, 1978.

12. ANALYST

1. Jack Bogaczyk, "Baseball Voice Heard in Announcer Selection," *Roanoke (VA) Times & World-News*, October 6, 1979.
2. Gary Deeb, "Luciano 'Gag' Reveals NBC Timidity," *Chicago Tribune*, September 28, 1979.
3. Jack Bogaczyk, "Luciano Criticized, Praised as Umpire," *Roanoke Times & World-News*, October 8, 1979.
4. Rudy Martzke, "Networks Ready for Post Season," *Rochester Democrat and Chronicle*, September 12, 1979.
5. Fred Rothenberg, "Luciano 'Called Out' for TV," *Dallas Morning News*, September 23, 1979.
6. "A.L. Announcing Ban Prompts Luciano Suit," *Boston Herald American*, September 24, 1979.
7. "Luciano Wants TV Job, Says He'll Sue," *Binghamton Press*, September 24, 1979.
8. John Fox, "NBC Brushes Off Luciano," *Binghamton Press*, September 28, 1979.
9. Bob Drzewiczewski, "Alpha Bits," *Rutland (VT) Daily Herald*, October 9, 1979.
10. Gary Deeb, "Pleasure and Pain Highlight TV Year," *Chicago Tribune*, December 21, 1979.
11. Bob Dolgan, "Logic Gets Thumb," *Cleveland Plain Dealer*, October 2, 1979.
12. Bogaczyk, "Baseball Voice Heard in Announcer Selection."
13. Peter Gammons, "Umps: Honest, Human," *Boston Globe*, December 23, 1979.
14. "What Makes a Good Ump?," *Boston Globe*, December 23, 1979.
15. Jon Fox, "Nobody'll Equal HER Placid," *Binghamton Press*, January 11, 1980.
16. "Pitching Staff Appears Settled," *Washington Star*, February 26, 1980.
17. Stan Isle, "All Major Umps Will Be Color-Coordinated," *Sporting News*, March 8, 1980.
18. "Cub Clouts," *Chicago Tribune*, March 16, 1980.
19. Jack Craig, "Luciano Being Tempted to Work as Analyst," *Sporting News*, April 5, 1980.

20. Randy York, "Worst Pitch in Baseball," *Lincoln (NE) Journal*, January 30, 1981.
21. "Luciano Deserting to Booth?," *Binghamton Press*, March 28, 1980.
22. Willie Schatz, "Luciano: Miked and Dangerous," *Washington Post*, May 11, 1980.
23. Craig, "Luciano Finds Job."
24. Dick Young, Young Ideas, *New York Daily News*, April 17, 1980.
25. Young Ideas, April 17, 1980.
26. Hal Bock, "Luciano Seeks Fortune as Announcer," *Poughkeepsie Journal*, April 25, 1980.
27. Merrill and Dent, *You're out and You're Ugly, Too*, 212.
28. Luciano and Fisher, *Strike Two*, 108.
29. "Insiders Say," *Sporting News*, May 3, 1980.
30. Bob Rubin, "NBC Gets Big, Bubbling Ump," *Miami Herald*, April 11, 1980.
31. Mark Wolf, "NBC's Luciano: 'Bride' or 300-Pound Lemon?," *Charlotte Observer*, April 18, 1980.
32. William Taaffe, "Ron Luciano: Is Mr. Inside on Way Out?," *Washington Star*, May 2, 1980.
33. Bud Wilkinson, "Ex-Ump Turned Sportscaster Knows the Meaning of Chatter," *Phoenix Arizona Republic*, July 7, 1980.
34. Carter Cromwell, "Luciano Strikes Back," *Austin American-Statesman*, April 13, 1980.
35. Ken Nigro, "Luciano Finds a Home on TV," *Baltimore Sun*, April 27, 1980.
36. Ed Barfield, "No One Fines Ex-Ump for Talking Too Much Anymore," *Atlanta Constitution*, April 25, 1980.
37. Murray Chass, "'Umpires Warned to Lay Off Spitballer Perry'—Luciano," *Sporting News*, May 3, 1980.
38. Leonard Shapiro, "Luciano Brushed Back after Bad Booth Call," *Washington Post*, June 21, 1981.
39. Bob Wisehart, "Umpire Gets a Hit—on TV," *New Orleans Times-Picayune*, July 30, 1980.
40. Nigro, "Luciano Finds a Home on TV."
41. Jim Hawkins, "The Man Who Loves to Talk Loves Life as an Announcer," *Detroit Free Press*, April 24, 1980.
42. John W. Fox, "No Dead Air with Loosh," *Binghamton Sunday Press & Sun-Bulletin*, April 27, 1980.
43. Alan Pergament, "Ex Ump Enjoys TV Role," *Buffalo News*, May 24, 1980.

44. Paul Henniger, "Batter up for Monday Night," *Los Angeles Times*, May 31, 1980.
45. Jack Lang, "We'll Suspend Madlock Friday, Umps Tell Feeney," *New York Daily News*, June 1, 1980.
46. Garagiola, "Premeditated Ejection," *Meriden (CT) Record and Journal*, June 3, 1980.
47. "Umps Threaten Daily Madlock Ejection Unless NL Acts," *Binghamton Sunday Press & Sun-Bulletin*, June 1, 1980.
48. Luciano and Fisher, *Strike Two*, 3.
49. Doug Grow, "Now Luciano Calls 'Em for NBC," *Minneapolis Star*, July 28, 1980.
50. Gary Deeb, "Piersall Broadcasts Add Color, Controversy," *Lexington (KY) Sunday Herald-Leader*, June 1, 1980.
51. Grow, "Now Luciano Calls 'Em."
52. Steve Wulf, "The Ump's Getting Some Lumps," *Sports Illustrated*, July 14, 1980.
53. Gross, "An 'Umpire Strikes Back.'"
54. Joe McGuff, "Phillies' Drug Story Distorted," *Kansas City Star*, July 23, 1980.
55. Ron Miller, "Burly Umpire Getting His Turn at Bat," *Kansas City Star*, August 3, 1980.
56. Jim Henneman, "A's Finley Finally May Be Out," *Baltimore Evening Sun*, August 22, 1980.
57. Jim Henneman, "Weaver, Luciano Confab More Civil Than Past Rhubarbs," *Baltimore Evening Sun*, August 23, 1980.
58. *NBC Game of the Week* pregame show, August 23, 1980, https://www.youtube.com/watch?v=P-tLFqZa-VA.
59. Bud Lea, "Luciano Likes Speaking Out," *Milwaukee Sentinel*, August 25, 1980.
60. Ray Benson, "Luciano Is Just as Funny in Booth as on the Field," *Columbia (SC) State TV Weekly*, October 12, 1980.
61. Lee Winfrey, "Series TV: Garagiola's Big Fall Hit," *Philadelphia Inquirer*, October 14, 1980.
62. Bob Rubin, "Garagiola, Seaver Save Face for NBC," *Miami Herald*, October 17, 1980.
63. Paul Henniger, "World Series Comes to Light," *Los Angeles Times*, October 18, 1980.
64. John W. Fox, "Loosh's 'Auto' Nears Publisher," *Binghamton Press*, December 20, 1980.

65. Jack Craig, "From Umpire to Announcer," *Boston Globe*, May 3, 1981.
66. William Taaffe, "Remark Places Barry's Job in Jeopardy," *Washington Star*, June 7, 1981.
67. Shapiro, "Luciano Brushed Back."
68. Thomas Boswell, "Both Sides Violate Baseball's Cease-Fire," *Washington Post*, February 7, 1981.
69. Paul Henniger, "Baseball's TV Drought Continues," *Los Angeles Times*, July 25, 1981.
70. Scott Ostler, "Some Circus," *Los Angeles Times*, August 20, 1981
71. Ryan Fagan, "Baseball Strikes and Lockouts," *Sporting News*, May 2, 2018.
72. Erik Brady, "Baseball Finally Shows Some Sense with Slate Loophole," *Buffalo Courier-Express*, August 17, 1981.
73. Gene Quinn, "McCarver Goes Prime Time Friday," *Philadelphia Daily News*, September 1, 1981.
74. Peter King, "NBC Grabs Reds' Seaver For Playoffs," *Cincinnati Enquirer*, October 4, 1981.
75. Leonard Shapiro, "Sports: A Diamond-Studded Dial for Hardball's Diehards," *Washington Post*, October 4, 1981.
76. Jack Craig, "Montgomery, Celtics Collide in His Debut," *Boston Globe*, March 22, 1982.
77. Sandy Schwartz, "Here's Why the Umpire Struck Out," *Peoria (IL) Journal Star*, June 2, 1984.
78. Alan Greenwood, "Luciano Gave the Game Life," *Nashua (NH) Telegraph*, January 20, 1995.
79. James M. Odato, "Luciano Regales Vestal Students," *Binghamton Press*, December 2, 1981.

13. AUTHOR

1. David Fisher, interview by author, April 24, 2023.
2. Richard Keyes Rein, "Ron Luciano Is a Showboat in Blue—Baseball's Most Outrageous Umpire," *People*, August 29, 1977.
3. Fox, "Loosh's 'Auto' Nears Publisher."
4. Fisher interview.
5. Andrew Jacobs, "The Thrills Are over at Mount Airy Lodge," *New York Times*, November 1, 2001.
6. Fisher interview.
7. Display ad, *Sporting News*, April 10, 1982.

8. Glenn Dickey, "Umpires Strike Back Again," *San Francisco Examiner*, June 24, 1984.
9. Hal Lebovitz, "The Ump Strikes Back—Again?," *Cleveland Plain Dealer*, June 20, 1982.
10. Roger Grooms, "Killing the Ump Is Annual Rite of Spring," *Cincinnati Enquirer*, April 4, 1982.
11. Benner, "Ump Ron Luciano's Best Call."
12. Peter Richmond, "Ex-Ump Luciano Sees Them Way He Calls Them," *San Diego Union*, May 20, 1982.
13. Dick Young, "More Trades for Yankees," *Pensacola News*, April 6, 1982.
14. Woodley, "'I've Been Wearing a Mask All My Life,' Says Ron Luciano, but Now the Umpire Strikes Back," *People*, July 12, 1982
15. John Fox, "Loosh's Book Is Tame Fare," *Binghamton Press*, April 4, 1984.
16. "Sports," *Library Journal*, April 15, 1982.
17. Cawley, "Luciano Book Hits Funny Bone."
18. Max Norris, "Diamond in the Rough," *Sacramento Bee*, April 11, 1982.
19. Freedman, "A Former Umpire."
20. Luciano and Fisher, *The Umpire Strikes Back*, dedication page.
21. Fox, "Loosh a Riot."
22. "Quotebook," *Los Angeles Times*, September 6, 1982.
23. "Ron Luciano 'Strikes Back,'" *Buffalo Courier-Express*, March 18, 1982.
24. Tom Cawley, "Book Mines Baseball Rich Lore," *Binghamton Press*, August 16, 1984.
25. Author's copy, inscribed following an interview for the *Peninsula Times Tribune* (Palo Alto CA), May 1982.
26. Richard Sandomir, "Ghost Stories," *Los Angeles Times*, May 11, 1990.
27. John W. Fox, "For Luciano, the Pen Is Almost as Mighty as the Mouth," *Binghamton Press & Sun-Bulletin*, September 23, 1987.
28. Furman Bisher, "The Ump Strikes Backs with a Pen," *Atlanta Journal*, June 9, 1982.
29. Jim Henneman, "AL Boss Has to Spank Anderson," *Baltimore Evening Sun*, May 15, 1984.
30. John W. Fox, "Earl Bugged Luciano, So Did FBI," *Binghamton Sunday Press*, February 28, 1982.
31. David Fisher, "Goodbye Ronnie, We'll Miss You," *New York Daily News*, January 22, 1995.
32. Fisher interview.

33. Michael Janofsky, "Three Swings for Baseball: Two Hits and an Out," *Miami Herald*, May 9, 1982.
34. Retrosheet, "Game Played on Tuesday, September 23, 1975 (N) at Royals Stadium," https://www.retrosheet.org/boxesetc/1975/b09230kca1975.htm.
35. "Luciano Plays Safe, But His Drink's Out," *Binghamton Press*, July 25, 1978.
36. Dick Young, "Weaver Driving toward Self-Imposed Retirement," *Palm Beach Post*, April 2, 1982.
37. "Locker Room Perspective," *Binghamton Press*, April 1, 1982.
38. John Hillyer, "Giants' VP Still Optimistic about Downtown Stadium," *San Francisco Examiner*, June 2, 1982.
39. Scott Ostler, "To Him, Baseball Was Just a Game," *Los Angeles Times*, June 22, 1982.
40. Bob Dolgan, "Ex-Umpire Luciano Calls 'Em Write," *Cleveland Plain Dealer*, April 23, 1984.
41. Advertisement, *Chicago Tribune Book World*, March 18, 1984.
42. Fox, "Loosh's Book Is Tame Fare."
43. Jerome Holtzman, "Luciano Unmasks the Men in Blue," *Chicago Tribune*, April 19, 1984.
44. Fox, "Loosh's Book Is Tame Fare."
45. "Luciano Hits a Home Run," *Fresh Air with Terry Gross*, April 26, 1984, https://freshairarchive.org/guests/ron-luciano.
46. Steve Grimley, "Luciano Calls One for Laughs," *Orange County Register*, March 18, 1984.
47. Holtzman, "Luciano Unmasks."
48. Kathleen Dawson, "Sequel about Baseball Destined to Be a Hit," *Dayton Daily News*, April 29, 1984.
49. Cawley, "Book Mines."
50. Lawrence A. Jenkins, "Summer Reads," *Binghamton Press*, July 6, 1984.
51. Jack Batten, "A Literary Sophomore's Jinx," *Toronto Globe and Mail*, March 24, 1984.
52. Sam Pollak, "Luciano Not so Lucky with this Book," *Tucson Arizona Daily Star*, June 10, 1984.
53. Hochman, "He Umpired by His Own Rules."
54. Harold Raker, "Luciano: Ballplayers Now Greet Him," *Sunbury (PA) Daily Item*, August 28, 1984.
55. Luciano and Fisher, *The Fall of the Roman Umpire*, 73.
56. Luciano and Fisher, *The Fall of the Roman Umpire*, 75.

57. Scott While, "New Book from the Ump," *Lethbridge (ALB) Herald*, August 23, 1986.
58. Edvins Beitiks, "Interviews Save Luciano's Latest Book," *San Francisco Examiner*, May 6, 1986.
59. Review, *The Fall of the Roman Umpire*, *Publishers Weekly*, May 1, 1986.
60. Daniel Neman, "The Luciano Curse? Don't You Believe It," *Richmond Times-Dispatch*, May 4, 1988.
61. Luciano and Fisher, *Remembrance of Swings Past*, 4.
62. Barbara Reynolds, "Play Ball!," *People*, April 7, 1988.
63. Review, *Remembrance of Swings Past*, *Library Journal*, June 1, 1988
64. Review, *Remembrance of Swings Past*, *Publishers Weekly*, April 1, 1988.
65. Red Barber, "The Worse Thing about a Spitball," *New York Times Book Review*, May 15, 1988.
66. "Bob Huckabone Television Show."
67. Guy Curtright, "Knuckleballing Niekro Brothers Write More than Baseball Book," *Atlanta Journal and Constitution*, August 7, 1988.
68. Victor Lee, "Braves Buys Bulk Up Bench," *Palm Beach Post*, March 26, 1989.
69. Jim Fox, "Ron Luciano Promotes Fourth Baseball Book," *Springfield Republican*, April 9, 1989.
70. Luciano and Fisher, *Baseball Lite*, back cover.
71. Hamilton, "The Clown Prince of Baseball."
72. Luciano and Fisher, *Baseball Lite*, 239.
73. Sandomir, "Ghost Stories."

14. HOMEBODY

1. Jim Meddleton, "Wallets Open for Softball's Mania in Area," *Binghamton Press*, April 21, 1982.
2. Richard A. Smith, "Luciano's Store Story Contained Errors," letter to the editor, *Binghamton Press*, August 17, 1984.
3. Kevin Maney, "Sell Out," *Binghamton Press*, February 27, 1983.
4. Barry Meisel, "Luciano, the Man," *New York Daily News*, January 24, 1995.
5. Rosenbaum, "The Tackle Who Became an Umpire."
6. Hubert Mizell, "Luciano, the Promoter Hits All the Bases," *St. Petersburg Times*, March 9, 1983.
7. Chapin, "The Man in Black."
8. Brian Schmitz, "Unmasking Luciano: An Oddball Who Called Strikes," *Orlando Sentinel*, March 8, 1983.

9. Meece, "Luciano Has Answer."
10. Larry Rumley, "Ump Tub-Thumps," *Seattle Times*, May 15, 1983.
11. Richard Woodley, "'I've Been Wearing a Mask All My Life.'"
12. Eric Mink, "Former Ump's Views," *St. Louis Post-Dispatch*, June 30, 1980.
13. John W. Fox, "Ron Luciano to Ump Game in Oneonta," *Binghamton Press*, July 31, 1983.
14. Geoff Hobson, "Luciano Loose in NY-P Stint," *Binghamton Press*, August 2, 1983.
15. "Saturday Night Live S09E07—The Smothers Brothers," https://archive.org/details/saturday-night-live-s-09-e-07-the-smothers-brothers-big-country.
16. Michael Olesker, "Ghosts Fill End Zones of Baseball," *Baltimore Sun*, April 3, 1984.
17. Laura Charles, "They Made the News," *Baltimore Sun*, December 30, 1984.
18. Devin Gordon, "It's a Really Weird Time to Be an Umpire," *New York Times Magazine*, March 30, 2023.
19. Ira Winderman, "SportsWeek/Etc.," *Fort Lauderdale News*, March 20, 1985
20. Winderman, "SportsWeek/Etc."
21. Luciano and Fisher, *The Fall of the Roman Umpire*, 306.
22. Tom Cawley, "Each Politician Has His Own Style," *Binghamton Press*, June 27, 1978.
23. Jonathan Rand, "Now Voters Can Throw the Ump Out," *Kansas City Times*, May 31, 1986.
24. "Anderson Responds," *Binghamton Press & Sun-Bulletin*, June 8, 1986.
25. E. J. Conzola, "Luciano Decides against Running," *Binghamton Press & Sun-Bulletin*, June 6, 1986.
26. Barry Hill, "Thanks to Luciano," letter to the editor, *Binghamton Press & Sun-Bulletin*, July 5, 1986.
27. Barbara Reynold, "Play Ball!," *People*, April 7, 1988.
28. Jonathan Rand, "Luciano Has Advice for Baseball," *Kansas City Times*, April 26, 1988.
29. Ron Musselman, "Luciano Sounds Off Again," *Wausau (WI) Daily Herald*, May 12, 1988.
30. Ian Hamilton, "Former Umpire Knows Whereof He Speaks," *Brandon (MB) Sun*, May 29, 1989.
31. Postema and Wojciechowski, *You've Got to Have Balls to Make It in This League*, 191.

32. Gene Collier, "For the Extra $7, Fans Won't See Spinks and Tyson Drop the Gloves," *Pittsburgh Press*, May 16, 1988.
33. Kenneth Zimmerman, "Viewpoint/Letters: Baseball Doesn't Need Wonder Woman," *Los Angeles Times*, May 28, 1988.
34. Jim Litke, "You're Out!," *Cleveland Plain Dealer*, December 15, 1989.
35. Dave Newhouse, "Blue Woman in Blue," *Oakland Tribune*, December 17, 1989.
36. Dave Hyde, "Umps: Pallone Couldn't Walk Away," *Miami Herald*, May 5, 1988.
37. Neman, "The Luciano Curse?"
38. Ron Musselman, "Luciano Sounds Off Again," *Wausau (WI) Daily Herald*, May 12, 1988.
39. Brian Schmitz, "Luciano: Giamatti Missed Call When Rose Got 30 days for a Bump," *Orlando Sentinel*, May 8, 1988
40. Lowitt, "Donatelli Rebuts Luciano."
41. "Former Players Provide Laughs," *Martinsville (IN) Daily Reporter*, June 30, 1988.
42. "Will Ernie Play 2 in Flyball Debut?," *Chicago Tribune*, May 9, 1989.
43. Bob McCoy, "Looking for Mr. Zagnut?," *Sporting News*, August 7, 1989.
44. Laurie Luebbert, "Luciano Tells Diamond Tales," *Binghamton Press & Sun-Bulletin*, July 22, 1991.
45. Glenn Miller, "Folklore Springs to Life," *Fort Myers News-Press*, March 4, 1993.
46. J. Cardene Johnson, "Ron Luciano Visits Canton High School," *Towanda (PA) Daily Review*, April 24, 1993.
47. Kirst, "Old Syracuse Buddies."
48. Bob Snyder, "Game Ends for the Gentlest Giant," *Syracuse Herald-Journal*, January 20, 1995.
49. Author interview, October 5, 2023.
50. "Population of Endicott, NY," accessed July 24, 2023, https://population.us/ny/endicott/.
51. C. J. Hughes, "A Renewal for IBM Campuses Once Home to Punch Cards and Circuit Boards," *New York Times*, July 20, 2021.
52. Ellen Goodman, "Have Carbon Monoxide, Will Travel," *Binghamton Press & Sun Bulletin*, May 22, 1994.
53. Murray Chass, "No Runs, No Hits, No Errors: Baseball Goes on Strike," *New York Times*, August 12, 1994

54. Bob Nightengale, "1994 Strike Most Embarrassing Moment in MLB History," *USA Today*, August 11, 2014.
55. Bill Madden, "Luciano: The Ump Always Wore a Mask," *New York Daily News*, January 22, 1995.

15. YORICK

1. Dave Philips, interview by author, June 27, 2023.
2. David Fisher, interview by author, April 24, 2023.
3. Richard Goldstein, "Ron Luciano, a Former Umpire in Big Leagues, a Suicide at 57," *New York Times*, January 20, 1995.
4. Barry Meisel, "Luciano, the Man," *New York Daily News*, January 24, 1995
5. Joe Donnelly, "Remembering Ron," *Newsday*, January 22, 1995.
6. Mark Winheld, "Umpire Luciano's Death Ruled a Suicide," *Binghamton Press & Sun-Bulletin, January 20, 1995.*
7. Rick Stefano, interview by author, October 5, 2023.
8. Ron Agostini, "Hot Shots and Pot Shots," *Modesto Bee*, January 28, 1995.
9. Alex Morris, "They Played Football as Children. Now Their Families Mourn," *Rolling Stone*, September 9, 2023.
10. Ken Belson and Benjamin Mueller, "Collective Force of Head Hits, Not Just the Number of Them, Increases Odds of C.T.E.," *New York Times*, June 20, 2023. For more information, see "Researchers Find CTE in 345 of 376 Former NFL Players Studied," Boston University Chobanian & Avedisian School of Medicine, February 6, 2023, https://www.bumc.bu.edu/camed/2023/02/06/researchers-find-cte-in-345-of-376-former-nfl-players-studied/.
11. Gross, "Luciano Hits a Home Run."
12. Stefano interview.
13. Kirst, "Old Syracuse Buddies."
14. David Fisher, author interview, April 24, 2023.
15. Snyder, "Game Ends for the Gentlest Giant."
16. Gregory Cerio et al., "Behind the Mask," *People*, February 6, 1995.
17. Charlie Vascellar, email to author, December 8, 2023.
18. Merrill and Dent, *You're out and You're Ugly, Too*, 227.
19. Author interview, June 27, 2023.
20. Phillips and Rains, *Center Field on Fire*, 141.
21. David Phillips, interview by author, June 27, 2023.

Bibliography

Armour, Mark. "Emmett Ashford." SABR BioProject, sabr.org/bioproject.

Aswad, Ed, and Suzanne M. Meredith. *Images of America: Endicott-Johnson*. Portsmouth NH: Arcadia, 2003.

Bacchia, John. *Augie: Stalag Luft VI to the Major Leagues*. Bloomington IN: iUniverse, 2011.

Cherry, Don. *Don Cherry's Sports Heroes*. Toronto: Anchor Canada, 2017.

Clark, Al, with Dan Schlossberg. *Called Out but Safe: A Baseball Umpire's Journey*. Lincoln: University of Nebraska Press, 2014.

Conlan, Jocko, and Robert W. Creamer. *Jocko*. Lincoln NE: Bison, 1997.

Corbett, Warren. "Earl Weaver." SABR BioProject, sabr.org/bioproject.

Eisenberg, John. *From 33rd Street to the Camden Yards: An Oral History of the Baltimore Orioles*. London: McGraw-Hill, 2002.

Eisenstadt, Peter, and Laura-Eve Moss, eds. *The Encyclopedia of New York State*. Syracuse NY: Syracuse University Press, 2005.

Fallon, Michael. *Dodgerland: Decadent Los Angeles and the 1977–78 Dodgers*. Lincoln: University of Nebraska Press, 2006.

Gerlach, Larry R. *The Men in Blue: Conversations with Umpires*. Lincoln: University of Nebraska Press, 1994.

Gerlach, Larry R., and Bill Nolan, eds. *The SABR Book of Umpires and Umpiring*. Phoenix: Society for American Baseball Research, 2017.

Gorman, Tom, and Jerome Holtzman. *Three and Two!* New York: Charles Scribner's Sons, 1979.

Gutkind, Lee. *The Best Seat in Baseball, but You Have to Stand!: The Game as Umpires See It*. Carbondale: Southern Illinois University Press, 1999.

Kaiser, Ken, and David Fisher. *Planet of the Umps: A Baseball Life from Behind the Plate*. New York: St. Martin's, 2003.

Leeke, Jim. "Ron Luciano." SABR BioProject, sabr.org/bioproject.

Luciano, Ron, and David Fisher. *The Fall of the Roman Empire*. New York: Bantam, 1986.

———. *Remembrance of Swings Past*. New York: Bantam, 1988.

———. *Strike Two*. New York: Bantam, 1984.

———. *The Umpire Strikes Back*. New York: Bantam, 1982.

MacPhail, Lee. *My 9 Innings: An Autobiography of 50 Years in Baseball*. Westport CT: Meckler, 1989.

Merrill, Durwood, with Jim Dent. *You're Out and You're Ugly, Too: Confessions of an Umpire with Attitude*. New York: St. Martin's, 1998.

Miller, Jeffrey J. *Rockin' the Rockpile: The Buffalo Bills of the American Football League*. Toronto: ECW, 2007.

Motley, Bob, and Byron Motley. *Ruling over Monarchs, Giants & Stars: True Tales of Breaking Barriers Umpiring Baseball Legends, and Wild Adventures in the Negro Leagues*. New York: Sports Publishing, 2007.

O'Malley, Martin, and Sean O'Malley. *Game Day: The Blue Jays at SkyDome*. Toronto: Viking, 1994.

Pallone, Ron, and Alan Steinberg. *Behind the Mask: My Double Life in Baseball*. New York: Viking, 1990.

Palmer, Jim, and Jim Dale. *Together We Were Eleven Foot Nine: The Twenty-Year Friendship of Hall of Fame Pitcher Jim Palmer and Orioles Manager Earl Weaver*. Kansas City: Andrews and McMeel, 1996.

Phillips, Dave, with Rob Rains. *Center Field on Fire: An Umpire's Life with Pine Tar Bats, Spitballs, and Corked Personalities*. Chicago: Triumph, 2004.

Postema, Pam, and Gene Wojciechowski. *You've Got to Have Balls to Make It in This League: My Life as an Umpire*. Lincoln: University of Nebraska Press, 2003.

Referee. "Interview: Ron Luciano." September–October 1976, 7–12.

Robinson, Frank, with Dave Anderson. *Frank: The First Year*. New York: Holt, Rinehart and Winston, 1976.

Ryan, Nolan, and Harvey Frommer. *Throwing Heat: The Autobiography of Nolan Ryan*. New York: HarperCollins, 1990.

Shropshire, Mike. *Seasons in Hell: With Billy Martin, Whitey Herzog and "The Worst Baseball Team in History"—The 1973–1975 Texas Rangers*. Lincoln: University of Nebraska Press, 1996.

Vincent, Fay. *It's What's Inside the Lines That Counts: Baseball Stars of the 1970s and 1980s Talk about the Game They Loved*. New York: Simon & Schuster, 2010.

Weaver, Earl, and Berry Stainback. *It's What You Learn after You Know It All That Counts: The Autobiography of Earl Weaver*. Garden City NY: Doubleday, 1982.

Weber, Bruce. *As They See 'Em: A Fan's Travels in the Land of Umpires*. New York: Scribner, 2009.

Zimmerman, Paul. "The Glutton's Guide to Eating Out." In *Junk Food*, edited by Charles J. Rubin, 142–44. New York: Dell, 1980.

———. *The New Thinking Man's Guide to Pro Football*. New York: Simon and Schuster, 1984.

Index